YALE ORIENTAL SERIES

RESEARCHES
VOLUME XXIV

PUBLISHED WITH THE PERMISSION OF THE LIBRARIAN
OF YALE UNIVERSITY, AND BY THE AID OF A GRANT
FROM THE AMERICAN COUNCIL OF LEARNED SOCIETIES

YALE ORIENTAL SERIES · RESEARCHES · VOLUME XXIV

PALESTINE—MOHAMMEDAN HOLY LAND

BY

CHARLES D. MATTHEWS, Ph.D.

With a Foreword by
JULIAN OBERMANN

NEW HAVEN
YALE UNIVERSITY PRESS
LONDON · GEOFFREY CUMBERLEGE · OXFORD UNIVERSITY PRESS
MDCCCCXLIX

THIS VOLUME IS RESPECTFULLY DEDICATED TO

PROFESSOR CHARLES CUTLER TORREY

NOTED SCHOLAR AND TEACHER IN THE FIELD OF BIBLICAL AND SEMITIC
LANGUAGES AND LITERATURES, INCLUDING ARABIC AND ISLAMICS

*The first Director of the American School of Oriental Research in Jerusalem,
in 1901–1902, at the outset of his brilliant and long career, in which he
has now, continuing his labors, attained his eighty-fifth year.*

FOREWORD

The title of this volume might create the impression that it is controversial in purpose. A random glance at the Introduction might even appear to strengthen that impression. A scholar less guileless or less sanguine than Dr. Matthews would probably have taken into account the hazard of exposing his work to misapprehensions of this kind. He might have considered that, at the present time, a book on Palestine which focuses attention on its character as a "Mohammedan Holy Land" would run the risk of being classed as partisan and, worst of all, of being disregarded by those who favor a purely realistic, political-economic approach to the study of the Near East.

In a very special sense, the present volume does bear on the intricacies of present-day Palestine. But it is to be hoped that its "timeliness" will not detract from its scholarly value, which is essentially divorced from those intricacies. Rather, it should be judged as a contribution to the history of the interdependence of Judaism, Christianity, and Islam: It makes available to scholarly scrutiny two Arabic documents dealing, respectively, with two religious centers of very great antiquity, Jerusalem and Hebron; and it endeavors to appraise their intrinsic significance in terms of Jewish-Christian-Moslem interrelations.

Indirectly, the present volume helps us understand why it should have been Palestine rather than one of the great imperial areas of Islam—such as Syria, Iraq, Egypt, Spain—that was elevated to the rank of "holiness" second only to that of the Hejaz, if not indeed on a par with the Hejaz; and how it retained this rank through all the vicissitudes of the Moslem community. Indirectly, too, we are made fully aware of a remarkable historical situation that has not been sufficiently noted hitherto: that pious lore and edifying legend of Judaism continued to exercise their influence in Islam not only long after the time of Muhammad but long after the major development of post-Koranic religious literature.

A case in point is the cycle of pious sayings and stories, in form of *ḥadīt*, centered around the Cave of Machpela, which forms the central theme of one of the Arabic documents and of the last chapter of the other. It seems obvious that this entire cycle must have developed under the impact of Christian pilgrimage, and may have been further stimulated as a reaction to the Crusades, with the materials supplied by the lore and tradition surrounding the Cave among both Peoples of the Book. Hence, no doubt, the frequency with which the Moslem cycle will be seen to fall back on the authority of Wahb ibn Munabbih and Ka'b al-'Aḥbar, considered the greatest authorities on *Isrā'īlīyāt*, on Jewish learning and practice, in Islam. The important thing is that, although the narratives of Abraham constantly recur in the revelation of Muhammad—narratives saturated with biblical and midrashic substance—and invariably occupy in the mind of the Prophet a position of highest veneration, there is no reference whatever to the Patriarch's burial place at Hebron either in the Koran or, as far as one can see, even in the far-flung standard Sunna.

Dr. Matthews' work offers but a single illustration of the vast fabric of ideas, of thought and belief, woven jointly by the three world religions. Studies of this kind, of which a goodly number have been made in recent times but of which a far greater number still remain in the realm of mere desiderata, are of inestimable value for the cultural history not only of the medievalism of the East but also of the modernism of the West. Eventually such studies are bound to be enhanced rather than hampered by the trends that of late have brought the problem of the Near East into new relief. Their common object is the interpenetration of the three social bodies involved during the period preceding and following the rise of Islam. Their common goal is to discover the deepest roots of Western culture and civilization: not in one of the three world religions, nor in all of them combined, but precisely in the indebtedness as well as the influence of each in relation to the two others.

JULIAN OBERMANN

New Haven, Conn.
May, 1949

CONTENTS

		PAGE
Foreword		V
Introduction		xi

PART I — *THE BOOK OF AROUSING SOULS*

Preface		1
Chapter First:	On the Beginning of the Building of the Mosque al-Aqsa	2
Chapter Second:	On Setting Out for Jerusalem; and the Merit of Going There and Lighting Its Lamps; and How One Should Enter the City of Jerusalem; and How One Should Enter Its Mosque; and the Merit of Going to Bethlehem and Praying There	4
Chapter Third:	On the Merit of Prayer in Jerusalem, and the Merit of Pilgrimage and Prayer in the Mosque of Medina and the Mosque al-Aqsa in the Same Year	10
Chapter Fourth:	On the Merit of Putting on the *Ihrām* from Jerusalem, and of Giving the Call to Prayer There	13
Chapter Fifth:	On the Merit of Giving Alms in Jerusalem, and Fasting There, and Witnessing the Pilgrimage Assembly	14
Chapter Sixth:	On the Merit of the Rock, and How It Is from Paradise	14
Chapter Seventh:	On the Black Marble, and How One Enters the Rock	18
Chapter Eighth:	On the Dome of the Ascension, the Dome of the Prophet, the Gate of Mercy, the Mihrāb of Zechariah, the Rocks to the Rear of the Mosque, the Gate of the Shekinah, the Gate of Forgiveness, the *Mihrāb* of 'Omar, and the Remaining *Mihrābs*, and the Door of the Prophet, the Mount of Olives, the Dome of the Chain, and the Gate of Repentance	19

PAGE

Chapter Ninth: On the Spring of Siloam, and the Water of Jerusalem, and the Well of the Leaf...... 23

Chapter Tenth: On the Plain *as-Sāhirah*, and the Merit of One Who Dies in Jerusalem............ 25

Chapter Eleventh: On Whether One Should Believe, or Not, That a Circuit of These Places Should Be Performed........................ 26

Chapter Twelfth: On the Merits of Jerusalem (and Palestine) in Summary........................ 27

Chapter Thirteenth: On the Merit of Pilgrimage to the Tomb of the Friend of God, Abraham, and the Adjacent Tombs of the Prophets............ 34

PART II — *THE BOOK OF INCITING DESIRE*

Preface 43

Chapter First: On Abraham's Genealogy, and the Length of His Life........................ 44

Chapter Second: The Birth and Infancy of Abraham...... 47

Chapter Third: His Going Forth from the Cave; His Remonstrance with His People; His Being Thrown into the Fire; with an Account of the Tower (of Nimrod) 52

Chapter Fourth: On His Migration to Canaan............ 64

Chapter Fifth: Account of the Birth of Ishmael, and His Migration (to Mecca) with His Father Abraham; and the Story of Zamzam...... 67

Chapter Sixth: On the Beginning of the Building of the Ka'bah, and Description of It from Its Building unto This Our Time............ 75

Chapter Seventh: The Story of the Sacrificing of Ishmael, and an Account of the Disagreement on the Matter........................ 78

Chapter Eighth: The Story of Isaac, and Record of the Disagreement upon Whether He Was the One Sacrificed 84

PAGE

Chapter Ninth: How Abraham Was Given the Annuncia-
                    tion of Isaac; and the Story of Abraham
                    and the Angels...................... 85

Chapter Tenth: The Story of Jacob, and the Extent of His
                    Life, and His Death.................. 88

Chapter Eleventh: The Story of Joseph, and a Description of
                    Him, and the Extent of His Life, and His
                    Death 89

Chapter Twelfth: The Story of Lot, and What Happened to
                    His People, and the Place of His Tomb... 92

Chapter Thirteenth: Record of the Sons of Our Lord Abraham
                    al-Khalīl, and His Wives, and the Wives of
                    His Sons, and Their Children.......... 98

Chapter Fourteentth: Account of the Death of Abraham....... 99

Chapter Fifteenth: Account of the Cave in Which Are the
                    Noble Tombs, and Which of the Prophets
                    Are in It; and a Description of Them and
                    of Their Tombs; and the Purchasing of the
                    Cave 103

Chapter Sixteenth: How Solomon the Son of David Built the
                    Enclosure around the Cave, by Revelation
                    of Allah; and an Account of Solomon..... 111

Chapter Seventeenth: On Visions of the Places of the Pious Ones
                    and Saints, Agreeing with What Has Pre-
                    ceded of Accounts of the Prophets and
                    Descriptions of Their Tombs........... 113

Chapter Eighteenth: On the Tomb of Joseph the Trustworthy,
                    and How His Coffin Was Borne from
                    Egypt, and Its Burial Near His Fathers.. 115

Chapter Nineteenth: On the Merit of Visiting the Tomb of
                    Abraham al-Khalīl, and His Noble Sons;
                    and the Reward and Recompense for So
                    Doing............................. 118

Chapter Twentieth: Accounts of His Hospitality, and of the
                    Merit and Noble Qualities with Which
                    Allah Hath Distinguished Him.......... 121

PAGE

Chapter Twenty-first: How He Was Graced by Divine Friendship and Love............................   123

Chapter Twenty-second: On Traditions Handed Down Concerning His Being Clothed on the Day of Judgment   128

Chapter Twenty-third: A Description of His Palace in Heaven...   129

Chapter Twenty-fourth: How He Came to See Grey Hairs; and His Circumcision; and His Being Given Trousers   130

Chapter Twenty-fifth: Description of Him, and the Splendid Qualities Which Allah Gave Him; and His Rank; and an Account of the Sacred Books (Revealed to Him)   133

Chapter Twenty-sixth: On the Noble Characteristics with Which Allah Distinguished Him, and the Pleasing Precedents Which Were of No One before Him, and Which Became Sacred Law and Polite Usage to Those after Him.........   135

Notes to *The Book of Arousing Souls*............................   139

Notes to *The Book of Inciting Desire*............................   149

Glossary   154

Bibliography...   157

Index   159

Historical and Religious Map of Palestine   *follows Index*

INTRODUCTION

Palestine, with Jerusalem the Holy City, is universally regarded by the Mohammedan world as a sacred land. To more than 275 million Moslems from the Philippines and China to Morocco, its sanctity is only below that of the homeland of the Prophet Mohammed in the Arabian Hejaz, the cradle of Islam itself, with its holy cities of Mecca and Medina. Still not realized or duly taken into account in Western countries, this historic attachment of thirteen centuries has an important bearing upon the future of the land of the Bible and of the peace of the world.

As a contribution to sources of information on Islam in Palestine and Palestine in Islam, the present volume offers a popular translation of two interesting and very old Arabic manuscript books on the subject. Both are in the nature of pilgrims' guides to the holy places, recounting stories and legends of Biblical and of later events and personages in connection with the shrines, and setting forth the religious merits to be gained there by visiting, praying, fasting, and giving alms.

The treatises are:

The Book of Arousing Souls to Visit Jerusalem's Holy Walls, or, in Arabic, the *Kitāb Bā'ith an-Nufūs ilā Ziyārat al-Quds al-Mahrūs*, and

The Book of Inciting Desire to Visit Abraham the Friend of Allah, etc., or, the *Kitāb Muthīr al-Gharām li-Ziyārat al-Khalīl, 'alaihi 's-salām!*

Both the basic texts of the small works represented are preserved in the Landberg Collection of Arabic Manuscripts at Yale University. This treasure was acquired by the University in 1900 through the generosity of Morris K. Jessup, from the Orientalia of Count Landberg which have gone to enrich a number of libraries in Europe and America.

Both texts are largely made up of extracts selected from such works as were considered suitable for the pious purpose of the compilers.

The author of *The Book of Arousing Souls*, a general and quite

typical book for the spiritual guidance of Moslem pilgrim-visitors in
Palestine, was Burhān ad-Dīn ibn al-Firkāh al-Fazāri. Ibn al-Firkāh
was born in 660 A. H./1262 A. D., in Damascus, the former capital of
the Islamic world (during the Omayyad era, 661-750 A. D.). He followed the scholarly way of his father, who had been author, teacher,
leader of the Shāfiʻite sect, and mufti of Syria. For a short time he was
preacher (khatīb) in the celebrated Omayyad Mosque of Damascus.
He died in 729/1329. The date of the composition of his work here
translated is not known. It was one of several by him.

Ibn al-Firkāh, like most Arab authors of former times, utilized the
works of his predecessors to a very great extent. But this does not
detract from his importance as a Moslem leader in letters and religion
in his time, especially in view of his literary influence, through his
judiciously selected extracts concerning a subject of great popular
interest, on many writers after him. The number of extant manuscripts
of *The Book of Arousing Souls*, surviving after six centuries and to be
found in both Oriental and in Occidental collections, proves the popularity and widespread influence of the little book. It was republished
by hand copying many times.

Popular interest led later copyists to add other material, including
familiar Jewish-Moslem legends of King Solomon (Suleimān) and of
Nebuchadnezzar (Bukht-un-nasar), and a section on the merits of the
once noted "border" city of Ascalon. The Yale copy appears to be
the earliest and best extant, having been made in 882 A. H./1477 A. D.
According to the judgment of the noted Dutch Arabist De Goeje, the
Leiden copy, used here for basic collation, is of the next century. The
Bibliothèque Nationale in Paris has a later manuscript in a beautiful
hand, with chapter titles of gold. There are other exempla in the
Preussische Staats-Bibliothek in Berlin, in the libraries of Istanbul
and of other Oriental cities, and in that of the British Museum. While
engaged in collating in the last named library, I discovered an additional copy lacking the title, which I was able to supply for the purpose
of recataloguing.

Copies of another work by Ibn al-Firkāh on the merits of Syria,
al-ʻIlām fī Fadāʼil ash-Shām, are to be found at Cambridge and in
Berlin.

The Yale manuscript is a separate volume bound in Oriental style with a flap edge cover. It has thirty-six sheets or seventy-two pages, and is 6¾ inches x 5 inches in size. The title, chapter headings, and practically all the chains of reference for traditions are written in red ink, although the copyist evidently once ran out of this embellishing material and used plain black ink for several pages. It is an unusually clear manuscript, written in a large and legible (although not elegant) hand. The Leiden text is more attractive calligraphically, but the Yale copy is freer from incorrect, popular forms which often, through the fault of less educated copyists, mar the classical Arabic of the original authors.

Our copyist made several slips, but in almost all cases corrected himself in the margin or, in a few instances, in the text itself. The little book has been remarkably preserved. The reader may see clearly where the reed pen was overloaded with ink, or where, in the formation of ligatures peculiar to the language, the pen became too dry and had to be raised from the paper to be dipped again. The general excellence of the text makes it a pity that this copy has found no mention in many important works of reference to Islamic literature and religion and was not edited and published until 1930-35.

The second treatise, *The Book of Inciting Desire*, a considerably longer work, was written in 1351 by Abu 'l-Fidā' of Hebron itself, the city with whose shrines the book is concerned. Abu 'l-Fidā, who died in 1429, was of a family which earlier lived in Tadmor or Palmyra, so that his full name carries the gentilic at-Tadmuri. He served, as had several of his family before him, as preacher of the Hebron mosque over the supposed tombs of the patriarchs.

The scope of the work by Abu 'l-Fidā' of Hebron is wider than that of the smaller book by Ibn al-Firkāh of Damascus. The former, because of its specific purpose as a pilgrim's handbook, excluded the legendary and historical material on the early ages of the world (*al-awā'il*) with which many Arab — and earlier Christian — writers were wont to begin. Abu 'l-Fidā', desiring to give a proper historical background to his work on Hebron and its shrines, starts with the familiar stories of "the beginnings" and of the early patriarch-prophets, especially Abraham and his family, because of their connections which gave incentive to his composition.[1]

---

[1] These accounts, which are usually derived from Biblical and from popular Jewish sources,

The focus of interest in *The Book of Inciting Desire*, however, is on the tombs of the patriarch-prophets in Hebron. Several accounts are given of actual penetrations by privileged visitors into the " Cave of Machpelah " itself (beneath the mosque), as well as of visions of the prophets resting in peaceful slumber upon their biers. These are of such importance, for their own interest and for the fact they were copied almost verbatim by many later authors, that Sir Guy Le Strange translated them (p. 320 ff.) in his *Palestine under the Moslems* (London, 1890—out of print and rare!) and in an article in *The Journal of the Royal Asiatic Society*, XIX (new series, 1887).[2]

It is most natural that a Moslem writer should include in a work on Hebron and its great patriarch Abraham stories of the building of the Ka'bah in Mecca. For, according to Moslem popular lore, Abraham and Ishmael—legendary progenitor of the north Arabs—built that primary shrine of Islam! Inclusion of the Ka'bah in the accounts is significant also in that it shows that Moslems regard Palestine as worthy to be ranked with the most holy places of their history and faith. It was necessary and natural also to give full place in such a work to the career of the beloved prophet Abraham, the first Moslem, whose faith Mohammed himself asserted he was only renewing. He and his prophetic family, it is said in effect, were the great and godly

are best known in the Mohammedan world through the work by ath-Tha'labi entitled *Stories of the Prophets* (*Qisas al-Anbiyā'*), which is often quoted here, and which I hope to translate and publish in English. Another work of similar nature and identical Arabic title, by al-Kisā'i, was published under the Latin title *Vita Prophetarum*, by Eisenberg (Brill, Leiden, 1922-23). It is therein indicated that a translation into German was at least intended. For this second reference I am indebted to my friend Dr. George S. Rentz, who loaned to me in Saudi Arabia in 1948 a copy presented to him by Dr. S. M. Zwemer in the summer of 1938 at Princeton.

The work by ath-Tha'labi, following the style of the two authors whose books are here translated, is cited generally below as *The Book of Brides*. This is a short, popularized form of the full title, *The Book of the Brides of the Assemblies on the Subject of Stories of the Prophets*, in Arabic: *Kitāb 'Arā'is al-Majālis fī Qisas al-Anbiyā'*. Brockelmann, in his *Geschichte der Arabischen Litteratur*, lists manuscript copies in Berlin, the Bodleian at Oxford, and the British Museum.

[2] Le Comte Riant gave in the *Archives de l'Orient Latin*, II (1884), a bibliography of more than twenty accounts of visits to the sepulchres beneath the Mosque of Abraham, including that of the then Prince of Wales in 1862. See also Dean Arthur P. Stanley, *Lectures on the History of the Jewish Church* (new edition, New York, Scribner's, 1892), I, 431 f. (Appendix II). See also Harry Emerson Fosdick, *A Pilgrimage to Palestine* (New York, Macmillan, 1933), pp. 105 f.

men of the history of the faith who came as pioneers to the land and made it sacred by their associations and memorials.

It is strange that the author made no use of the many well-known stories of the grant of Hebron and its territory by the Prophet to the Tamīmi clan, accounts of which are given in *The Book of Arousing Souls* and other works on Palestine. But since the latter just as strangely omits relations of visits to the actual tombs beneath the mosque, the two guides to the shrines of Palestine complement each other well.[3]

The Yale manuscript of *The Book of Inciting Desire* is one of 70 folios or 140 pages, in size $6\frac{3}{4}$ inches x $5\frac{1}{4}$ inches. It is well preserved, and is written in a good, clear *naskhi* hand.

These, then, the two most interesting and typical Moslem guide-books to the holy places of Palestine, are the works here translated. The first was edited and translated in 1930-31 as a dissertation for the Ph. D. degree at Yale which was conferred in 1932. Thus ended three years of study, the first in 1923-24 for the M. A. degree, under direction of Professor Charles Cutler Torrey, renowned student of Dr. and Mrs. George Foote Moore and Professor Theodor Noeldeke. Those years which had included an individual seminar in Dr. Torrey's home in New Haven terminated with a historic *dernière classe* on his retirement after over thirty years of teaching at Yale. Fifteen years and more of fruitful labor have since been added to his career.

It was while engaged in work upon the first text on Palestine in general, with the privilege of handling the original manuscript, that I found in the Yale Landberg Collection the companion volume on Hebron. I transcribed it and began editing it, with the aid of a photostatic copy of the Leiden text for collation, in 1931-32. Then, in 1933-34, on the way to the Near East for a year of study, particularly in Jerusalem at the Newman School and the American School of Oriental Research, there came the rare opportunity to collate my

---

[3] Several accounts of the purported grant occur in Maqrīzi's little treatise, the *Kitāb Dau' as-Sāri li-Ma'rifah Khabar Tamīm ad-Dāri* or *Light of the Night-Traveller for Information concerning Tamīm ad-Dāri*. My edition of this, based on the Yale Landberg text (which was annotated by the hand of Maqrīzi himself!), was finally published in *JPOS*, Nos. 3-4 (1941), after several years of delay due to civil war in Palestine, and with no opportunity for correction of many typographical errors. The subject is discussed also by F. Krenkow in "The Grant of Land by Muhammad to Tamīm ad-Dari," in *Islamica*, I (1924-25), 529.

copies of both texts with copies in the British Museum and the Bibliothèque Nationale. During a busy year of study in two schools, of visiting archaeological sites in Palestine and Trans-Jordan under the leadership of Professor William F. Albright, and of practising spoken Arabic with the family of Mr. Assaf Wehbe with whom I was residing (a family whose friendship many have known), the final texts were made. I possess the handwritten text of *The Book of Arousing Souls*, as it was kindly returned to me by the German Orphanage Press in Jerusalem, with the embellishment of printer's smudges on the sheets.

Both texts (the Arabic only) were later published in Jerusalem in *The Journal of the Palestine Oriental Society*, that of *The Book of Arousing Souls* in 1934-35 (Vol. XIV, No. 4, and Vol. XV, No. 1) and that of *The Book of Inciting Desire* in 1936-37 (Vol. XVI, No. 4, and Vol. XVII, No. 1). But such materials, so representative and typical, so rich for the history of popular religion in Palestine, could not be left accessible only to a few specialists. Therefore, in the midst of resumed college teaching and of continued work on Arabic texts on Palestine, far from research materials, I undertook a popular translation. Such a work should be of interest and value as long as Palestine and veneration for Palestine hold the unique place which they have always maintained in the world. I was enabled to complete the work while attending the three sessions of the Seminar in Arabic and Islamics at Princeton University, held under the auspices of the American Council of Learned Societies in the summers of 1935, 1938, and 1941. For this opportunity my thanks are gladly given to the Council and to the moving spirit of the seminars (and of much else in American Islamic studies), Professor Philip K. Hitti. At the last session I had the benefit of the generous aid of Mr. I. R. Khalidi of Jerusalem.

An attempt has been made to give an ancient flavor appropriate to the translation by the use of the older English style employed in the Authorized Version of the Bible. Following Biblical style, also, quotation marks have been used rarely — mainly in cases of direct quotation from the Koran. Indeed the involved method of citing authorities in giving traditions makes this almost necessary in order to avoid a confusing piling up of quotation. For the convenience and interest of the reader a running guide has been provided in the form of marginal headings. Almost all the universally used phrases of pious respect after the names of titles of Mohammed the Prophet, Jesus, Abraham, and other worthies have been omitted as repetitious and artificial in an English translation.

It is hoped that Muslim friends will understand and condone appearance in the title of " Mohammedan." More proper usage, such as " Muslim (or Islamic) Holy Land " would to occidentals still be unfamiliar. Effort has been made to present the correct forms in the notes and the glossary.

The religion of Islam in its sacred book the Koran (properly *al-Qur'ān*, " the reading " or " the proclamation ") , just as in its authoritative tenets and in its folk belief and practice, is naturally much in debt to official and popular Judaism and Christianity. This fact by no means reduces Islam to merely a Judeo-Christian sect or heresy, as has often been asserted. But the Koran itself retells many Biblical stories and accepts most of the Biblical worthies as prophets in the long succession before Mohammed. And the historic and popular faith has borrowed much from the Scriptures and from the two " peoples of (or having) Scripture," *ahl al-kitāb*. The Prophet Mohammed learned much, directly and indirectly, from Jewish and Christian informers and teachers. He adapted much (along with the misconceptions and anachronisms of his popular sources!) in his preaching and teaching.

New study of the subject, especially by Professor Julian Obermann of Yale, is making even clearer the relationships between popular Judaism in Arabia (before the Jews and the Christians were expelled) and the Biblical material in the Koran — especially that dealing with the Pentateuch or Torah. In an article on " Koran and Agada " (*The American Journal of Semitic Languages*, Vol. LVIII, No. 1 [January, 1941] Dr. Obermann says:

Through more than half of his life-span . . . he [Mohammed] was a diligent disciple in the institution in which nearly all the intellectual and spiritual life in the Near East has been fashioned for many centuries, the institution of oral tradition received by oral instruction (that is, the Biblical interpretations and teachings of the rabbis) . . . Here he, a son of pagan Arabia, acquired agadic learning that is truly imposing in its amount, its variety, and its soundness.

Mohammed the Prophet freely and repeatedly acknowledged his

indebtedness to the bearers and recipients and preservers of revelation before him. In two places (surah 2, verse 130, and surah 3, verse 78), as a notable example, the Koran says (Rodwell's translation):

Say ye: We believe in God, and that which hath been sent down to us, and that which hath been sent down to Abraham and Ishmael and Isaac and Jacob and the tribes; and that which hath been given to Moses and to Jesus, and that which was given to the prophets from their Lord. No difference do we make between any of them; and to God are we resigned (as Muslims).

It was only natural that such a sincere seeker as Mohammed, discontented with ancient tribal paganism and no doubt influenced by the spirit of seeking of the times, should be attracted by the readily available doctrines of the historic Scriptural religions, especially Judaism and Christianity. The earnest mystic seeker had abundant opportunity to learn through Jewish and Christian communities among the Arabs and perhaps through contacts also on caravan journeys into Byzantine Southern Syria. It was natural too that that unsophisticated genius should lay hold upon, and should treasure and develop in his own growing system, popular religious lore (which is an inevitable departure and a universal accompaniment of all religion), such lore as his Jewish and Christian neighbors willingly contributed to his eager ears. This Biblical lore, in its midrashic Jewish form [4] and in the dress given it also, for example, in Christian apocryphal writings, had become widely current in the Arabian peninsula. As mentioned above, there were Christian and Jewish communities there. In addition there had recently been Jewish rule in the Yemen. And there was lively contact between the Arabs of the Hejaz and both Abyssinia and Syria.

It is only from realization of this familiarity with Biblical matters that the elliptical nature of many Koranic references to Biblical material can be understood. For although there are many instances in the Koran of Biblical stories skilfully retold with dramatic detail because of their very interest, there are also a great many instances of brief and cryptic allusion, especially in connection with the divine mission of earlier prophets to their unbelieving generation. Each such allusion

---

[4] On similarities between the popular Islamic and Jewish idealization of Biblical personalities, see note to *The Book of Arousing Souls* (p. 140 below), where Ginzberg's excellent work, *The Legends of the Jews*, which is both convenient and fertile for such comparisons, is cited.

was a sufficient word to the wise — a reference to sacred story with which the speaker knew his hearers in Mecca or in Medina to be adequately if not perfectly familiar.

Adaptation of Jewish and Christian material naturally thereafter continued in the age of written commentaries upon the Koran. Multitudes of such Biblical references had to be accounted for and explained in writing, for the sake of complete clarification of the text and for the guidance of the studious faithful in all succeeding ages.

In his *Religion of the Crescent* (London, 1895, p. 190), the Reverend St. Clair-Tisdall, in a typically polemic approach (which it is to be hoped may soon lack followers among liberal Islamic and Christian and Jewish students of religion!), points out the following as sources of Islamic teaching, in addition to Mohammed's "own character and pronounced personality": (1) Pre-Islamic beliefs among the Arabs; (2) Talmudic Judaism; (3) heretical Christianity and apocryphal Christian traditions, and (4) Zoroastrian ideas emanating from Persia.

Because of his propagandistic purposes St. Clair-Tisdall devotes considerable space to pointing up the "blunders of Mohammed" by way of anachronisms and confusion of persons and places in sacred story. Such "blunders," however, were usually due not to the ignorance of the new prophet of the Arabs but to the nature and the source of his instruction. (See the quotation from Professor Obermann, below p. xx f.) Biblical students will recall that there are many instances of uncorrelated tradition and of details derived from popular lore or other noncanonical sources in the Bible. For example, according to Judges 1. 8, the tribe of Judah captured Jerusalem long before the time of the conquerors David and Joab. Again, Professor Torrey has several times pointed out (most recently in his *Apocryphal Literature* [New Haven, 1945], pp. 51, 53, 88) that in Daniel and Ezra and several of the Old Testament Apocrypha an unhistorical doctrine of the succession of Persian kings is maintained. Familiar in the New Testament is the popular notion that Abraham purchased the burial cave not from Ephron the Hittite in Mamre-Hebron but from Hamor in the northern shrine city of Shechem. (See Acts 7. 16, and compare Genesis 23 and 25. 8-10 with Genesis 33. 18-20 and Genesis 34.) Satan falling "as lightning from heaven" (Luke 10. 18), a saying reported from Jesus himself, is manifestly from Jewish popular lore. And Christ

preaching "to the spirits in prison" (I Peter 3. 19) is likewise from
some popular source in early Christianity.

The Koran, like the Old Testament and the New Testament, is a
book of religion, not of factual history. And everlasting insistence upon
literal accuracy would have been a stultifying criterion in any of the
three. The legitimate criterion for the judgment of a religion and of a
book of religion, on the other hand, is the use of ideas, including their
appropriation from whatever source, and the universalizing of them.

There is an approach, without apologetic or controversy, for fruitful
consideration of the development of Islam in the Koran, in the community and state, and in the vast literature of the religion. That approach has again been followed up by Professor Obermann (who is
continuing it elsewhere) in his essay on "Islamic Origins, A Study in
Backgrounds and Foundations" (in *The Arab Heritage*, edited by
Dr. Nabih A. Faris [Princeton, 1944], pp. 58-120) . From this important
study I quote the following, which is as significant as it is appropriate
(p. 94) :

. . . Western scholars have been led to the recognition that Muhammad
cannot possibly have had direct, firsthand acquaintance with Scripture—
notwithstanding his constant appeal to matters and persons of biblical history and the bona fide implications that his familiarity with things biblical
was of the most intimate kind. "Not only the Hebrew original but any
sort of a translation would surely have precluded the gross discrepancies,
inaccuracies and delusions he exhibits, almost invariably, when his revelation involves data from the Old Testament or, for that matter, from the
New Testament." The decisive thing, however, is that in a great many
instances where a biblical element appears misrepresented or distorted in
the revelation of Muhammad, the very same misrepresentation and dis-
tortion can be shown to recur in postbiblical sources as homiletical or
expository embellishments characteristic of the treatment of Scripture
both in the Jewish Synagogue and in the Christian Church. Indeed, his
"recounting" of biblical materials, while entirely out of keeping with their
corresponding Scriptural prototypes, agrees with the exposition of the same
materials in noncanonical literature so often and so closely that his knowledge of this literature, especially of rabbinical Agada, would seem to be
astonishingly wide, solid and versatile. Yet, it is altogether out of the question that Muhammad had direct access to the written works of the Agada
or any other branch of postbiblical literature, either rabbinical or patristic . . .

The situation becomes clear once we recognize that Muhammad had acquired his entire store of knowledge about Scripture, and about Judaism and Christianity in general, through oral channels and personal observation during a long period of association with the People of the Book . . .

Islam, therefore, began and has continued as the third of three "Biblical" religions, the first being Judaism, the second Christianity, which is of course built upon Judaism, and the third Islam, which is based upon both its predecessors. It is true that the Prophet, when chided with errors and confusion in his accounts of Biblical matters drawn from such popular sources, asserted that the Jews and the Christians had falsified their books of revelation and "changed words from their places" (an apologetic which is still often used by Moslems). But the relationship between his religion and theirs is always indirectly or directly acknowledged, and the Prophet continued to distinguish Jews and Christians from the unbelieving world by the honorable designation of "people of the book" or people possessing a divine revelation in holy Scriptures like the revelation vouchsafed to him. This was to set them apart *with* the Moslems, his own people.

The religious genius of Mohammed, his truly prophetic career, his personality which through difficulty and danger won a following of men ready to die for him and for the faith which he brought to them, made Islam a genuine religion in its own right. And it is one which has continued as a living force in the lives of millions in many lands. Yet the borrowings from Judaism and Christianity continued beyond the initial sources for the Koran. Converts from Judaism like Wahb ibn Munabbih and Ka'b al-Ahbār (who are cited often in the two books here presented) gave and sometimes manufactured Biblical information regarding references in the new holy book, or concerning Palestine and the holy places after Islam and the Arabs had come there. Such sources from Judaism and from Christianity are much used by Koran commentators, traditionists, historians, and geographers —of all of whom Islam has a great company.

It was thus natural that Islam, as a Biblical religion, should take over the holy places in the Biblical land and make them its own shrines—just as Judaism and Christianity had in succession taken over the sacred places of history and tradition. In fact, as most of the Palestinian Moslems were (and still are) of the continuing population of the land (see below, p. xxix), veneration for the shrines of the country persisted with them as a part of their very life.

Moslem reverence for Palestine, thus built upon a Biblical foundation, was deepened by the Jeroboam-like policies of the Omayyad caliph 'Abd al-Malik (685-705). At a time of serious political division in the Islamic world he feared the Meccan pilgrimage as a too ready means of propaganda on the part of 'Abdullah ibn az-Zubeir, a rival caliph in the Arabian holy land of the Hejaz. 'Abd al-Malik, therefore, wishing to keep his people from the politically influenced pilgrimage and to retain in his own undisputed realm the great amount of pilgrims' gold, built the beautiful structure known as the Dome of the Rock (and incorrectly called the Mosque of Omar) on the site of the ancient Hebrew-Jewish temples, and he rebuilt and embellished the Aqsa Mosque, also in the Temple enclosure, on the ruins of a Byzantine Christian church. Thus Ya'qūbi, a noted geographer-historian of the ninth century, says: "The people took the custom of circumambulating the Rock even as they had performed the circuit of the Ka'bah, and the custom continued all the days of the dynasty of the Omayyads." (See pp. 115 f., Le Strange, *Palestine under the Moslems*, cited above, p. xiv.) The great pilgrimage to Mecca and Medina of course resumed its supreme importance. But many of the faithful continued to visit Palestine on a lesser pilgrimage.

Affection of Moslems for Palestine was heightened also by its temporary loss to the Crusaders, and by the necessity of the Moslem struggle against the invaders to redeem it—which constituted or included counter-crusade and propaganda. Indeed, the Moslem reaction to the Crusades was a potent factor in the development of the Islamic literature on the "merits" of Jerusalem and Palestine. This is made evident by Professor A. S. Atiyah, Egyptian historian, in *The Crusade in the Later Middle Ages* (London, Methuen, 1938). He (pp. 468 f.) says: "The abundance of such literature is a notable feature of the fourteenth century"—which is the era of both of our writers.[5]

[5] Dr. Atiyah cites (p. 469) and quotes from another of the works of Ibn al-Firkāh, author of our *Book of Arousing Souls*. In his excellent bibliography he also includes the work of Abu 'l-Fidā' of Hebron which is translated here. His omission of reference, however, to the *Book of Arousing Souls* itself shows how fitting it is to rescue the work from oblivion. It was a pleasure, so much as a reception introduction allowed, to discuss this material with Dr. Atiyah at Cairo in 1946.

Atiyah continues with the following certainly justifiable statement:

" The history of this interesting and important movement, rich in Arabic documentary evidence, is worthy of a special study covering the period from the great Saladin to Muhammad the Conqueror [of Turkey]. Much has been written on the crusade, yet little is to be found on the 'counter-crusade' save isolated and disconnected references . . ." [6]

Thus on the basis of religious history, continuing popular custom, and political and patriotic motivation, there arose in Islam universal veneration for Palestine and pilgrimages or devotional visits to its holy places.

In his essay, " Crusade and Jihad," in *The Arab Heritage* (pp. 158-198; cited above, p. xx), Dr. John L. La Monte has shown again that the fundamental motivation of both East and West in the Crusades was economic and political, not religious. However, the religious factor in the minds of the masses was, as he acknowledges, considerable. It is after all doubtful that the Crusades would have been possible, and certainly they could not have been so long continued or renewed, had not the religious urge been present. And as to the Moslem reaction, religion is not so artificial a force as to have been absent from the patriotic fervor which inspired defense of homelands.

A document of interest and significance in this connection is furnished by the words and the fervent spirit of a historic sermon, preached at the direction of Salāh ad-Dīn himself by the celebrated judge and litterateur Muhyī ad-Dīn ibn az-Zaki of Damascus, within the newly redeemed area of the Temple in Jerusalem itself, in 1187, in thankful celebration, with the victorious sultan and " all the chief men of the empire" in attendance. The revealing address may be read in De Slane's translation of the *Biographical Dictionary* (cited below in

[6] Another Arabic document of the counter-crusade and of Moslem veneration of Palestine is the second *Muthīr*, the *Muthīr al-Gharām ilā Ziyārat al-Quds wa-'sh-Shām* (" Inciter of Desire to visit Jerusalem [or Palestine] and Syria "), written in 1350 by Jamāl ad-Dīn Ahmad al-Maqdisi (of Jerusalem). I have had a microfilm copy of the excellent Princeton Garrett Collection text for some years, and obtained from Paris at the beginning of the war additional copies for collation. But going beyond making a preliminary text, several years ago, has been prevented by military and government service abroad and by lack of research facilities even when there has been a little leisure. Professor Jibrail Jabbour of the American University of Beirut was working upon similar materials during a year of study in 1946-47 at Princeton on an exchange fellowship provided by the United States Government.

note 9 to *The Book of Arousing Souls*) by Ibn Khallikān (whose account is in II, pp. 633-642).

Islamic pilgrimages to such places as the Temple area and the mosque of the tombs of the patriarch-prophets in Hebron, and such ceremonies as those of the Nabī Mūsā festival with its annual pageantry and excited religious and patriotic emotions, are not, therefore, mere adaptations from the great Mecca-Medina hajj, for this itself came out of the *Pilgerfahrt* of Semitic and general religious history. And such visitations in Palestine have as their particular and direct basis the familiar practices of the Old and New Testament eras, and of continuing popular Judaism and Christianity. Reference need only be made, for the Bible, to the law of appearing before God at the great festivals (Deuteronomy 16; Exodus 23. 14, and 34. 22-23; Leviticus 23; Numbers 28-29); to the familiar story of Hannah's pilgrimage and the devotion of young Samuel (I Samuel 1-3); pilgrimage hymns in the Book of Psalms (e. g., Psalms 65, 84, 122); the presentation of Jesus in the Temple (Luke 2. 22 f.), and the Passover at his twelfth year; Paul's pilgrimage to Jerusalem after a vow made upon his missionary journeys (Acts 21. 6 and sequel). In addition, the custom of pilgrimage by Jews of the diaspora is well known. After the second war against Rome (132-135 A.D.) the Jews were for a time excluded from the Holy City, which had been rebuilt upon its ruins as the Roman city of Aelia Capitolina. But after Constantine they resumed their visits and pilgrimages of worship and mourning, which have been continued ever since.[7]

The historically immediate precedents for Moslem visitation of the holy places in Palestine include also early Christian pilgrimages from lands afar, especially during the era of the Byzantines, from whom the Moslems acquired Palestine and much else in the Near East in 634-636. The throngs of Christian pilgrims made it necessary as well as desirous for the Christian temporal and spiritual authorities to build shrines, churches, and hostels throughout Palestine. The enormous building activity, many famous monuments of which have survived

[7] The late Dr. Cyrus Adler prepared for the Special Commission of the League of Nations, appointed to study Jewish-Arab clashes over the " Wailing Wall," or the " Wall of al-Burāq," after the uprisings of 1929, a useful document entitled *Memorandum on the Western Wall*. The chapter or section, " The Ruins Always Holy to the Jews," pp. 14 f., is especially apropos. Dr. Adler kindly supplied me with a copy, but the volume was privately printed and so far as I know was never made available to the general public.

numerous wars and destructive earthquakes, was associated especially
with Constantine and his mother Helena in the fourth century, the
Empress Eudocia (wife of Theodosius II) in the fifth, and the Emperor
Justinian I in the sixth. Thus many of the holy places of Jewish and
Christian history, and a number of piously manufactured ones, were
rediscovered and glorified and the pilgrimage became an established
feature of Christianity.

It was no less the case with the Christians of the West (e. g., the
"Bordeaux Pilgrim" of 333 A. D.) —that is, Italy, Gaul, and other lands
which eventually became the domain of the Roman Catholic Church,
as distinguished from Eastern Roman or Byzantine Christendom around
the Eastern Mediterranean. Paula and the two Melanias lived in Palestine, as did Helena and Eudocia, and devoted their fortunes and efforts
to building churches and shrines. Saint Jerome (as his very name
Hieronymus, "the man of Jerusalem," denotes) passed many years in
devoted work on the Latin Scriptures at Bethlehem in the vicinity of
the Holy City.

It may be said with justice that the pilgrimage custom, although it
became a factor in the Crusades, helped measurably in the civilizing
of the Western Christian world and in holding all Christendom more
or less together for several centuries. Even when the unity was broken
by the definite and final cleavage between Eastern and Western Christianity in 1054, the pilgrimages, with their mutual influences on people
of differing lands and faiths and with the inevitable broadening of
mind of the devoted travellers, contributed hardly less beneficial results
than the Crusades themselves—those military expeditions which often
involved lengthy residence by Western Christians in Moslem or Greek
lands.[8]

The literature of pilgrimages to Palestine and of veneration for the
holy places there is vast in both Western and Greek Orthodox Chris-

---

[8] In Henry L. Savage's essay, "Fourteenth Century Jerusalem and Cairo through Western
Eyes," pp. 199-220, in *The Arab Heritage* (cited above, p. xx), compare the noble and devout
pilgrim Ogier, Baron d'Anglure. The author declares (p. 219) that his contacts in the Orient,
with Moslems as well as with Christians of other divisions of the church than the Roman
Catholic, "opened his eyes, enlarged his tolerance, and broadened his charity. . . . Thus
much had the East done to one man of unimaginative mind and quite conventional habits.
If we multiply many, many times what the East had changed in Ogier, we shall be able to
imagine, even though vaguely, what its effect upon the West had been and was continuing
to be . . ."

tianity and in Islam. For the Christian material typical sources are readily available in the following:

Thomas Wright, *Early Travels in Palestine* . . . (London, 1848), containing the narratives of eight travellers; E. Carmoly (tr.), *Itinéraires de la Terre Sainte*, of the thirteenth to the seventeenth centuries (Brussels, 1847); the various volumes of the Palestine Pilgrim's Texts Society (London, 1896, etc.), which include also some of the Moslem pilgrim handbooks, e. g., that of the celebrated poet-geographer Nāsir-i-Khusraw the Persian, eleventh century (translated by Le Strange in Vol. IV of the series, 1886); Titus Tobler and Augustus Molinier (editors), *Itinera Hierosolymitana et Descriptiones Terrae Sanctae* (Geneva, 1879, published by La Société de l'Orient Latin); and Michaud's *History of the Crusades*.

For Moslem material the sources are admirably brought together by Sir Guy Le Strange in his *Palestine under the Moslems* (cited above, p. xiv), with translations of excerpts from numerous writers. There should be mentioned also, for those who read Arabic, the *Biblioteca Geographorum Arabicorum*, edited by De Goeje (Leiden, 1870, etc.), and the standard commentators, historians, and traditionists of Islam.

It is my belief, however, that in none of the very numerous Moslem works on Palestine is there found more of interest in and of clear insight into the Moslem veneration for the land of the Bible and the prophets than in the two presented here for the first time in English. It is indeed a pity that two such typical works have not been better known by students of the land and of Islam. Le Strange, as noted above, made some use of the *Muthīr* on Hebron, but he overloked or had no room for *The Book of Arousing Souls* on Jerusalem and Palestine in general. Together they give a nearly complete and quite satisfying picture.

Such books are now replaced by shorter tracts (in addition to brochure guides in English) which are available to visitors to al-*Haram ash-Sharīf*, the Temple area in Jerusalem, like the following: *Guide for the Visitor and Director for the Rites and Visits to the Sacred Places of Jerusalem and Hebron* (al-*Murshid li-'z-Zā'ir wa-'d-Dalīl fī Manāsik wa-Ziyārat Amākin al-Quds wa-'l-Khalīl*) by al-Hājj Mustafā al-Ansāri; and (a smaller one) *The Rites in Holy Jerusalem* (*Manāsik al-Quds ash-Sharīf*) by Yūsuf Diā' ad-Dīn ad-Danaf al-Ansāri.[9]

[9] Cited by Dr. Tewfik Canaan, noted Jerusalemite Christian physician and student of Pales-

The Arabic term for such works is *kitāb faḍā'il* (plural, *kutub faḍā'il*), books of "merits" or "excellencies," i. e., they are books which inform the pilgrim of the religious merits possessed by the land and by its shrines, and guide him in his visitation and worship by indicating the specific merits he may gain with Allah by performing certain acts of prayer, almsgiving, fasting, etc., in various spots.

Thus the Moslem pilgrims' guides follow very closely the Christian models of earlier times and of their own era. Wright (*Early Travels in Palestine*, p. viii) says: "Every mile on the road was believed to count in heaven for so much towards the redemption of past crimes and offences, however great, of the traveller." Just as the Christian pilgrim hoped for pardon, absolution, indulgence, Heaven, as reward for his visit and devotion, so also the Moslem pilgrim hoped for forgiveness, merit with Allah, answer to his prayer for whatever need, and eventual entrance into Paradise. The popular Jewish attitude of devout pilgrimage was of course similar.

The likeness of the religious points of view may be clearly seen by reference to such Christian pilgrim accounts as the anonymous *Guide-Book to Palestine*, written in 1350, just about the time of the two Moslem devotional works here given. This, as will be clear after comparison with the present material, has a corresponding devotional tone, gives directions for visitation and worship, and points out the indulgences to be gained as reward.[10] The story of the pilgrimage of Saint Paula in the last quarter of the fourth century is a pious account which, had it been that of a Moslem visitor, would undoubtedly have become popular in Islam. The story of the pilgrimage of Saint Antonius, in the early part of the seventh century, on the eve of the Moslem conquest, contains marvels fully on a par with those recited by the writers of Islam.

In answer to the natural question whether the pilgrims, Christian, Moslem, and Jewish, sincerely believed all they read and were told of

---

tinian folkways, in his *Mohammedan Saints and Sanctuaries in Palestine* (London, Luzac & Co., 1927) (Luzac's Oriental Series, V; reprinted from *The Journal of the Palestine Oriental Society*).

[10] One of the many anonymous Christian guide-books, this was published in Vol. VII of the Palestine Pilgrim's Texts, 1894, in a translation by J. H. Bernard, from a Latin manuscript in the library of Trinity College, Dublin, based partly on an account of the Holy Land by Philippus Brusserius Saronensis.

the marvels and merits of the holy places, it must be conceded that, being people of their time and environment and authoritative religious training, they themselves would have been greater marvels had they not believed. It is of such idealizing stuff, otherwise known as " superstition," that popular religion has largely been made through all centuries and in all civilizations.

It is of course well known that among both Christians and Moslems the marvels did not fail to increase with time, and changes in location of shrines were wont to occur (in spite of both history and geography), if for no other reason than destruction of the original structure or even the better convenience of the pilgrims. There was also a natural tendency to accumulate relics, and even "sites," within the bounds or the neighborhood of important holy places. Examples are the conglomerations within the rambling structure of the Church of the Holy Sepulchre (properly the Anastasis, or Church of the Resurrection), or within the sacred enclosure of the Temple. In his introduction to the account of the *Bordeaux Pilgrim* in the Palestine Pilgrim's Texts, Stewart points out that the pilgrims of times later than those of that noted visitor in 333 A.D. were no longer satisfied with quiet activity of prayer and devotion, and of course with the realization that they were in the sacred atmosphere of the Bible where such and such events of holy history had taken place. He says: " . . . The necessary aids to faith were provided in gradually increasing numbers, until, in the sixth century, we find not only the true cross, but the crown of thorns, the reed, the sponge, the lance, the cup used at the Last Supper, the stone that was rolled away from the sepulchre, and other relics of minor importance, such as the 'charger' in which John the Baptist's head was carried."

The Bordeaux Pilgrim made (unique) mention in his time of a crypt in Jerusalem in which Solomon used to torment devils—a note which is characteristic also of later Moslem writers on that glorious king of men, of animals, and of nature, Suleimān son of David! Parallel with these in Moslem accounts are the actual ring in the Western wall of the Temple area by which Mohammed and Gabriel are supposed to have tied up their magical mount al-Burāq (which transported them from Mecca to Jerusalem and back in one night), some hairs from the Prophet's beard, and several tracks made by him —which at least formerly were shown in Jerusalem.

Genuine devotional pilgrimage, however, is not dependent upon such marvels and relics. Christian leaders in earlier Palestine endeavored, against the lively credulity of flooding pilgrims, to lessen the marvellous and to exalt the spiritual. Moslem attendants at the Dome of the Rock and at other shrines today significantly allude to the pious legends only to disclaim crassly literal belief in them. More intelligent veneration remains and deepens. This is indicated by the burial within the Temple area in Jerusalem, in 1931, of two noted Moslems, Muhammad 'Ali of India and the former King Husein of the Hejaz.

Jewish veneration for Palestine is attested by the long-continued custom of burying pious folk there, the use of a little soil from Eretz Israel for burial with the dead in other lands, the ceremony of lamentation at the Wailing Wall, the intercessory petitions to Abraham which are stuck into a niche in the wall of the Mosque of Abraham in Hebron, and the whole aura of idealism surrounding the venture of modern Zionism.

Christian affection for the land of Palestine is shown by the continued popularity of pilgrimages there (and more secularized tours, which in rare times of security are an important source of income for government and people), and by the maintenance of innumerable pious and philanthropic foundations — churches, monasteries, shrines, orphanages, schools, hospitals, etc. Such institutions are paralleled by many Moslem *awqāf* (singular, *waqf*) or pious foundations for various good purposes, as well as by laudable institutions supported by the Jews.

Palestine will remain what it has been for these thirteen centuries— a holy land of three great world religions, despite the present resumption of strife over its political control. Because the view is often held and expressed by sincere people that the "Arabs are mere interlopers in Palestine" and ought to give way to the "return" of the rightful and historic Jewish "owners" of the land of the Bible, a further word may be said regarding the ethnology of the land. The simple fact is that the majority of the "Arab" people of Palestine are not descendants of those "new arrivals" who intruded with the Islamic-Arab conquest in the seventh century. The majority of native Palestinians, both Christian and Moslem Arabs, are of a mixed race whose connection with the land reaches back into very early history. There is a natural tendency for history to be simplified by the concept that all the Moslems of the conquered lands came in, and assumed control, from the outside; and it is an understandable fancy for most of the Moslem population to believe that their ancestors were of the conquering race. Of course considerable numbers of real Arabs from Arabia did settle in the new possessions, and there are in the voluminous general and local histories of history-minded Islamic peoples records of such settlement. But the conquerors and the settlers who followed in the wake of military success and political control were only a small minority compared to the masses of the continuing, historic population. The designation of "Arab" was gradually accepted by the majority along with the new religion, and the Arabic language was adopted by all. The change in religion was in most cases voluntary, for the sake of preferment and advantage, to escape the higher taxes on non-Moslems, and in a natural process of following the predominant environmental influence and practice. The simplicity and the virility of the new faith, in contrast with the often violent theological controversies over complex philosophical-religious doctrines of Christianity, also had their influence. Therefore the "Arabs" of Palestine are the historic people of the land, and the country has always been theirs; but Palestine still is, and will remain, the holy land of *three* religions. Each of the three groups in Palestine needs what the others have to contribute to the common welfare. A common and mutual welfare can be achieved—if no group will seek undue aggrandizement; but for such a goal all of the people of Palestine need the informed sympathy and understanding of the hundreds of millions of the three great world religions to which the land is sacred.

This volume is sent forth, therefore, with a sincere echo of the plea of the Psalmist, "Pray for the Peace of Jerusalem!"

I wish to thank the Committee of the Faculty on the Yale Oriental Series who have maintained their interest and helped me to maintain my hope for the publication of this volume, which was accepted for the Series in 1942. I express my gratitude also to the American Council of Learned Societies for a considerable grant in aid, which helped to make publication possible, to the donors of the Kohut Fellowship at Yale for enabling me to spend two years in study, to Professor Obermann for writing the Foreword, and to Mr. Vincent Quinn for the map.

Dhahran, Saudi Arabia,
    December, 1948.

CHARLES D. MATTHEWS.

Part I

THE BOOK OF AROUSING SOULS

By the Sheikh and Imām and Mufti of the Muslims, Burhān ad-Dīn Ibn al-Firkāh al-Fazāri, of Damascus

PREFACE

In the name of Allah the Merciful, the Beneficent! [1] O Lord, prosper and perfect with good, Thou Gracious One!

Praise be to Allah, Lord of the two worlds! And I witness that there is no god but Allah, alone, having no partner; and I witness that Mohammed is His servant and apostle! May Allah bless him, and his family, and his wives, and his seed altogether; and grant them lasting peace forever until the Day of Judgment; and may Allah accept his Companions, and his Helpers, and his Followers! The Author's Invocation

As for what follows: This is a compendium on the merits of Jerusalem and of the tomb of the Friend of God, Abraham (in Hebron). The greater part is from the book *al-Mustaqsa*,[2] by the hāfiz Behā' ud-Din ibn 'Asākir. Somewhat of it is from the book (*Fadā'il al-Quds wa-'sh-Shām*) of the sheikh Abu 'l-Ma'āli al-Mushrif ibn al-Murajja of Jerusalem. What I have quoted from the book of Abu 'l-Ma'āli is made apparent; and the remainder is from *al-Mustaqsa*. I have elided the isnāds [3] in so far as convenience required. His Subject and His Sources

This compendium, if Allah so will, may be to the profit of these: whoever closely regards and approves it, and follows its excellent instructions; he from whom the veils of obstinacy have been removed, and to whom the ways of the pious of Allah's servants have been revealed; he who conforms to the true doctrine, has a soul, lends an ear, and bears witness. O Allah! I beg that it may not disappoint him who hopes from it profitable, beneficial, and excellent results! His Intended Audience

I have arranged the matter in thirteen chapters.

Chapter first, On the beginning of the building of the Mosque al-Aqsa.[4]

1

Chapter second, On the merit of setting out to it, and the merit of going there and lighting its lamps; and how one should enter Jerusalem, and how one should enter its mosque; and the merit of going to Bethlehem and praying there.

Chapter third, On the merit of prayer in Jerusalem, and of pilgrimage and prayer in the Mosque of Medina and the Mosque al-Aqsa in the same year.

Chapter fourth, On the merit of putting on the *ihrām* from Jerusalem, and the merit of giving the call to prayer there.

Chapter fifth, On the merit of giving alms there, and fasting.

Chapter sixth, On the merit of the Blessed Rock, and how it is from Paradise.

Chapter seventh, On the merit of the Slab of Black Marble; and how one should enter the Rock.

Chapter eighth, On the Dome of the Ascension, the Dome of the Prophet, the Gate of Mercy, the Mihrāb of Zechariah, the Rocks which are to the rear of the Mosque, the Gate of the Shekinah,[5] the Gate of Forgiveness, the Mihrāb of 'Omar, the other mihrābs, the Gate of the Prophet, the Mount of Olives, the Dome of the Chain, and the Gate of Repentance.

Chapter ninth, On the water of Jerusalem, and the Spring of Siloam, and the Pool of the Leaf.

Chapter tenth, On the Plain as-Sāhirah; and the merit of dying in Jerusalem.

Chapter eleventh, On whether one should believe, or not, that a circuit of these places should be performed.

Chapter twelfth, In summary on the merits of Jerusalem (and all Palestine).

Chapter thirteenth, On the merits of the Tomb of Abraham al-Khalīl,[6] and those matters and precincts connected with it.

The Table
of Contents

CHAPTER FIRST

On the Beginning of the Building of the Mosque al-Aqsa

Al-Bukhāri relates in his *Sahīh*,[7] on authority of Abu Dharr, the following: I said, O Apostle of Allah, which mosque was stationed in the earth first? He said, The Sacred Mosque of Mecca. I said, Then which one? He said, The Mosque al-Aqsa (in Jerusalem). I said, How much time intervened? He said, Forty years. Then he said, Wherever the time of prayer overtakes you, then pray; for truly there is merit in it. I quote this from al-Bukhāri.

The hāfiz Behā' ud-Din (Ibn 'Asākir) relates, with his authorities, in his book, *al-Mustaqsa*, from Abu Dharr: I said, O Apostle of Allah, which mosque was stationed in the earth first? He said, The Sacred Mosque. I said, Then which one? He said, The Mosque al-Aqsa. I said, How much time intervened? He said, Forty years. And al-Farrā' adds: Then he said, Wherever prayer time overtakes you, then pray; and it is as a mosque.[8]

This is a sound tradition. The two *Sahīhs* include it in their selections, and an-Nasā'i and al-Qazwīni have it.[9] I quote this from the chapter, Which Mosque Was Founded First, from his (Ibn 'Asākir's) selections on the merits of Jerusalem.

He afterward relates a tradition in the chapter, On the Building of the Temple on an Old Foundation, saying on authority of Ka'b al-Ahbār:[10] Solomon built the Temple on an ancient foundation, just as Abraham al-Khalīl built the Ka'bah (in Mecca) on an ancient foundation. And as to the older foundation which the Temple had, Shem the son of Noah laid it; then David and his son Solomon built the Temple upon that foundation.[11]

I say: It has been mentioned that Shem must needs have been the one who founded it, on a previous structure, according to the sound tradition above. For al-Azraqi relates on authority of Mujāhid the following: Allah created the place of this House, i. e., the Ka'bah, the Sacred House, a thousand years before He created anything of the world; and its pillars go down to the seventh nether world. Then he relates on authority of 'Ali ibn al-Husein: Verily, the Sacred House is of the construction of angels. Then, on authority of Ibn 'Abbās: Verily, Adam was the first to found the House; and he prayed in it and performed the circuit. Then, lo! the location of the House disappeared by reason of the Flood, until Allah sent Abraham and Ishmael, and they raised up the pillars; and then the matter stood thus. And there were between its founding and that of the Mosque al-Aqsa forty years.

So the commencement of the Mosque al-Aqsa was before Shem. And it is said in the *Kitāb al-Mughni fī Gharīb al-Muhadhdhab* [12] that there were between Adam and Noah a thousand and two hundred years. And the imām al-Khattābi notes in his book, *al-I'lām*, that some of the saints of Allah built the Mosque al-Aqsa before David and Solomon; then David and Solomon rebuilt it and made it larger and wider — and for this reason its construction is attributed to them. And Allah knows best!

David and Solomon only Rebuilders of the Temple

CHAPTER SECOND

On Setting Out for Jerusalem; and the Merit of Going There and Light-ing Its Lamps; and How One Should Enter the City of Jerusalem; and How One Should Enter Its Mosque; and the Merit of Going to Bethlehem and Praying There

On authority of Abu Sa'īd al-Khudri it is related: The Apostle of Allah said, Set out only for three mosques, the mosque of Medina, the mosque of Abraham, and the mosque of Jerusalem. Ibn 'Asākir says that al-Bukhāri and Muslim relate this. Then he mentions in another citation: The Sacred Mosque (in Mecca), and the Mosque al-Aqsa, and my mosque (in Medina).

The Three Paramount Mosques

And in a citation on authority of Abu Hureirah from the Prophet, it is said: Set out for three mosques, the Sacred Mosque, the Mosque of the Prophet, and the Mosque al-Aqsa. And in another tradition: The Prophet said: Ye shall ride your mounts only to three mosques— and mentions them. In another tradition: Ye shall only ride your beasts to three mosques—and mentions them.

In a tradition on authority of Ibn 'Abbās it is related: The Prophet said, Ye shall set out only for three mosques, the Sacred Mosque, and the mosque of Medina, and the Mosque al-Aqsa. And a prayer in the Sacred Mosque is worth a hundred thousand prayers, and a prayer in my mosque is worth a thousand prayers, and a prayer in the Mosque al-Aqsa is worth ten thousand prayers.

The Value of Prayer in Them

And a tradition from the Prophet says: Ye shall set out only for four mosques, the Sacred Mosque, and this mosque (in Medina), and the Mosque al-Aqsa, and the mosque of al-Janad.[13]

I quote all this from the chapter, Setting Out.

It is related of Dhu 'l-Asābi' that he said: O Apostle of Allah, if we are sorely tried when we are left after thou art gone, where dost thou command us to go? He said, Incumbent upon you is Jerusalem; and perhaps Allah will give food for those who will go there and return. *A Portent of the Conquest of Jerusalem* Abu Ayyūb says he meant the mosque of Jerusalem. He quotes this in the last part of (the chapter), Portent of the Chosen One (Mohammed) on the Conquest of Jerusalem.

A tradition is given on authority of Meimūnah, a freed-woman (and one of the wives) of the Apostle of Allah, saying: I said, O Apostle of Allah, give us a precept as to Jerusalem! He said, Go there and pray there. I said, But how is that possible? For the Greeks at that time were there. He said, If ye cannot, then send some oil to light its lamps. *Oil for the Lamps of Jerusalem* Abu Da'ūd and al-Qazwīni quote this. I take it from the chapter, The First Merit of Prayer in Jerusalem.

On authority of Anas ibn Mālik [14] it is related: Who comes to the mosque of Jerusalem, there is pardon for him, and elevation by four degrees. I quote this from a tradition cited in, The Merit of Prayer in Jerusalem. And there will come, if Allah will, two traditions of like tenor on the merit of prayer there.

On authority of Ka'b al-Ahbār a tradition is given: Verily, there stands unto Allah the Glorious and Mighty an open door in the nearer heavens facing Jerusalem, where there descend every night seventy *Seventy Thousand Interceding Angels* thousand angels, interceding for pardon for those who come to Jerusalem to pray there. I quote this from the chapter, On the Descending of Angels upon Jerusalem.

On authority of Anas ibn Mālik it is related: The Apostle of Allah said, Who makes pilgrimage to Jerusalem, counting upon merit, Allah will give him the reward of a thousand martyrs. He cites the tradition also: The Apostle of Allah said, Who makes pilgrimage to a learned *Rewards of Pilgrimage* man, it is as if he made pilgrimage to Jerusalem; and who makes pilgrimage to Jerusalem, counting upon merit with Allah, verily Allah will make him inviolable, flesh and body, against Hell-Fire.

On authority of Ka'b al-Ahbār, also: Who comes to Jerusalem for the sake of some (religious) need, not asking Allah for anything but that, he will grant it. I quote this from the chapter, On Making Pilgrimage to Jerusalem.

On authority of Khuleid ibn Du'laj, it is reported that Safīyyah, wife of the Prophet, went to Jerusalem and prayed there, and ascended the Mount of Olives and prayed there, and stood on the crest of the mount, and said, From this very place shall mankind be separated on the Resurrection Day unto Paradise and unto Hell-Fire. I quote this from the chapter, On the Mount of Olives.

Olivet and the Judgment

On authority of Meimūnah, daughter[15] of al-Hārith, wife of the Prophet, it is related: She said, O Apostle of Allah! give us a rule as to Jerusalem. And he said, It is the land of the Resurrection and the Judgment assembly; go there and pray. For indeed a prayer there is worth a thousand elsewhere. She said, O Apostle of Allah! Is he who cannot accomplish it held accountable? He said (If one cannot), then let him send there oil to light its lamps; for indeed one who sends is as he who prays there. Al-Qazwīni preserves this tradition. I quote it from the chapter, Lighting Lamps in Jerusalem.

Oil for the Lamps Again

On authority of Ka'b it is related: When Solomon finished building the temple, he placed the offering in the court of the temple, and stood on the Rock, and said, after offering praise and thanks, O Allah! I beseech Thee for whoever enters this mosque five favors—that there not enter it a guilty soul earnestly seeking only forgiveness, but that Thou accept his repentance and forgive him and pardon him; and that there not enter here an affrighted soul seeking only assurance, but that Thou give him assurance from his fear and forgive his guilt; and that there not enter here one who is sick earnestly seeking only remedy, but that Thou heal him from his disease and forgive him his guilt; and that there not enter here one afflicted with drought earnestly praying for rain, but that Thou give rain to his land; and that Thou not turn Thy regard from him who enters here until he go forth! O Allah! if Thou hast answered my prayer, then grant my request; and give as a sign of that the acceptance of mine offering!—And fire descended from Heaven and bore up the offering.[16]

Solomon's Prayer at the Temple Dedication

I quote this from the last chapter, Solomon's Building the Holy Temple.

On authority of 'Abdullah ibn 'Omar it is related: The Apostle of Allah said, When Solomon built the temple, he asked of his lord three boons, and He gave him two; and I indeed wish that He had given him the third! He asked of Him a kingdom no one should deserve

Not Fully Granted

after him, and He gave him that; and he asked of Him wisdom and knowledge no one should deserve after him, and He gave him that; and he asked Him that no one should come to this temple and pray there without returning to his sinlessness as he was on the day his mother bore him! And I would that He had granted him that!

It is related from the Prophet: When Solomon finished building the Holy Temple he asked of Allah three favors—wisdom like unto His own, and a kingdom not deserved by anyone after him, and that no one should come to this temple concerned about nought but prayer there, without Thou absolving him from guilt as he was on the day his mother bore him. And the Prophet said, As for two of the favors, He granted them; as for the third, I indeed wish that he had been granted it! This is termed "the prayer of a prophet and the wish of a prophet."

In a citation from the Prophet also on authority of 'Abdullah ibn 'Omar it is related: When Solomon son of David finished building the Holy Temple, he asked of Allah wisdom comparable with His own, and a kingdom not deserved by anyone after him, and that there not come to this mosque anyone wishing only to pray, without he be absolved from his sins as he was on the day his mother bore him. And the Apostle of Allah said, As to two of them, He granted them; and I indeed wish He had granted the third! An-Nasā'i and Ibn Mājah quote this tradition.

On authority of Abu 'l-'Awwām this tradition is given: We were told that when the Prophet of God, Solomon, finished building the Holy Temple, he sacrificed three thousand (oxen) and seven thousand sheep. Then he said, O Allah! whoever of the guilty comes here, pardon his guilt! Or whatever victim of distress, relieve his distress! And the tradition says, No one came there without obtaining abundantly of what was prayed for by Solomon son of David. I quote this from the chapter, The Prayer of Solomon When He Finished Building the Holy Temple.

Solomon's Dedicatory Offering, and Prayer

TRADITIONS OF THE NIGHT-JOURNEY

The imām al-Beihaqi cites in the chapter, The Night-Journey, of his book, *Dalā'il an-Nubūwah*,[17] with his chain of references, an account on authority of Shaddād ibn Aus:

The Prophet's
Night-Journey
to Jerusalem
and Paradise,
the " Isrā' "

We said, O Apostle of Allah, how wert thou taken upon the Night-Journey? He said: I had prayed the twilight prayer at nightfall with my companions in Mecca. And Gabriel came to me with a white male mount (or a white female mount), larger than an ass but smaller than a mule. And he said, Mount! But she was unmanageable for me. So he twisted her mouth with a ziwār and grasped her by the ears, and set me upon her. And she started ahead quickly with us, her hoofs falling as far as her eye could reach, until we came to a land of palm trees. And he caused me to descend; then he said, Pray! And I prayed.

Halts for
Prayer in
Medina

Then we mounted; and he said, Knowest thou where thou hast prayed? I said, Allah knoweth best! And he said, Thou didst pray in Yathrib; thou didst pray in Teibah.[18]

And she started swiftly ahead with us, her hoofs falling as far as the eye could reach. Then we came to another place; and he said, Descend and pray! (Or, Descend!) And I dismounted. Then he said, Pray! And I prayed. Then we mounted; and he said, Knowest thou where thou hast prayed? I said, Allah knoweth best! He said, Thou

In Midian

didst pray in Midian, at the trees of Moses.[19]

Then she started quickly forward with us, her hoofs falling as far as the eye could reach. Then we came to a land whose palaces were distinguishable to us. And he said, Descend! and I descended. And he said, Pray! and I prayed. Then we mounted; and he said, Knowest

In Bethlehem

thou where thou hast prayed? I said, Allah knoweth best! He said, Thou didst pray in Bethelehem, where was born Jesus the Messiah, son of Mary.[20]

Then he went on with me until we entered the City (of Jerusalem) by its southern gate. And we came to the south side of the mosque, and he tied up there his mount. And we entered the mosque by one of its doors through which the sun and moon shine at setting.[21] And I prayed in the mosque where Allah willeth. And there came upon me a

Arrival and
Devotions in
Jerusalem

thirst stronger than I had ever felt. And there were brought to me two vessels, one with leban and the other with honey, both sent to me together. And I hesitated between them. Then Allah guided me, and I chose the leban; and I drank it until I emptied it. And there appeared before me an old man, leaning on his staff, who said to Gabriel, Thy companion hath taken on religion; verily, he is rightly guided![22]

Then we went on until we came to the Valley (of Gehenna), and behold! Gehenna spread out before me as a carpet! And I (Shaddād, the questioner) said, O Apostle of Allah, how didst thou find it? He said, Like the vehemence of fever! A Vision of Hell

Then he (Gabriel, after the Prophet's visit to Paradise) turned back with me. And we passed by, in a certain place, a caravan that belonged to the Koreish; and they had let stray a camel of theirs, which a certain man had brought back. And I greeted them; and one of them said, That is the voice of Mohammed! Then I came to my companions in Mecca.[23] The Return to Mecca

And Abu Bekr [24] came to me and said, O Apostle of Allah, where wert thou last night? For I sought thee in thy wonted places. I said, Thou must know, I went to Jerusalem last night! And he said to me, O Apostle of Allah, verily, it is a month's journey! Now, describe it to me. He (Mohammed) said, The path is as clear to me as if I were looking upon it! No one shall ask me a thing about it but I can inform him. And Abu Bekr declared, I bear witness that thou art the Prophet of Allah! Abu Bekr Believes

But the unbelievers said, Look at "Ibn Abu Kabshah," [25] asserting that he went to Jerusalem last night! The Hostile Scoff

And he said, As a sign of proof, I say to you that I passed by a caravan of yours in a certain place, and they had let stray a camel of theirs, and a certain man had brought it back. They shall come on the march to alight (tonight) at such and such a place; and they will arrive among you on such and such a day, in their van a red camel on which there rest a black hair-cloth and two large grain-sacks. Irrefutable Proof

And, indeed, when that day came the people were in a high state of expectancy, until, as it drew near mid-day, the caravan approached —in its van that camel which the Apostle of Allah had described! [26]

This I saw in an account by the imām al-Beihaqi. And 'Oqbah says: This is a sound chain of reference. I saw this tradition in the book, *Fadl al-Khail*,[27] and in others. And there was mention there of a white female mount (without the uncertainty above). Also, it says first: . . . Until we reached a land of palm trees; and he said, Descend! and I descended. Then he said to me, Pray! and I prayed. Then it has after the words, "as far as the sight of the eye could reach," until we came to a white land; and he said to me, Descend! and I descended. Then he said to me, Pray! and I prayed. Then it has: Then we passed Parallels from Another Account by a land whose palaces were distinguishable; and he said, Descend! and I descended. Then he said, Pray! and I prayed. Then we mounted; and he said, Knowest thou where thou didst pray? I said, Allah knoweth best! He answered, Thou didst pray in Bethlehem, where was born Jesus son of Mary, etc., as the tradition continues.

CHAPTER THIRD

On the Merit of Prayer in Jerusalem, and the Merit of Pilgrimage and Prayer in the Mosque of Medina and the Mosque al-Aqsa in the Same Year

It is related of 'Abdullah ibn 'Amr ibn al-'Āsi [28] that he said: I heard the Apostle of Allah say, Prayer in Jerusalem is better than a thousand prayers elsewhere, except in the Sacred Mosque (in Mecca) and this my mosque (in Medina).

Various Traditions on the Value of Prayer in Jerusalem

On authority of Abu 'd-Dardā', it is related of the Prophet that he said: The merit of prayer in the Sacred Mosque exceeds all else by a hundred thousand prayers, and my mosque by a thousand prayers, and in the Holy Temple by five hundred prayers.

In another tradition on authority of Abu 'l-Muhājir it is reported: The Apostle of Allah said, Prayer in Jerusalem is worth five hundred prayers; and joining with the faithful there increases it by twenty-five.

On authority of Abu Hureirah it is related: The Apostle of Allah said: Who prayeth in Jerusalem, all his guilt is forgiven him.

On authority of Anas ibn Mālik it is reported: The Apostle of Allah said, The prayer of a man in his house is worth a prayer; and his prayer in the mosque of the tribes is worth twenty-five; and his prayer in the mosque where the people are wont to gather is worth

Compared with Other Shrines

five hundred prayers; [29] and his prayer in the Mosque al-Aqsa is worth fifty thousand prayers; and his prayer in this my mosque is worth fifty thousand; and his prayer in the Sacred Mosque is worth a hundred thousand.

Also on authority of Anas the tradition is given: The Apostle of Allah said, Who prays in Jerusalem five voluntary prayers, with four rak'ahs in every prayer, reciting in the prayers ten thousand times,

"Say, He is One God!"[30] then Allah will have redeemed his soul, and the Fire hath no power over him.

And in a tradition on authority of Ibn 'Abbās it is related: The Apostle of Allah said, Prayer in the Sacred Mosque is worth a hundred thousand prayers; and a prayer in my mosque is worth fifty thousand prayers; and a prayer in the Mosque al-Aqsa is worth twenty thousand prayers.

And on authority of Abu Umāmah al-Bāhili it is reported: The Apostle of Allah said, Who makes pilgrimage to Jerusalem and performs the ceremonies and prays, and engages in the jihād, and perseveres, he hath become perfect in fulfilling my laws.

On authority of Makhūl it is reported: Who goes forth to Jerusalem, not for any ordinary necessity, but rather to pray there, and prays five prayers—in the morning, at noon, in the afternoon, at sunset, and at nightfall—he is absolved from his guilt as on the day his mother bore him. *The Five Stated Daily Prayers*

Also on authority of Makhūl it is reported: Who makes pilgrimage to Jerusalem by riding there,[31] he shall enter Paradise carefully guided, and shall visit all the prophets in Paradise; and they shall envy him in his relationship with Allah. And whatever company sets forth to go to Jerusalem, there shall attend them ten thousand angels, interceding for them and praying for them, and serving as their agents, when they set out for Jerusalem. And they shall have for every day in which they steadfastly stand in prayer seventy kingdoms. And whoever enters Jerusalem cleansed from grievous sin, Allah will meet him with a hundred mercies, not a one of them but is a mercy so great that had it been vouchsafed to all creatures, it would have enriched them. And whoever prays in Jerusalem a prayer of two rak'ahs, reciting during them the Fātihah, and, Say, He is One God! he shall be absolved from his guilt as he was on the day his mother bore him.[32] And he shall possess goodness in every hair of his body. And he who prays in Jerusalem a prayer of four rak'ahs shall pass along the Path (of Judgment) to Paradise like al-Burāq; and he shall be given safeguard from the greatest of terrors on the Day of Judgment. And he who prays in Jerusalem six rak'ahs, there shall be granted to him a hundred prayers surely answered, the least of them freeing him from Hell, and making him worthy of Paradise. And he who prays in Jerusalem eight rak'ahs *Merit of Pilgrimage from Distance, or in Company with Others* *The Merit of Prayers of Varied Length* shall be the boon companion of Abraham, the Friend of the Merciful. And he who prays in Jerusalem ten rak'ahs shall be the boon companion of David and Solomon in Paradise. And whoever intercedes three times (in prayer) in Jerusalem for the believers, male and female, shall share in the merit of their good works; and there shall come to every believer, man and woman, because of his prayer seventy pardons; and there shall be forgiven him all his faults.

On authority of Muhammad ibn Shu'eib it is related: I said to 'Othmān al-Khorāsāni, son of 'Atā', What sayest thou about prayer in Jerusalem? He said, Yea; go there and pray. Verily, David founded it, and his son Solomon built it. And he paved it with gold and silver— a brick of gold and a brick of silver. And there is not a span of it but there has worshipped upon it an angel or a prophet; so perhaps thy forehead may touch a place (touched by that) of an angel or a prophet!

And on authority of Sufyān ath-Thauri[33] it is related that a man in Mecca asked him, saying, O Abu 'Abdullah, what sayest thou of prayer in this city? He said, It is worth a hundred thousand prayers. He asked, And in the mosque of the Apostle of Allah? He said, Fifty thousand. He asked, And in the mosque of Jerusalem? He said, Forty thousand. He asked, And in the mosque of Damascus? He said, Thirty thousand.

It is related on authority of Ibn 'Abbās: Whoever makes pilgrimage and prays in the mosque of Medina and the Mosque al-Aqsa in the same year, he shall be absolved from his faults as he was on the day his mother bore him. It is reported that this is a doubtful tradition. I quote it from Ibn 'Asākir's (chapter on) The Merit of Prayer in the Three Mosques.

And in the book of Ibn al-Murajja [Abu 'l-Ma'āli, one of his sources], on authority of Abu 'l-Hasan ibn Muslim, in an oral tradition, it is related: There came to our sheikhs (i. e., to Sahil ibn 'Abdullah and others) four travellers of the families of Abu Bekr, 'Omar, 'Othmān, and 'Ali, and greeted them; then they went to 'Abbādān, and fasted there the month of Ramadān.[34] And when they had finished the fast, they went to Mecca on pilgrimage with the people; then they came from Mecca to Jerusalem, and prayed there. This was their custom in every year. He mentions this in the chapter, The Sending Down of the Table (the Eucharist).

The Precious Pavement, and Associations of Angels and Prophets

A Doubtful Tradition

But Supported by a Pious Precedent of Four Great Families

Chapter Fourth

On the Merit of Putting on the Ihrām[35] *from Jerusalem, and of Giving the Call to Prayer There*

On authority of Umm Salimah[36] it is related: The Apostle of Allah said, Who goes on pilgrimage or pious visitation from the Mosque al-Aqsa to the Sacred Mosque, there shall be covered for him the faults he has committed and those he may later; and he shall be duly granted Paradise. This is mentioned from an account by ad-Dāraqutni.

Merit of Jerusalem as Starting Point of Pilgrimage to Mecca

And in another citation from her it is related: The Apostle of Allah said, Who puts on the ihrām in pilgrimage or pious visitation from Jerusalem, he is absolved from his sins as he was on the day his mother bore him. And in another account: Allah shall forgive him his past sins. It is mentioned that Abu Dā'ūd and an account of al-Qazwīni cite this.

On authority of Umm Hakīm it is related: Who goes on sacred visitation from Jerusalem, he shall be forgiven. And on authority of Ibn 'Omar it is reported: The Apostle of Allah said, Who puts on the ihrām from Jerusalem and comes to Mecca, there is forgiveness for him.

On authority of Ibn 'Omar also it is reported: Who puts on the ihrām in pious visitation from Jerusalem in the month of Ramadān, it is equivalent to ten campaigns with the Apostle of Allah.

Especially in Ramadan

On authority of Jābir,[37] it is related that a man said: O Apostle of Allah, what creatures shall be first to enter Paradise? He said, The prophets. He asked, O Prophet of Allah, then who? He answered, Then the martyrs. He said, O Prophet of Allah, then who? He said, Then the muezzins of my mosque. He asked, O Prophet of Allah, then who? He said, Then the muezzins of the Mosque al-Aqsa. He asked, O Prophet of Allah, then who? He said, Then the rest of the muezzins, according to their good works.

Merit of the Muezzins of Jerusalem

Chapter Fifth

On the Merit of Giving Alms in Jerusalem, and Fasting There, and Witnessing the Pilgrimage Assembly

On authority of al-Hasan al-Basri [38] it is related: Whoever gives alms in Jerusalem to the value of a dirham, it is his ransom from the Fire. And who gives alms to the value of a loaf of bread, he is as one who gives alms to the value of mountains of gold.

"The Widow's Mite"

The Merit of Fasting

On authority of Muqātil it is related: Who fasts in Jerusalem a day, he has freedom from Hell.

The Ever-living Saints Fast in Jerusalem in Ramadan

In the book by Ibn al-Murajja it is reported on authority of as-Suddi: Elias and St. George fast the month of Ramadān in Jerusalem, and frequent the pilgrimage assembly every year.[39] This is noted in the chapter, The Merit of Him Who Lights Lamps in Jerusalem.

Chapter Sixth

On the Merit of the Rock, and How It Is from Paradise

On authority of Rāfi' ibn 'Amr it is related: I heard the Apostle of Allah say, The Rock (in Jerusalem) and the 'Ajwah date are from Paradise.

On authority of 'Ali ibn Abu Tālib,[40] he (Mohammed) used to say: The greatest of places is Jerusalem; and the greatest of rocks in the Rock of Jerusalem. And on authority of Ibn 'Abbās it is said: The Rock of Jerusalem is from Paradise.

The Divine Origin of the Rock in Jerusalem

On authority of Ka'b it is said: Verily, the Ka'bah is in an equivalent position to the Frequented House in the Seventh Heavens, to which the Angels of Allah make pilgrimage. And if rocks fell from it, they would have fallen on the place of the rocks of the Temple of Mecca. And, indeed, Paradise is in the Seventh Heaven in an equivalent position to the Holy Temple (in Jerusalem) and the Rock; and if a rock had fallen from it, it would have fallen upon the place of Rock there. And for this cause the city is called Urushalīm,[41] and Paradise is called Dār as-Salām.

On authority of Wahb it is related: Allah said to the Rock of Jeru-salem, In thee is my Paradise and my Hell; and in thee is my reward and my punishment.[42] And blessed is he who visits thee! Again, blessed is he who visits thee! Again, blessed is he who visits thee!

Its Sanctity and Import- ance for the Two Worlds

And on authority of 'Ubādah ibn as-Sāmit it is related: The Apostle of Allah said, The Rock! the rock of Jerusalem is over a palm tree; and the palm tree is by one of the rivers of Paradise; and under the palm tree are the nurse of the wife of Pharaoh, and Miriam the daughter of 'Imrān,[43] arranging the vestments of the people of Paradise against the Resurrection Day.

Miriam and the Nurse of the Wife of Pharaoh

On authority of Abu Hureirah, the Prophet said: All the rivers and the clouds and the winds come from under the Rock of Jerusalem. And in another citation he says: The Apostle of Allah said, Verily, the sweet waters and the rain-bearing winds issue from the base of the Rock of Jerusalem.

The Rock the Source of Clouds, Winds, and Water

On authority of Ubayy ibn Ka'b he said: There is no sweet water but issues from the Rock which is in Jerusalem.

On authority of Nauf al Bakāli he said: The Rock! there issue from it the four rivers of Paradise—Sihon, Gihon, the Euphrates, and the Nile.[44]

And of the Four Rivers of Paradise

And on authority of Ka'b it is related he said: Allah the Mighty and Glorious said to the Rock of Jerusalem, Thou art my nigher throne, and from thee have I spread out the earth, and from thee have I ascended unto Heaven; and I have made to flow from beneath thee every fresh stream which rises on the mountain peaks.

On authority of Abu Hureirah it is related: The Apostle of Allah said, When I was carried on the Night-Journey to Jerusalem, Gabriel took me to Jerusalem and went with me to the Rock. And he said, from hence thy Lord ascended into Heaven. And Allah inspired me to say, We are on the place whence my Lord ascended! And I prayed among the prophets.[45]   Then I was taken up to Heaven.

The Prophet at the Rock

I quote this from the chapter, The Coming Down of the Rock. His statement, I was taken up, does not intend what is understood by similar expressions in the case of one of us. Nay, it is something more befitting the glory of Allah!

On authority of Abu Idrīs al-Khaulāni it is related: Allah will change the Rock of Jerusalem on the Day of Judgment into white coral,

The Judgment to Be There

as broad as Heaven and earth. Then He will set upon it his Throne, and establish his scales (of judgment); and He will judge between his servants, and some will go from thence into Paradise, and some to Hell.[46]

On authority of Abu Ishāq al-Buhturi,[47] the qādi, it is related: Prayer is unacceptable at seven places—on the Ka'bah, on the Rock of Jerusalem, on the Mount of Olives, on Mount Sinai, on as-Safa and al-Marwah, on al-Jamrah, and on Mount 'Arafat.

Too Sacred to Be Mounted for Prayer?

On authority of Abu 'l-Hasan 'Ali ibn Ahmad al-Wāhidi:[48] In the words of the Exalted, "Then, when with a summons He shall summon you from the earth, lo! ye shall come forth," (it is meant) that Israfel shall give summons from the Rock of Jerusalem, when "the trumpet shall be blown," by the command of Allah for the awakening after death.

Israfel and the Last Trumpet

On authority of Abu Sa'īd al-Khudri: The Apostle of Allah said, On the night I was taken on the journey to Jerusalem, I worshiped west of the Rock.

Position and Procedure for Devotions There

On authority of 'Abdullah ibn Salām it is related: Who prays in Jerusalem a thousand rak'ahs on the right of the Rock and on the left of it, he shall enter Paradise before his death. Meaning, he shall see it in his dreams.

A Foretaste of Paradise

On authority of al-Haushabi it is said: When ye enter unto the Rock, go so that it is placed on your right. On authority of Ka'b al-Ahbār it is related: Who comes to Jerusalem and prays on the right of the Rock or on its left, and prays at the Place of the Chain, and gives alms of little or much, his prayers will be answered; and Allah shall visit his distress, and he shall be absolved from his sins as he was on the day his mother bore him. And if he asks Allah for martyrdom, He will give it to him.[49]

Abu 'l-Ma'āli al-Mushrif ibn al-Murajja says in his chapter, What Is Fitting for the Worshiper When He Enters unto the Rock: It is considered fitting for him who enters unto the Rock that he place it on his right, so that he is in the reverse position to the circuit around the Sacred House of Allah. And let him come to where the people pray, and put his hands upon it, but not kiss it; then pray. And then he says: It is indeed most fitting that he descend underneath the Rock; and let him do so. And he must fortify himself, and repent toward Allah, and be instant in prayer and sincere in invocation. And when he goeth beneath, let him pray as long as he may wish, using the invocations mentioned above. And it is necessary that he be instant in prayer underneath the Rock; for verily, prayer in that place will be answered, if Allah the Exalted will!

I say, the prayers referred to have nothing in them peculiar to this place; but they are blessed prayers, if Allah Most High will. For wherever one of Allah's servants prays, he is answered there.[50]

But Prayer Has Value Anywhere!

On authority of Ka'b it is related: The most beloved thing about Syria in the sight of Allah is Jerusalem; and the most beloved thing about Jerusalem in the sight of Allah are the Rock and the Mount of Olives. I quote this from the the chapter, Jerusalem the Choice of Allah among His Lands.

Sanctity of the Rock and Olivet

On authority of Zeid ibn Aslam it is related: The key to the Rock of Jerusalem was in possession of Solomon son of David, and he trusted no one with it. But one day he arose to open it, but he could not. Then he called mankind to his aid, but they were not able; then he sought aid of the Jinn, but they were not able; so he sat down in distress and sadness, thinking that his Lord had forbidden him His House. And lo! while he was in this state there approached him an old man, walking with his staff, advanced in age—and he had been one of the companions of David.

Story of Solomon and the Key to the Rock

And he said, O prophet of Allah, I see thou art in sadness. And he answered, I came to this door to open it, but was not able; and I called mankind to aid, but they did not open it; then I called the Jinn to aid, but they did not open it!

And the old man said, shall I not teach thee the words which David thy father used to say in his distress, and Allah would give him relief? He said, Yea, indeed! He said, Say, O Allah! by Thy light am I guided, and by Thy grace am I enriched; and in Thee I (live) morning and evening; and my sins are before Thee, and I ask Thy forgiveness, and repent toward Thee, O Thou merciful and gracious One!

And when Solomon said these words, the door came open for him.[51]

Abu 'l-Ma'ali says: So it is considered fitting for one to pray this prayer when he enters the door of the Rock, and likewise the door of the mosque. I quote this from the chapter, The Prayer of Solomon When the Doors of the Mosque of Jerusalem Were Closed.

Abu 'l-Ma'āli relates on authority of Muhammad ibn Shihāb az-Zuhri [52] the following: Allah hath not sent a prophet to the earth since the descent of Adam (from Paradise) who hath not set as his point to face in prayer the Rock of Jerusalem. Our Prophet prayed thus for sixteen months. He cites this in the chapter, How Long the Prophet and the Muslims Prayed toward Jerusalem.

The Rock Mohammed's First Qiblah

CHAPTER SEVENTH

On the Black Marble, and How One Enters unto the Rock

On authority of Ibrāhīm ibn Mihrān it is related: Nuheilah, who was a devotee of the Rock of Jerusalem, tells us this:—On a certain day, which I do not remember, there entered where I was, from the northern door, a man having on the garb of travel. He entered—and I said, Elias! Then he prayed two rak'ahs, then four; and then he started forth. And I clung to a part of his garment, and said, O such an one! I saw thee do something, but I know not what it signified. He said to her, I am a man of the people of Yemen.[53] I started forth to come to this temple; and when I passed by Wahb ibn Munabbih, he said to me, Whither goest thou? I said, I go to Jerusalem. He said, When thou enterest the mosque, enter the Rock from the northern door; then stand before the qiblah, and there will be on thy right a pillar and a column. So look between the pillar and the column for a piece of black marble. Verily, this is one of the gates of Paradise! So pray blessing upon it! and pray unto Allah the Mighty and Glorious! For verily, prayers said there will be answered.

A Pilgrim's Story

Of Abu 'Othmān of the Ansār it is related that he would come by night after the conclusion of his term of prayer in the month of Ramadān, and would pray at the slab of Black Marble.

Chapter Eighth

On the Dome of the Ascension, the Dome of the Prophet, the Gate of
Mercy, the Mihrāb of Zechariah, the Rocks Which Are to the Rear
of the Mosque, the Gate of the Shekinah, the Gate of Forgiveness,
the Mihrāb of 'Omar, and the Remaining Mihrābs, and the Door
of the Prophet, the Mount of Olives, the Dome of the Chain, and
the Gate of Repentance [54]

Al-Mushrif says: It is fitting that one go to the Dome of the
Ascension and pray there, being instant in prayer; for it is a place
where the answer to prayer is met. And it is fitting that one go to the
Dome of the Prophet, behind the Dome of the Ascension, and pray
there, being instant in prayer.

> Spots for Further Devotions

He says further: Then one should go to the Gate of Mercy and
pray there, inside the wall. Then one should make invocation and ask
Allah in this place for Paradise, and seek refuge in Him from Hell;
and there will be granted more than that.

And verily, the valley to the rear (of the eastern wall) is the Valley
of Gehenna. And this is the place about which Allah said: "And there
shall be set between them a wall with a gate, on its inside Mercy, and
without, in front of it, Punishment." [55]

> The Valley and Wall Mentioned in the Koran

He says: Then one should go to the mihrāb of Zechariah and pray
there. Let him do so, and be instant in prayer, and ask Allah for
Paradise, and seek refuge in Him from Hell. Because it is likewise
within the mosque enclosure. Then one should go to the Rocks which
are to the rear of the mosque, adjacent to the Gate of the Tribes, and
pray in the place which is called the Throne of Solomon; and one should
face the qiblah and be instant in prayer. This is the place where
Solomon prayed when he finished building the Temple, and Allah gave
him answer there. [56] Then one should go to the Gate of the Shekinah
and do likewise; and as well at the Gate of Forgiveness.

> Spots for Prayer around the Haram

Then one should enter the interior, roofed mosque (al-Aqsa itself),
and go to the mihrāb of 'Omar and pray there, and be instant in prayer;
and likewise to the mihrāb of Mu'āwiyah, and all the mihrābs which
are in the mosque. And he should go down to the Gate of the Prophet

Worship in
al-Aqsa,
Including the
Mihrab of
Mary
and pray there, and make invocation. Then he should go to the mihrāb of Mary, and be instant in prayer. And, verily, prayer there is answered. So one should pray there, and recite the Sūrah of Mary,[57] for the sake of her connection with it. And he should worship meanwhile, as did ʿOmar in the mihrāb of David, when he recited there the Sūrah Sād,[58] worshiping meanwhile, because of its connection with David. And let him pray as long as he will. Let him be instant in prayer, for verily it will be answered. More than one man has tested it and found it so. And the best prayer there is the prayer of Jesus, which he prayed when Allah took him up from the Mount of Olives.[59]

The Pilgrim's
Devotional
Attitude
And it is fitting for one, when he does all this, that he repent toward Allah, and desist from sin, and thank Allah in that He hath enabled him to visit this holy place, and be instant in obedience and prayer and invocation and almsgiving. And in this there is indeed great merit! And if one does this, he is absolved from his sins, and becomes as his sinless condition was on the day his mother bore him. So let him begin.

The Station of
Mohammed's
Steed
And let him go down to the place where Gabriel made a hole with his finger and tied up al-Burāq there. It is without the Gate of the Prophet. And let him be instant in prayer, and ask Allah for the best things of this world and the next.[60]

Olivet
And one should ascend as-Sāhirah, which is the Mount of Olives.[61] So let him do this. And there is there a track made by Safīyyah, wife of the Prophet; for she came to Jerusalem and ascended the Mount of Olives. And let him be instant in prayer.

Angels and
Prophets with
Mohammed
in Jerusalem
It is related on authority of Kaʿb: The Prophet, when he was taken to Jerusalem on the Night-Journey, stopped al-Burāq at the station where the prophets had stopped previously, then he entered by the Gate of the Prophet, with Gabriel before him, shining like the shining of the sun. Then Gabriel went before him until he was on the north of the Rock. And Gabriel pronounced the call to prayer, and the angels descended from Heaven, and Allah gathered unto him the prophets. Then he stood in prayer; then he stood before them (as their
Mohammed's
Ascent to
Heaven
imām), and the prophet prayed among the angels and the prophets. Then he went forward from that place, to where were set before him a ladder of gold and a ladder of silver, and that was the place of his ascent. So Gabriel and the Prophet ascended unto Heaven.

'Abdu 'r-Rahmān says: It is the nearer dome on the right of the Rock. And he who comes to the dome with a specific request, having any need of this world or the next, and prays here two or four rak'ahs, there shall be revealed unto him the swiftness of His answering, and he shall know the blessedness of the place. For the Prophet prayed there, and it is called the Dome of the Prophet. *The Dome of the Prophet*

On authority of Abu Hudheifah, muezzin of Jerusalem, it is related as told by his grandmother, that she saw Safīyyah, wife of the Prophet, as Ka'b was saying to her: O Mother of the Faithful, pray here! for verily, the Prophet prayed with the prophets when he was taken on the Night-Journey to Heaven, and he prayed with them here, for they were assembled unto him.—And Abu Hudheifah pointed out with his hand the farther dome to the rear of the Rock. *Where His Wife Safiyyah also Prayed*

On authority of Wahb ibn Munabbih it is related: When evil and evidence of idolatry had increased among the Children of Israel, Allah gave David a chain for testing guilt. It was a chain of gold, suspended from Heaven to the earth, before the Rock which is in Jerusalem,— and so on, according to the tradition.[62] *The Golden Chain of Testing*

On authority of Ahmad ibn Mohammed ibn Ka'b it is related: David asked Allah to give him a means of evidence, through which the truthful man might be known from the liar. And Allah sent down a chain of light from Heaven, suspended between Heaven and earth— and so on, as the tradition says. He says further: The Dome was built later; 'Abdu 'l-Malik built it in the place which is called the Dome of the Chain, on the east of the Rock. And it is the dome in which the Prophet met with the houris at the time he was brought on the Night-Journey. The dome which is north of the Rock was also built later.[62a] *Origin of the Dome of the Chain* *Houris Seen Here by the Prophet*

Then the author counsels that prayer is fitting at the Dome of the Chain. And Allah knoweth best!

There is a citation in the chapter, Jerusalem the Choice of Allah, where on authority of Ka'b it is reported: The most beloved thing of Syria before Allah is Jerusalem; and the most beloved thing of Jerusalem before Allah is the Rock and the Mount of Olives.

On authority of Ibn 'Abbās it is said: In the words of the Most High, "And when We said, Enter this city," Jerusalem is meant. And, "Eat of it bountifully as ye wish," is meant, the amount is at your volition. And, "Enter the gate worshiping," is meant the gate of *Jerusalem Again in the Koran?*

Jerusalem.[63] And His expression (in this part of the Koran) "Hittah" means, There is no god but Allah (Lā ilāh illa 'llāh!), because it is a term which unburdens the load of sin.

Merit of the Gate of Forgiveness

And on this subject also: It used to be said, Who prays at the Gate of forgiveness a prayer of two rak'ahs, he shall have a reward of the measure of (what would have been) his to whom the Children of Israel said, Enter! but he did not enter.[64]

On authority of 'Abdu 'r-Rahmān ibn Mohammed ibn Mansūr ibn Thābit ibn Istanbād it is related: My father told me on authority of his father, on authority of his grandfather, this: It was the custom in the time of the Children of Israel, that when one of them sinned, his

Repentance Here in Ancient Times

sin was written on his forehead and on the threshold of his house, Behold, So and So sinned on such and such a night! And they would drive him out and banish him. But he would come to the Gate of Repentance, which is the door at the mihrāb of Mary, from which sustenance was brought to her;[65] and he would weep, and make humble entreaty, and stand in prayer for some time. And if Allah forgave him, that (accusation) was erased from his brow, and the Children of Israel would receive him. But if He did not forgive him, they drove him out and banished him.

On authority of 'Abdullah ibn 'Omar it is related: The wall which Allah mentions in the Koran, "And there shall be set between them a wall with a gate, on the interior Mercy, and on its exterior Punish-

Gehenna to East of the Sacred Place of the Temple

ment," means (that wall by) the Valley of Gehenna.[66]

From Ziyād ibn Abu Saudah it is related that he saw 'Ubādah ibn as-Sāmit at the eastern wall of Jerusalem, and he was weeping. And some one said to him, What causeth thee to weep, O Abu 'l-Walīd? And he said, From right here the Prophet told us he saw Gehenna! And in another citation: Verily, he saw here Gehenna! And in another: I heard the Apostle of Allah say, This is the valley of Gehenna.[67]

CHAPTER NINTH

On the Spring of Siloam, and the Water of Jerusalem, and the Well of the Leaf [68]

On authority of Abu Hureirah it is related: The Apostle of Allah said, Verily, Allah hath chosen of all cities four—Mecca, which is the Sacred City; Medina, which is the place of palms; Jerusalem, which is the place of olives, and Damascus, which is the place of figs. And He hath chosen of all frontiers four — Alexandria of Egypt, Qazwīn of Khurāsān, 'Abbādān of Irāq, and Asqalon of Syria. [69] And He hath chosen of all fountains four (He saith in His clear Book, "In it are two flowing springs, and in it are two bubbling springs.") [70] — and as for the flowing springs, they are the spring of Beisān and the spring of Siloam; and as for the bubbling springs, they are the spring of Zamzam and the spring of 'Akka. And He hath chosen of all rivers four—Sihon, Gihon, the Nile, and the Euphrates.

Allah's Chosen Cities, Frontiers, and Fountains in Palestine

On authority of Khālid ibn Ma'dān it is related: Zamzam and the spring of Siloam in Jerusalem are each a spring of Paradise. On his authority also: Two springs of Paradise in this world are Zamzam and Siloam.

Sanctity of Siloam

On authority of Yazīd ar-Raqāshi it is related: Who wishes to drink water in the night, let him say, O water! water of Jerusalem! He pronounceth peace upon thee! Then he shall drink (in spirit); and verily, it is a security (from thirst) by the will of Allah.

Concerning Sharīk ibn Hubāshah an-Namīri it is related: He went to get water from the Pool of Solomon which is at Jerusalem, and his bucket came loose. He went down into the pool to get it—and while he was seeking for it there, lo! he was by a tree! And he plucked a leaf from the tree, and behold, it was not from a tree of this world! And he took it to 'Omar ibn al-Khattāb. [71] And he said, I witness that this is the truth! I heard the Apostle of Allah say, A man of the people shall enter Paradise before his death. And 'Omar took it and placed it between the leaves of the Book.

The Marvellous Story of the Well of the Leaf

On authority of 'Atīyyah ibn Qeis is related this: The Apostle of Allah said, A man of my people shall indeed enter Paradise walking on his feet and still alive. Now a company came to Jerusalem to pray there, in the caliphate of 'Omar. And there was sent a man of the Banu Tamīm, called Sharīk ibn Hubāshah, to get water for his fellows. And his bucket fell into the pool. And when he went down to get it he found a door in the pool, opening into a garden. So he entered the door into the garden, and walked about in it. And he took a leaf from a tree there, and placed it behind his ear. Then he went outside, into the pool, and came up. And he went to the governor of Jerusalem and told him about what he had seen in the garden, and how he entered it. So he sent some people with him to the pool, and he went down, and the people with him. However, they did not find a door, or enter the garden.

Now he (the governor) wrote to 'Omar about that matter; and 'Omar wrote back confirming it with this tradition, saying, A man of this people shall enter Paradise walking on his feet and still living. And 'Omar said in his letter, Look at the leaf; for it is become dry and altered, then it is not from a tree of Paradise; for anything from Paradise does not become altered. And it is recorded in the account, Verily, the leaf was not altered!

And in another citation: Indeed, as he was going down into the pool, a being appeared to him, and said to him, Go down with me! And he took his hand (and helped him) into the pool, and carried him into the garden. And Sharīk plucked some leaves. Then he brought him back, and he went unto his fellows. And this adventure reached the ears of 'Omar. And Ka'b gave a citation: Verily, a man of the people shall enter Paradise while he is alive among you. And he said, Look at the leaves; and if they be altered, then they are not leaves from Paradise. And 'Atīyyah said, And they were not altered. In this citation also it was Sharīk ibn Hubāshah who entered the garden and plucked the leaves.

On authority of a company who went to Sharīk ibn Hubāshah, living in Salamīyyah,[72] it is related: We came to him and made inquiry of him; and he told us about his entering the garden and what he saw

Proof from Sharik Himself there, and about his taking the leaves therefrom. And he had only one leaf left, which he had treasured for himself. We asked him to show it to us. So he called for his Koran, and took it out from the leaves of the Book, green and luxuriant. And he kissed it; then he laid it on his eyes, and then he replaced it between the leaves of the Book.

It is related further: And when he was at the point of death, he willed that it be placed on his breast beneath his shroud. And they say: The last one who testified to us about it said they did place it on his breast, and then his winding sheets were placed upon it.

Then it is recorded: Verily, they likened it to the peach leaf, the size of the hand, sharp at the top.[73]

CHAPTER TENTH

On as-Sāhirah, and the Merit of One Who Dies in Jerusalem

On authority of Hudheifah and Ibn 'Abbās and 'Ali it is related: We were seated one day in the presence of the Apostle of Allah, and he said, Mankind shall be assembled! (etc., according to the tradition). They shall go to a land called as-Sāhirah. This is the region of Jerusalem. It shall become widened for mankind, and shall contain them, by the will of Allah.

Jerusalem and the Judgment Assembly

On authority of Abu 'Ablah it is related: In the words of Allah, "And behold, they are in as-Sāhirah," and, the valley "on the side of the mount," (both) mean the Mount of Olives.

Mentioned in the Koran?

On authority of Abu ibn Ibrāhīm it is related: A tradition widely taught and well known in Jerusalem is that as-Sāhirah is the Mount of Olives. A place used as a burial ground, near the Oratory of 'Omar, is called as-Sāhirah.

On authority of Abu Hureirah it is related: The Apostle of Allah said, Who dieth in Jerusalem, it is as if he died in Heaven. On authority of Ka'b al-Muslim it is related: Allah says in the Bible, to Jerusalem, Who dieth in thee, it is as if he died in Heaven; and who dieth near thee, it is as if he died within thee!

The Bible Quoted?

On authority of Ka'b al-Ahbār it is related: Who is buried in Jerusalem, he hath gone over the Path to Heaven. And on his authority also: Who is buried in Jerusalem shall not be punished.

A Happy Place for Death and Burial

On authority of Wahb ibn Munabbih it is related: Who is buried in Jerusalem hath escaped from the calamity and misfortunes of the grave.

On authority of Khuleid ibn Du'laj it is related: I heard al-Hasan say, Who is buried in Jerusalem in the olive-garden of the Christians, it is as if he were buried in the nearer Heavens. And Khuleid says: And I did not know what was meant until I went to Jerusalem.[73a]

On authority of 'Abdu 'r-Rahmān ibn 'Adi al-Māzini it is related: 'Abdu 'r-Razzāq asked me about my home; and I told him, Verily, I am from Jerusalem. And he said, Knowest thou the olive-garden of the Christians? I said, Yea! He said, The report hath come to me that it is one of the luxuriant gardens of Paradise.

On authority of Ahmad ibn Khalaf al-Hamdāni it is related: A friend of mine, a man of veracity and self-restraint, told me that he started out to Ramleh on a matter of importance, and he passed the night in the village of al-'Aneb,[74] in the caravanserai. And he saw in a dream, as if there were brought near a coffin, with a dead man in it. And there met it before it entered the village, two companies, one of which said, We are the Angels of Mercy! and the other said, We are the Angels of Punishment! And they contended together over who should take him. And the Angels of Mercy overcame the Angels of Punishment, saying, He hath entered the land of Jerusalem; ye have no power over him! And when it was dawn, and the door of the caravanserai was opened, lo! some people had come with a coffin, in it a dead man, from Egypt. And I said to the people who were with it, Who is this deceased? And they mentioned that he was a man connected with the sultan, a man of great power, who had made it his will that he should be buried in Jerusalem.

He says further: And I returned to Jerusalem, and prayed over him, and was present at his burial.

CHAPTER ELEVENTH

On Who Believes That One Should Perform the Circuit of the Above Places, and Him Who Does not

On authority of Ja'far ibn Musāfir it is related: I saw Mu'amil ibn Ismā'īl in Jerusalem, as he presented something to the people and they performed the circuit with it around and around these places. And his son said to him, O father, Wakī' ibn al-Jarrāh entered here, but he did not perform the circuit! He replied, O son, every man doth about it as he wisheth.[75]

Margin notes:

Especially the Olive-Grove of the Christians

A Story Showing the Redeeming Sanctity of the Land

The Circuit Not Binding

CHAPTER TWELFTH

On the Merits of Jerusalem in Summary

On authority of Abu Umāmah it is related: The Apostle of Allah said, The Koran was sent down unto me in three places, Mecca, Medina, and Syria—which means Jerusalem, as Walīd says.[76]

The Prophet Received Some Revelation Here

On authority of Abu 'l-Fath Salīm ar-Rāzi it is related: In explanation of the words of the Most High, "Ask those of Our messengers whom We have sent before thee if We have appointed another god beside the Merciful for them to worship,"[77] that when the Prophet was taken on the Night-Journey there were gathered unto him in Jerusalem the prophets; and when he was in anxiety (of doubt), he was divinely told, Inquire of them! But he did not (further) doubt, and so he did not ask. I quote this from the chapter, That Which Hath Been Handed Down to the Effect That Syria was the Place of Exile of Abraham, the Friend of the Merciful, and That It Is Among the Places Chosen for the Sending Down of the Koran.

Application of Another Koran Verse to Jerusalem

On authority of 'Āyeshah[78] it is related: Verily, Mecca is a land which Allah greatly honored, and He made great its sacredness. He created Mecca and encompassed it with His angels all in one day, a thousand years before He created anything else of the world. And He added to it Medina; and He added to Medina Jerusalem. Then He created the world entire, after one thousand years, by one act of creation.

Jerusalem, with Mecca and Medina, Created First

On authority of 'Ali ibn Abu Tālib it is related: The earth was of water.[79] And Allah sent a wind which blew strongly on the water. Then there appeared on the earth a scum, which He divided into four parts, creating from the first Mecca, from the second Medina, from the third Jerusalem, and from the fourth Kūfah. I quote this from the beginning of the chapter, Miscellany of the Merits of Jerusalem.

The Creation

On authority of 'Abdullah ibn 'Omar it is related: Verily, the Sacred Place (of the Ka'bah) is sacred in the Seventh Heaven in the same degree it is on earth; and the Holy City is holy in the Seventh Heaven in the same degree as on earth. I quote this from the chapter, Jerusalem, the Holy.

As on Earth, So in Heaven

One of Four
Cities of
Paradise

On authority of Abu Hureirah it is related: The Apostle of Allah said, Four cities on earth are of Paradise—Mecca, Medina, Jerusalem, and Damascus.

The Choice
Land to Allah
and to Men

On authority of Mu'ādh ibn Jabal it is related: The Apostle of Allah said, Verily, Allah said, O Rūshalīm! Thou art the choicest of My lands; and I cause to turn to thee the choicest of my servants. Who was born in thee preferreth thee, and in fault it shall avail him; and who was born otherwhere preferreth thee to his birthplace. And this is a mercy from Me!

The Bride

In this connection also (Allah said): Jerusalem, thou art holy by My light; and in thee is the assembling place of my servants. I shall lead thee on the Day of Resurrection as a bride to her husband. And who entereth thee shall have no need of oil or grain.[80] (And Rūshalīm is a name of Jerusalem.)

Mu'āwiyah's
Sermon

From Khālid ibn Ma'dān it is related: Mu'āwiyah ibn Abu Sufyān arose in the minbar at Jerusalem, and said, What is between the walls of this mosque is more beloved by Allah than all the remaining lands.[81]

Allah's Praise
of Jerusalem

From Ka'b it is reported: Allah said to Jerusalem, Thou art My paradise and My sanctuary, and My choice of the lands! Who dwelleth in thee, it is a blessing (to him) from Me; and who is outside thee without just reason, it is from Mine anger at him.[82]

Its People
Neighbors
of Allah

On authority of Wahb ibn Munabbih it is reported: The people of Jerusalem are neighbors of Allah. And it is incumbent upon Allah that He not punish His neighbors.

Moses in
Jerusalem!

From 'Abdullah ibn 'Amr ibn al-'Āsi it is reported: Moses saw, when he was in Jerusalem, a light from the Lord of Might descending and ascending upon Jerusalem.[83]

The Heavenly
Light on
Jerusalem

From Ibn 'Abbās: There is a door open from Paradise, from whose opening there goeth forth a light from the Gardens of Paradise, and rests upon its mosque, its mountains, and its rocks; and the Rock of Jerusalem is from Paradise.

Heavenly Dew

From Ka'b: There is a door open in the Heavens, one of the doors of Paradise, from which there descend upon Jerusalem grace and mercy every morning, until the Hour cometh. And the dew which descends upon Jerusalem is a remedy for every disease, because it is from the Gardens of Paradise.[84]

From Muqātil it is related that there descend every night seventy thousand angels from the Heavens unto Jerusalem, invoking Allah, *The Praising Angels There* and saying, Holy! Holy! of Allah, and praising Allah, and thanking Allah; and they shall not return until the Hour cometh.

From Anas ibn Mālik: Verily, Paradise yearneth toward Jerusalem; and the Rock is from the Garden of Paradise, and it is the treasure of the earth. I quote this from the chapter, Jerusalem, a Blessed Land.

The hāfiz Behā' ud-Dīn gives this citation on authority of Muqātil: The Rock of Jerusalem is in the center of the worlds; and if a believing *The Rock in Center of the World* servant said to his master, Let us go to Jerusalem! Allah would say, O ye My angels, give witness! Verily, I have forgiven them before they go forth from this land, if it be that they persist not in sin.

Behā' ud-Dīn also cites on authority of Muqātil the tradition: I have heard that the Apostle of Allah said, Prayer in Mecca is worth *The Value of Prayer There* a hundred thousand prayers; and a prayer in my mosque is worth fifty thousand prayers; and a prayer in the mosque of Jerusalem is worth twenty-five thousand prayers.

And he says: Verily, Allah assureth one who lives in Jerusalem of provisions, although wealth may have escaped him. And he who dieth while dwelling in Jerusalem, trusting in reward, it is as if he died in Heaven. And who dieth in the vicinity of Jerusalem, it is as if he died *Various Merits, Including Abundance* in Jerusalem. And what is scarce in the earth is provided in abundance in the land round about Jerusalem. All sweet waters issue from the Rock of Jerusalem. The first land in which Allah gave blessing was the land of Jerusalem. The Lord will take His stand on the Day of Judgment in Jerusalem. He hath made as His choice of all the lands the land of Jerusalem. The land which Allah mentioned in the Koran, saying, "The sanctified land in which we have blessed the worlds," is the land of Jerusalem.[85]

And Allah said to Moses, Go to Jerusalem, for in it are My light and My Fire and My *tannūr* (meaning, "the oven which boils").[86] *Moses There* And Allah spake to Moses in the land of Jerusalem. And the One who is Praised and Exalted revealed Himself in the Mount in the land of Jerusalem. Moses saw the light of the Lord of Might in the land of Jerusalem.

And the Rock of Jerusalem is the center of all the worlds. When

Merit of
Inviting to
Pilgrimage
a man says to another, Let us go to Jerusalem, and they do it, Allah
will say, Blessed! to the one who invites and the one invited.

He also cites on authority of Muqātil the following:[87] Allah forgave
David and Solomon in the land of Jerusalem. And Allah confirmed
unto Solomon his kingdom in Jerusalem. And Allah announced to
Various Popu-
lar Biblical
References,
from
Tradition
Abraham and Sarah the good news of Isaac in Jerusalem. And Allah
announced to Zechariah the good news of John in Jerusalem. Allah
subjected the mountains and the birds to the will of David in Jeru-
salem. The angels surrounded the mihrāb over David in Jerusalem.
The prophets continually made their offerings in Jerusalem.[88] The
angels descend every night unto Jerusalem. There was brought to
Mary the fruit of winter in summer and the fruit of summer in winter,
in Jerusalem. And Allah caused a river to flow from the Jordan to
Mary and Jesus
Jerusalem. And Allah planted the palm for Mary in Jerusalem. Jesus
spake, as a child, in Jerusalem. Jesus was born in Jerusalem. And
Allah took him up to the Heavens from Jerusalem. Jesus shall descend
from the Heavens unto Jerusalem. The Eucharist was sent down to
him in the land of Jerusalem.

Gog and Magog shall conquer all the world except Jerusalem. And
Gog and Magog
Allah shall destroy them in the land of Jerusalem.[89] Allah the Exalted
Mohammed
looks every day with favor upon Jerusalem. Allah gave the Prophet
al-Burāq, and she carried him to Jerusalem. Adam, when he died in
Adam
the land of Hind, willed that he be buried in the land of Jerusalem.
Mary died in Jerusalem. Abraham migrated from Kuthārabba to
Abraham
Jerusalem. And the Migration in the Last Day shall be to Jerusalem.
The ark and the shekinah were taken up from Jerusalem. The chain
The Ark and
the Holy
Presence
descended from Heaven to Jerusalem. And the chain was taken up
from Jerusalem.

The Prophet and the Muslims prayed for a time toward Jerusalem.
Malik, the
Angel of
the Fire
The Prophet, when he was taken on the Night-Journey, saw Mālik,
custodian of the Fire, in Jerusalem. The Prophet rode al-Burāq to
Jerusalem; and he was taken on the Night-Journey to Jerusalem. He
prayed with the prophets and the apostles in Jerusalem.

The resurrection and the judgment assembly will be in Jerusalem.
And Allah Most High and the angels shall come with darkness from
The Last
Things
the clouds unto Jerusalem. And Paradise shall be conducted as a bride
on the Day of Resurrection to Jerusalem. All creatures shall be turned

to dust except men and jinn in Jerusalem. The reckoning on the Day of Judgment shall be in Jerusalem. The Path to Paradise, over Hell, shall be set up in the land of Jerusalem. The serried ranks of angels, on the Day of Judgment, shall be in Jerusalem. Israfel shall blow the trumpet over the Rock of Jerusalem. He shall call out, O ye wasted bones and emaciated flesh and severed arteries, come forth to your reckoning! Your souls shall be breathed into you, and ye shall be recompensed for your works! This is the day which ye were promised! And mankind shall be separated forth from Jerusalem, unto Paradise and unto Hell. And that is what the Word of the Most High means, On that day shall ye be separated, and on that day shall ye be arraigned, a part unto Paradise and part unto the Flames.

Zechariah became surety for Mary in Jerusalem.[90] Jesus shall slay Anti-Christ in the land of Jerusalem. Allah endowed Solomon with **Anti-Christ** knowledge of the speech of birds in Jerusalem. Solomon asked of his **Solomon and** Lord a kingdom not deserved by anyone after him, and He granted **the Birds** that to him, in Jerusalem. Solomon asked Allah to forgive whoever prayed in Jerusalem.

The middle of the Great Fish,[91] on whose back rest the lands, whose head is in the rising of the sun and whose tail is in the place of its **The Great** setting, is under the Rock of Jerusalem. Who delights to walk in one **Fish** of the gardens of Paradise, let him walk under the Rock of Jerusalem. On the day of Summoning, the Summoner shall be in a place near the Rock of Jerusalem.

In the words of the Most High, "And We brought him (Abraham) **Abraham** and Lot to the land in which We blessed the worlds," is meant Jeru- **and Lot** salem. In His words, "And We settled the Children of Israel in a truly **The Israelites** settled abode," is meant Jerusalem. In the words of the Most High, "And We wrote in the Psalms, after the giving of the Law, Verily, **The Psalms** My righteous servants shall inherit the earth!" is meant Jerusalem.[92] In the words of the Most High, "Praise be to Him Who took His **Mohammed's** servant by night from the Sacred Mosque to the Mosque al-Aqsa!" **Night-Journey** is meant Jerusalem. And in the words of the Most High to the Children of Israel, "Enter this city, and eat of it abundantly as ye wish," is meant Jerusalem.

And in the words of the Exalted, "And we appointed you a meet- **Mary and** ing place on the right side of the mount," is meant Jerusalem. In the **Her Child** words of the Exalted, "We made the son of Mary and his mother a sign, and settled them in a lofty spot, quiet and watered with springs," is meant Jerusalem.

Noah; Isaac Noah presented his offering on the Rock of Jerusalem. Allah Most High rescued Isaac from being sacrificed in Jerusalem.[93]

Adam. David. Wife of Imran In the words of the Most High, "O ye people! enter the land which Allah decreed for you!" is meant Jerusalem. Adam presented his offering in Jerusalem. Allah confirmed to David his kingdom in Jerusalem. And he softened iron for him in Jerusalem.[94] And Allah accepted from the wife of 'Imrān her vow in Jerusalem. And Allah granted to **Jesus and John** David (pardon for) his sins in Jerusalem. Allah strengthened Jesus[95] with the Holy Spirit in Jerusalem. Allah gave to John wisdom in his childhood in Jerusalem. And Jesus raised the dead and performed miracles in Jerusalem.

Mohammed in Jerusalem There will remain no believer, man or woman, who shall not go to Jerusalem. The treasure of the world is Jerusalem. Who prays in Jerusalem, it is as if he prayed in the nearer Heavens. All the lands shall be destroyed, but Jerusalem shall prosper. Allah shall assemble Mohammed and his people unto Jerusalem. The first thing that was disclosed from the waters of the Flood was the Rock of Jerusalem. Allah shall assemble His creatures unto Jerusalem. Allah gathered the prophets unto His Apostle, and he prayed with them as their imām in Jerusalem. The angels are in serried ranks round about Jerusalem. **Hell-fire and Heaven** Allah forgives who comes to Jerusalem. The Apostle of Allah came with Gabriel and Michael to Jerusalem. Hell-fire is heated in Jerusalem. A door of Heaven is open unto Jerusalem.

Merit of the Muezzins Allah shall assemble the muezzins of the Sacred Mosque, and the muezzins of the Mosque al-Aqsa, and the muezzins of the mosque of His Apostle unto Paradise before the other muezzins, except Bilāl the muezzin of the Apostle of Allah.[96]

The Supreme Merit of Prayer in Jerusalem Who performs the ablutions seven times,[97] and prays a prayer of two or four rak'ahs in Jerusalem, there shall be forgiven him what was before that time. And who prays in Jerusalem shall be absolved from his sins as he was on the day his mother bore him; and he shall have for every hair of his body a hundred lights in the presence of Allah on the Day of Judgment; and he shall have a justifying and acceptable pilgrimage; and Allah shall give him a heart that is thankful, and a tongue that speaks His praise; and shall protect him from rebellious sins, and shall gather him with the prophets.

Whoever stays patiently a year in Jerusalem despite tiresomeness and discomfort,[98] Allah shall come to him with provisions, in front of him, on his right, on his left, above him, and under him; he shall eat abundantly; and if Allah the Exalted will, he shall enter Paradise.

Merit of Spending a Year There

The first spot that was created in all the world was the place of the Rock of Jerusalem. And Allah said to Solomon when he finished building the Temple, O Solomon, ask of Me what thou wilt! I will grant it. He said, O my Lord! I ask of Thee that Thou forgive my sins. Allah said, All that is thine. He said, O my Lord, and I ask of Thee a kingdom not deserved by anyone after me! Verily, Thou art the Bounteous Giver![99] Allah said, All that is thine. He said, O my Lord, and I ask of Thee for whoever comes to this Temple wishing only to pray here, that he be absolved from his sins as he was on the day his mother bore him! Allah said, All that is thine! He said, And I ask of Thee for whoever comes here in sickness that Thou heal him. Allah said, All that is thine. He said, And I ask of Thee that Thine eye be upon him unto the Day of Judgment. Allah said, All that is thine.

Allah Grants All Solomon's Requests

And he says: Allah looks in mercy every day unto Jerusalem. Moses' staff shall appear at the end of time in Jerusalem. Allah announced to Mary the good news of Jesus in Jerusalem. Allah showed unto Mary favor above all women in Jerusalem. Angels descend every night unto Jerusalem. Allah prevents the enemy of Allah, the Anti-Christ,[100] from entering Jerusalem. He shall conquer all the lands except Jerusalem and Mecca and Medina. Allah turned (with acceptance) toward Adam in Jerusalem. Who gives alms to the amount of a loaf of bread in Jerusalem, it is as if he gave alms to the weight of earthly mountains, all of them gold. Who gives alms to the value of a dirham, it will be his redemption from the Fire. Who fasts a day in Jerusalem, it will mean his immunity from the Fire.

The Annunciation to Mary There

Anti-Christ Kept Out

The choice of Allah of all His lands is Jerusalem, and in it are the chosen of his servants. And from it the earth was stretched forth, and from it shall be rolled up like a scroll. Allah directs his regard toward Jerusalem every morning, and showers upon its people His mercy and His benefits; then He showers them upon the rest of the lands.

In the Creation and the End of the World

The dew which descends upon Jerusalem is a remedy from every sickness, because it is from the gardens of Paradise. No one shall dwell in Jerusalem without there accompanying him seventy thousand angels unto Allah. Allah will say to him who is buried in Jerusalem, Thou shalt be My neighbor in My House; and is not My House Paradise! And only the generous and forbearing shall be My neighbors there.

The Prophet said to Abu 'Obeidah 'Āmir ibn al-Jarrāh,[101] The place to flee to when the rebellion occurs is Jerusalem. And he said, O Apostle of Allah, but if I cannot reach Jerusalem? He said, Then take heed for what is thine, and preserve thy religion! And likewise 'Ali ibn Abu Tālib said to Sa'sa'h, Yea! the place to dwell in on occurrence of rebellion is Jerusalem. He who remains there is as he who devotes himself to the way of Allah. And verily, the time is coming when one of them shall say, Oh, that I were a straw in a brick in Jerusalem![102]

The dearest part of Syria in the eyes of Allah is Jerusalem; and the dearest to Him of its mountains is (that on which is) the Rock. And it shall be the last of the lands to be destroyed, by forty years. It is one of the gardens of Paradise. Allah will say to the Rock of Jerusalem, My Might and My Majesty I confer upon thee, My Throne! I shall assemble unto thee all My creatures. And I shall make thy rivers to flow as rivers of milk and rivers of honey and rivers of wine and rivers of water.[103] On that day I shall be their Lord and their King.

Who drinks of four springs, Allah shall make his body inviolable to the Fire—from the spring al-Baqr which is in 'Akka, from the spring al-Fulūs which is in Beisān, from the spring of Siloam which is in Jerusalem, and from the spring Zamzam which is in Mecca the holy.

And Allah knoweth best!

CHAPTER THIRTEENTH

On the Merit of Pilgrimage to the Tomb of the Friend of God, Abraham, and the Adjacent Tombs of the Prophets

In the matter which I quote from the book of Abu 'l-Ma'āli, on authority of Abu Hureirah, he says: The Apostle of Allah said, When I was taken on the Night-Journey to Jerusalem, Gabriel went with me to the grave of al-Khalīl; and he said, Descend and pray here a prayer of two rak'ahs, for verily here is the grave of thy father Abraham!

In another tradition of the Apostle of Allah it is related that he said: Verily, Abraham was born in Irāq, in a place called Kūthārabba. But they forced him to migrate, and sent him forth from there. Then he came to Palestine, to the region of the Jordan. And he purposed to invoke evil upon them; but Allah gave him a revelation, Do not wish evil upon the people of Iraq; for verily, I have placed something of the store of My mercy among them, and have settled mercy upon their hearts! [104]

Abraham
Comes to
Palestine

On authority of Ka'b al-Ahbār it is related: The first person who died and was buried in Habra (or Hebron) was Sarah, whom Abraham buried; and she was his wife.[105] And on this subject also: Abraham sought of the king of that place that he sell him a plot of land to bury those of his people who died. And the king said, I give thee permission, so bury where thou wilt in my land. But he refused, except by purchase. And he had sought from him the Cave. So he said, I will sell it to thee for four hundred dirhams, five dirhams in each, altogether a hundred dirhams royal coinage. And he was purposely increasing the price to him, in order that he not find the money; so he maintained what he said. And Abraham went away. But Gabriel brought that amount and paid it to the king. So he bore Sarah unto the Cave, and buried her in it.

How Abraham
Bought the
Cave and
Buried Sarah

Then Abraham died, and was buried beside her. Then Rebecca, the wife of Isaac, died and was buried there. Then Isaac died, and was buried opposite his wife. Then Jacob died, and was buried inside the door of the Cave. Then Leah died, and was buried beside Jacob.[106]

Abraham and
Others Buried
There

Then the sons of Esau and his brothers connived, and said, Let us leave the door of the Cave open; and every one of us who dies, we shall bury him there. Then they quarreled; and one of the brothers of Esau lifted up his hand and struck Esau a hard blow, and his head fell into the Cave. And they bore away his body, and it was buried without the head, for his head remained in the Cave. And the people shut the door of the Cave, and walled it up.[107]

Only Esau's
Head There
Buried

And they placed in it grave-markers on every spot, writing upon them, This is the grave of Abraham, This is the grave of Sarah, This is the grave of Rebecca, This is the grave of Jacob, This is the grave of his wife Leah. And they went forth from it. Thereafter, whoever came there passed over it and failed to find it. And no one came upon

The Inscribed
Tombstones

The Byzantines
Build a Church
There it until the Greeks (Byzantines) arrived there later, and opened one of the doors, and entered it, and built a church there.[108]

A Summary
Account of
Abraham
In some books it is recorded: When Allah rescued Abraham from the fire, he came from Babylon to the Holy Land, and with him Sarah and Lot, the son of his brother, and the kindred of his people, as far as Harrān.[109] And they remained there for a time. Then they came to the Jordan (region). And they were compelled to go to a city in which there was a giant. He it was who dared to take Sarah, but Allah pre-
Sarah and the
Evil Tyrant
vented her being touched by him.[110] And that giant, it is said, went forth from that city, and Allah gave it to Abraham as an inheritance. So Abraham grew rich there, and Allah increased his possessions, and showered provisions upon him. So Abraham divided with his nephew Lot, and gave him half of it. And Abraham died and was buried in Habrūn, the city of the giants; and there was where Sarah was buried, in a field which Abraham had purchased.

On authority of 'Abdullah ibn Muslim it is related: Isaac lived a hundred and eighty years. And when he died he was buried near the
Summary of
the Patriarchs
grave of Abraham, in the field which Abraham had purchased. And likewise Esau and Jacob died, and were buried in the field near the grave of Abraham. And their ages were a hundred and forty-nine years.

On authority of Ibn 'Abbās it is related: When Allah Most High wished to take the soul of His Friend Abraham, He gave this revela-tion unto the earth, Verily, I shall bury in thee My Friend! And the earth moved itself with a mighty motion, and its mountains were heaved up on high, and there was depressed in it a vale called Habra.
Allah's
Message
to Hebron
Regarding
Abraham's
Burial
And Allah said to it, O Habra! thou art My brightness! thou art My brightness! thou art My sanctuary! In thee is the treasury of My wisdom, and upon thee I send down My mercy and blessing; and unto thee shall I assemble the choicest of My servants of the children of My Friend. Blessed is he who inclines his forehead in prayer to Me in
And the
Merit of
the Shrine
thee! I shall give him to drink of the immanence of My holiness, and shall protect him in the pouring out of My resurrection, and shall give him an abode in Paradise by My mercy. And blessed art thou! again, blessed! I shall bury in thee My Friend!

On authority of Ka'b it is reported: When Solomon son of David finished building the mosque of Jerusalem, Allah spoke to him by reve-lation, Construct a building over the grave of Abraham, My Friend, that it may be known! And Solomon went and built on a place called ar-Rāmah. And Allah spoke to him by revelation, This is not the place; but look unto the light descending from Heaven! So he looked, and behold! the light was over the vale called Habra! So he knew that was the intended place; and he built over that.[111] Solomon Builds the Shrine by Command of Allah

From Wahb ibn Munabbih: In the latter time there shall be a gulf between mankind and the Pilgrimage. And who has not made the Pilgrimage completely, he must go to visit the grave of Abraham. For indeed, a visit to it is equivalent to a Pilgrimage (to Mecca). Pilgrimage Here Like the Hajj to Mecca

From him also: Who visits the tomb of Abraham once in his lifetime, concerned only for that, he shall be gathered on the Day of Resurrection secure from the great distress; and he shall be protected from the two angels of the tomb.[112] And it is incumbent upon Allah that He join him and Abraham in the Abode of Peace. The Reward of Sincere Pilgrimage Here

From Ka'b: Who visits Jerusalem and goes (also) to the tomb of Abraham for prayer there, and prays five prayers there, then asks of Allah anything, He will give it to him; and all his sins will be forgiven. And who visits the graves of Abraham, Isaac, Jacob, Sarah, Rebecca, and Leah, He will give him for that visit lasting honor, and sufficient provisions during his life; and Allah shall cause him, while supplied with these things, to reach the Abodes of the Just. And he shall not return to his home without his sins having been forgiven; and he shall not go from the world until he sees Abraham, who shall give him the good news that Allah hath pardoned him. The Merit of Pilgrimage and Prayer, in Jerusalem and Hebron

And the author relates on authority of 'Abdullah ibn Salām this: Visiting the grave of Abraham and praying there is a pilgrimage for the poor, and a work of meritorious value for the rich. Like a Pilgrimage for the Poor

It is considered appropriate for one who wishes to visit (the graves of) al-Khalīl and Isaac and Jacob that he fortify himself, and that he ask of Allah success and assistance; and that he pray a prayer of two rak'ahs, and ask of Allah, after them, protection; and that he be cautious not to bring unto the Friend of Allah anything abominable or inappropriate in his visit. For verily, the prophets are in a living state in their tombs![113] Directions for the Pilgrim

Then he should go to the spot with humility and quietness, and mentioning the name of Allah, and praying for pardon. Then he should enter the mosque, beginning the entry with the right foot, and saying, The Ritual of Entering

In the name of Allah! and, Peace upon the Prophet of Allah! O Allah! bless Mohammed and the family of Mohammed! And forgive Thou me and have mercy upon me! And open for me the doors of Thy mercy, and also unto (all) the Muslims! And he should pray a prayer of two rak'ahs, saluting the mosque. Then he should enter unto the tomb of al-Khalīl, approaching it from any direction he may wish; then pronounce peace upon him, saying, Peace upon thee, O thou prophet, and the mercy of Allah and His blessings! Then he should pray blessing upon the Prophet (Mohammed), invoking Allah with whatever prayer he may wish, saying all this while he is standing still, facing the tomb.

Fitting Respect

It is not fitting for him to place his hand on the tomb, or embrace it. He must only stand, and pronounce peace upon him, as one does upon the living, with dignity and quietness and respect and reserve, as if he were in his living presence.

Abraham as Intercessor

And it is fitting that he say numerous prayers there, and make entreaty through him unto Allah; for verily, no one entreats through him without Allah answers.

And, he says, when thou hast finished that, thou passest to the tomb of Isaac, and performest what thou hast done at the grave of Abraham, in the way of praying and pronouncing peace upon the Prophet, and of invocation. And when one has completed the visitation at the grave of Isaac, he should come to the tomb of Jacob Israel of Allah, and repeat his former actions. And he should be earnest in prayer. For, he says, verily, prayers there are answered! More than one person has tried it, and found answer there.

The Women after the Men!

When one finishes that, he should pass on to the grave of Sarah, and pronounce peace upon her, and pray there, and pray blessing upon the Prophet. And he should do likewise at the grave of Rebecca, the wife of Isaac, and likewise at the grave of Leah. This is what is appropriate—that people begin the visitation with the men before the women, just as their lot hath been made.

Visiting the Tomb of Joseph

And when one has finished that, he should pass on to the tomb of Joseph as-Siddīq. It is outside the Cave, in the vale. And he should pronounce peace, and pray blessing on the Prophet, and upon his family, and his Companions, and make invocation.[114]

And he relates on authority of Abu Bekr ibn Ahmad and Abu 'Amr ibn Jābir:[115] Someone asked concerning the tomb of al-Khalīl, and

the certainty of its authentication. And he said, I have not seen
(record of) any of the sheikhs with whom the people of learning have
studied but who affirm that the sepulchre is that of Abraham al-Khalīl,
and Isaac, and Jacob, and their wives. They say no one disparages
that, except he be a man who is a perverter and a designer.

And the Prophet assigned (as a fief) the territory of Hebron, with
what pertained to it, to Tamīm ad-Dāri, before Allah gave the Muslims
the victory over Syria. And he gave him a written document to that
effect. So he brought it before Abu Bekr as-Siddīq, and he allowed it
as a valid document of the Apostle of Allah. And he likewise took it
to 'Omar ibn al-Khattāb, and he gave him his lawful due, after the
conquest, as the Apostle of Allah had executed it to him.

Then he relates on authority of Abu Hind ad-Dāri, this: We went
before the Apostle of Allah, six of us in a group, including Tamīm ibn
Aus, his brother Nu'eim ibn Aus, and Yazīd ibn Qeis, and Abu
'Abdullah — who is the source of the tradition — and his brother at-
Tayyib ibn 'Abdullah — whom the Apostle of Allah called 'Abdu
'r-Rahmān—and Fākihah ibn an-Nu'mān.[116]

And he greeted us. And we asked of the Apostle of Allah that he
assign to us a district of the land of Syria. And the Apostle of Allah
said, Ask where ye will!

And Abu Hind says: We arose from his presence, and went to a
place aside, where we took counsel about where we should ask. And
Tamīm said, I think we should ask for Jerusalem and its territory.
And Abu Hind said, I think best of the Persian territory (there); is it
not at present Jerusalem?[117] And Tamīm said, Yea! Then Abu Hind
said, And it will likewise be the property of the Arabs; so I fear he will
not grant all this to us. And Tamīm said, Then let us ask for Beit
Jibrīl and its territory.[118] And Abu Hind said, That is larger, and
more extensive! And Tamīm said, Then what thinkest thou best to
ask him for? He said, I think best that we ask him for the towns in
which our mats are made, with the relics of Abraham that are there.

And the Apostle of Allah said, O Tamīm! dost thou wish to inform
me what ye are talking about, or shall I inform you? Tamīm said,
Nay! inform us, O Apostle of Allah! for we are seeking after safety
and certainty! And he said, Thou dost wish, O Tamīm, so and so; and

this man (Abu Hind) wisheth so and so— And he approved the wish which was that of Abu Hind.[119]

And the Apostle of Allah called for a piece of red leather,[120] and wrote a document of which this is a copy:

The Prophet's
Writ of Grant In the name of Allah the Merciful and Compassionate! This is a record of what Mohammed the Apostle of Allah granted to the Dāris. When Allah shall have vouchsafed to him the land, he granteth to them Beit 'Ein, and Habrūn, and al-Martūm, and Beit Ibrāhīm,[121] with what is in the same, unto them forever. Witness: 'Abbās ibn 'Abdu 'l-Mutallib, Jahm ibn Qeis, and Shurahbīl ibn Hasanah.

And when the Apostle of Allah migrated to Medina, we went unto him and asked him that he renew the document for us. So he wrote for us a document, of which this is a copy:

The Writ
Renewed in
Medina after
the Hijrah In the name of Allah the Merciful and Compassionate! This is what Mohammed the Apostle of Allah granted unto Tamīm ad-Dāri and his fellows: Verily, I grant to you Beit 'Ein, and Habrūn, and al-Martūm, and Beit Ibrāhīm, with their protected population, and with everything in them, as a public grant. And I give and assure this unto them for The Great
Witnesses ever and ever. And whoever causeth them injury there, Allah will injure him! Witness: Abu Bekr ibn Abu Qahāfah, 'Omar ibn al-Khattāb 'Othmān ibn 'Affān, 'Ali ibn Abu Tālib, and Mu'āwiyah ibn Abu Sufyān.[122]

And when the Apostle of Allah died, and Abu Bekr succeeded him, and sent the troops on expeditions into Syria, he wrote for us a letter as follows: In the name of Allah the Merciful and Compassionate! Abu Bekr's
Letter From Abu Bekr as-Siddīq unto Abu 'Obeidah 'Āmir ibn al-Jarrāh. Peace upon thee! Verily, I thank Allah—than Whom there is no other god!—for thee! And now—I forbid whoever believeth in Allah and the Last Day from interfering in the towns of the Dāris. And if their people have left them, the Dāri wish them to be sown and tended; so let them be sown. And if their people return to them, then (the lands) are theirs, and they have the prior right. And farewell![123]

The Author's
Conclusion and
the Copyist's
Colophon Then says the sheikh, the imām, known as the preserver of the Sunnah, stay of the Sharī'ah,[124] Burhānu 'd-Dīn Abu Ishāq, son of the sheikh and imām known as Tāju 'd-Dīn Abu Mohammed ibn 'Abdu 'r-Rahmān ibn Ibrāhīm as-Sabbā' al-Fazāri ash-Shāfi'i (may Allah continue His care over him, and make him profitable and useful!), this is the end of what he by his hand prepared and assembled on the subject of the Merits of Jerusalem. We ask of Allah Most High that he make us profitable through it in this world and the next. Verily, He bestoweth success! There is no God beside Him! Him do we trust! He is the Lord of the Great Throne! There is no strength or power save in Allah Most High and Mighty.

And completion of this copy came to pass, with thanks unto Allah the Exalted,
Who made it a good success, on the evening of Thursday, the seventh
of the month Rabi' al-Awwal, of the year 882.[125] O Allah!
Make good the ending, and make good the beginning! Verily, Thou hast power
over all things!
Amen!

Part II

THE BOOK OF INCITING DESIRE

By the Sheikh and Imām Abu 'l-Fidā', Preacher of the Shrine of Our Lord Abraham [1]

PREFACE

In the name of Allah, the Merciful, the Beneficent! O Lord, make easy and aid in our task! Thus wrote the sheikh and imām known as Abu 'l-Fidā' Ishāq (Isaac), son of the sheikh and imām known as Abu 'l-'Abbās Ahmad, son of the sheikh known as Abu 'Abdullah Mohammed at-Tadmuri, of the Shāfi'ite school, preacher of the shrine of our lord Abraham (upon him blessing and peace! and may Allah forgive him in His mercy and good pleasure, with all the Apostles!): The Author's Invocation

I praise Allah that He hath made us neighbors of His prophet Abraham, His bosom-friend (al-Khalīl), and hath included all of us in his blessings every morn and eve, at every daybreak and nightfall. And I witness that there is no god but Allah, without companion, the Mighty Lord! And I witness that our lord Mohammed is His servant and apostle, calling us to the true faith, and guiding us to the straightforward path! May Allah bless him, and the rest of the prophets and apostles, eternally, without cessation or change!

As for what follows (and may the light of Allah be before me, and before thee, with the light of certainty! and may He be gracious unto me and unto thee, as unto His pious servants!): A petitioner whom I was duly concerned to answer, having been strengthened by the Divine will in his affection and companionship, asked that I put together a delectable lot of pertinent records and historical materials concerning the trustworthiness of the reports and accounts and reliques on the subject of the birth of our lord Khalīl ar-Rahmān, and his noble sons, and their wives, and the extent of their lifetimes, and their resting places in the Holy Land, and their deaths; with also mention of their children and their wives, and the places of their sepulchres; also, the merit of pious visitation unto them; and further, the evident miracles which Allah Most High granted His prophet and friend, and the manifest signs vouchsafed to him by Gabriel. Occasion for the Book: The Request of a Friend The Subject: Abraham, and Other Prophets Connected with Palestine

So I acceded to his request, hoping from Allah a good reward and recompense on the Day of Return to Him (Verily, He is generous and bountiful!). And I have composed the work under the title, *Muthīr al-Gharām li-Ziyārat al-Khalīl* ('aleihi 's-salāt wa-'s-salām!), arranging the material in twenty-seven chapters.

Chapter First

On His Genealogy, and the Length of His Life

Abraham's Pre-eminence

He is Abraham, Bosom-friend of the Merciful, father of the noble prophets, the first entrusted with the duty of apostleship. Allah revealed unto him ten books, all of them in the form of proverbs. He gave him a tongue of truth for all time, that is, for its beautiful praise. There is no one in all nations who does not love him. And He honored him by his special relationship as the Friend of God, and by the fact that He appointed most of the prophets from his seed, and set as the seal of them our prophet Mohammed.

Now the holy verses (of the Koran) concerning him are familiar and famous.

Abraham's Age, and His Station in the History of the Prophets

As for his age, an-Nawawi says in his *Tahdhīb al-Asmā' wa-'l-Lughāt*: It is said that his age came to a hundred and seventy-five years. There intervened between Noah and him a thousand, one hundred, and forty-two years, and between his birth and the Hijrah (of Mohammed) two thousand, eight hundred, and thirty-two years (or, according to the reckoning of Jewish history, two thousand, four hundred, and thirty-two years).

His Parents and Descent

He was the son of Āzar, whose name was that given him by his father Terah; though it is said that Āzar was the name and Terah the by-name, or vice versa, both opinions being well known. An-Nawawi reports in his *Tahdhīb* that Āzar was of the people of Harrān, and that the mother of Abraham was named Nūnah, or, as others say, Ayūnah, of the children of Ephraim ibn Ar'awa ibn Peleg; and her family was related (to that of Āzar and Abraham) through Ar'awa.[2]

The hāfiz ibn 'Asākir reports: When Terah reached seventy-five years of age, there were born to him Abraham, Nahor, and Haran; and there was born to Haran Lot. And they say that Abraham was the middle son of Nahor, son of Serug, son of Reu, son of Peleg, son of Eber, son of Salah, son of Arphaxad, son of Shem, son of the prophet of Allah, Noah. And he (Noah) was the foremost of the apostles.

Now (Noah) was the first of all the establishers of sacred law, and the first to call people unto Allah Most High, and the first warner of mankind. The author of the *Jāmi'u 'l-Usūl* says that there were between him and Adam a thousand and two hundred years, as one report has it; and he was the second Adam, for those who were with him in the Ark did not perish, and all mankind thereafter were from his three sons, Shem, Ham, and Japheth. The length of his prophetic mission was nine hundred and fifty years; and he lived after the Flood fifty years—or, as others say, two hundred years.

Pre-eminence of Noah

The Second Adam

Ath-Tha'labi relates, on authority of (Aus) ibn Shaddād, that he lived before the Flood a thousand years, less fifty — which he spent among his people — and after the Flood three hundred and fifty years. And according to this opinion the extent of the life of Noah would be a thousand and three hundred years. The majority of the 'ulemā' are of the view that he lived a thousand years but fifty, and that he was sent as prophet to the people of Qābīl when he was fifty years of age. And the duration of the Flood was six months, the last day of it being the Tenth of Moharram.[3] And the Ark went about the entire earth in that space of time; then it came to rest on Mount Jūdi, which is in the area of Mosul. The time of their embarkation was when ten days had passed of the month Rajab; and they disembarked on the Tenth of Moharram.

The Flood

And when Noah and those with him left the Ark, they took for themselves a spot in the district of al-Jazīrah,[4] and built there a town which they called Thamānīn ("Eighty"); because every man who was in his company built a house—and they were eighty. It is called today Sūq Thamānīn ("The Market of the Eighty").

Then, when death came, he placed matters in charge of his son Shem, blessing him to exclusion of his brethren; and all of the prophets were of his descendants. And now Shem had been born eighty-nine years before the Flood; and it is said that he was Noah's firstborn. Noah was the longest-lived of all the prophets, yet his strength did not diminish. And mankind after him was of his seed. Tradition relates that when death drew near, someone said to Noah, How dost

Life a House With Two Doors

thou regard thy life? And he said, Like a house with two doors, through one of which I entered, and left by the other!

Ath-Tha'labi gives an account from the Prophet to this effect: Noah had three sons, Shem, Ham, and Japheth; Shem was the father of the Arabs and the Persians and the Greeks; Ham was the father of the blacks; and Japheth was the father of the Turks, the barbarians, and Gog and Magog (Yājūj and Mājūj). He was son of Amalek, son

of Methuselah, son of the prophet of God, Idrīs, whose name was really Enoch (Khanūkh). He was called Idrīs because of his devotion to study (verb: *darasa*) of the books and scriptures revealed to Adam and Seth. He was born while Adam was still living—a hundred years before his death. He was the first prophet sent after Adam, Allah Most High having commissioned him two hundred years after Adam's

death. And he continued in his prophetic mission a hundred and fifty years, Allah sending down to him thirty books. Then Allah raised him up to a place on high, as some have said, to the fourth Heaven, and as others, to the sixth, and still others, to Paradise itself—than which there is no place more exalted! At the time he was four hundred and fifty years old. He was the first to write with the pen, and the first to sew together clothing and to wear sewed garments; he was the first to consider the matter of the stars and reckoning. Allah Most High sent him as prophet unto the sons of Qābīl.[5] And when Allah translated him, mankind disagreed, and revelation languished until Allah sent Noah son of Yarid, or, as some say, son of Yārid, son of Mahaliel, son of Qīnān, son of Unūs, son of Seth, son of Adam.

Now Adam was the father of mankind. Allah created him from earth, and honored him in having the angels bow before him. The author of the *Jāmi'u 'l-Usūl* says: Ibn Abu Khutheimah writes, that from the time Allah created Adam until He sent Mohammed there were five thousand and one hundred years—though others say it was longer. And there were between Adam and Noah a thousand and two hundred years. Adam lived nine hundred and sixty years. People in his lifetime were of one religion, holding to the scriptures which the angels had brought to them. So they continued, until Idrīs was translated; but thereafter they disagreed.

The hāfiz Ibn 'Asākir writes: There were between Adam and Noah ten centuries, and between Noah and Abraham ten centuries. So

Abraham was born at the end of two millennia after the creation of Adam. And an account by Ayyūb ibn 'Utbah, qādi in Yemen, says: There were between Noah and Abraham ten of the patriarchs—and that is a thousand years; and there were between Abraham and Moses seven patriarchs, the number of years for which he does not indicate; and there were between Moses and Jesus a thousand and five hundred years; and there were between Jesus and Mohammed six hundred years, which is the interval between the sending of prophets (al-fatrah). But the lack of agreement upon the matter is considerable.

What the author of the *Jāmi'u 'l-Usūl* certifies is that between the death of our lord Abraham and the Hijrah, according to the view of the Moslems, there were two thousand and six hundred and thirty-two years—allowing that he (Abraham) lived two hundred years. And this is the conservative opinion. For from the Hijrah to our present time is eight hundred and fourteen years. So that from the death of our lord Abraham to our present time would be three thousand, four hundred, and forty-six years.

An-Nawawi writes in the *Tahdhīb al-Asmā' wa-'l-Lughāt*: He (Abraham) died in the Holy Land, and was buried there. His tomb is well known, in the city called al-Khalīl, between which and Jerusalem is less than a day's journey.

And may the blessings and peace of Allah be upon him, and upon his sons and descendants!

CHAPTER SECOND

His Birth

The learned disagree upon the place where he was born. Ath-Tha'labi says his birthplace was in Sūs in the region of Ahwāz. Some of them say it was Babel in the region of Suwād, in the territory called Kūtha (or Kūthā-rabbā); then his father took him to the place where Nimrod dwelt, in the territory of Kūtha. At-Tabari, in his history, says: Some say his birthplace was in Harrān, but his father Terah carried him to the land of Babel. An-Nawawi says: We are told in the *History of Damascus* by the hāfiz Ibn 'Asākir, on authority of Ibn 'Abbās: Abraham was born in the Ghautah of Damascus, in a village

[marginal notes:]

The Great Prophets, from Adam to Jesus and Mohammed

Death and Burial of Abraham

Various Views of the Birthplace of Abraham

known as Barzah. So says he in this account. The truth is that he was born in Kūtha, in the region of Babel, in Irāq; and he is connected with this place (Barzah and Damascus) because he prayed there when he came on the expedition in aid of his nephew Lot.

Born in the Era of the Impious Nimrod

Most of the historians of antiquity say that Abraham was born in the time of Nimrod,[6] son of Canaan, son of Cush, son of Shem, son of Noah. And he (Nimrod) was the first who placed a crown on his head, and acted with impious pridefulness in the earth, calling upon the people to worship him. He had astrologers and diviners, who told him,

Predicted by Astrologers

Verily, there will be born in thy kingdom this year a youth who will have a religion different from that of the people of the land, and will be the cause of thy destruction and the end of thy rule! It is said that so they found in the books of the prophets.

The Four Kings of the Earth

Now it is said that the kings who ruled the earth were four, two believers and two heathen. The believers were Solomon son of David, and Alexander (He of the Two Horns) ; and the heathen were Nimrod and Nebuchadnezzar (Bukhtu-nassar).

Another Story of the Astrologers

Ibn Ishāq says: When Allah desired to send Abraham to remonstrate with his people and to be a prophet calling them to His service —and there had been no prophet in all the time between Noah and Abraham, except Hūd and Sālih [7] — Nimrod saw in a dream, as it were a star arising. It took away the brightness of the sun and the moon, until there remained no light in them. So he was greatly terrified. And he summoned his magicians and diviners and astrologers, and asked of the matter. And they said, It is (the sign of) a child born in thy region this year, by whose hands will come thy destruction and the destruction of the people of thy house. Thereupon, as it is said, Nimrod ordered the slaughter of every man-child born in that area that year. And he ordered the men to desist from their wives, placing over every twenty men a trusty guard. So when a woman came to her menses, the restriction was removed; but when she was purified, her

Abraham's Conception

husband was made to refrain from her. But it came about that Āzar, father of Abraham, came home and found his wife in a state of purification; so he lay with her thus, and she came to bear Abraham.[8]

Nimrod's Warning

An-Nawawi writes in his history: Before the birth of Abraham, Nimrod one day ascended his throne—and there came a great quaking, and he heard a voice saying, Woe unto him who disbelieves in the God of Abraham! So he said to Terah (or Āzar), who was standing at his head, Didst thou hear what I heard? He said, Yea! And he said, Now, who is Abraham? And he said, I know him not. So he sent to his magicians and asked them about Abraham, informing them of what he had heard. And they said, We know not either Abraham or his god! Then the voices came to him time and again; and animals and birds and beasts spoke in the same way.

He saw also visions in his sleep—one of them, as if the moon arose from Terah's loins, sending forth his light as a column stretching between heaven and earth. Also, he heard a voice saying, "The truth hath come!" And he beheld the idols, which were moved as if thunder- **Other** struck. So he awoke. And he related his vision to Terah, who said to **Portents** him, O King! I am indeed like the moon in the earth because of my **of Terah** devotion to the worship of these images! And he said to him, Thou hast spoken truth. So Terah turned aside and entered the idol temple; **The Idols** and behold, they were fallen from their pedestals, and were lying over- **Overturned** turned on their faces! Thereupon he ordered their attendants to give service to them, being in wonder about the matter.

An-Nuweiri also relates in his history as follows: Terah came one day unto the images, and they were struck a mighty blow, and were prostrated. And Allah endowed them with speech, to say, O Terah, "Truth hath come, and falsehood hath disappeared." And Nimrod will meet that of which he was warned! So he went forth, exceedingly afraid, and entered where his wife was, and told it to her.

And she said, I will tell thee of a marvel: I have ceased from the menses since such and such a time! (Or, she said, I have menstruated on this very day.) So he said, Conceal the matter, lest it reach the king! So when she was purified, a voice said to him, O Terah, hasten **The Sign of** unto they wife, that thou mayest send forth the light which is upon **the Light** thy face! And when he heard that, he ran away, as it were falling upon his face in flight; when, lo! an angel said to him, Where goest thou? Return, and restore the pledge which is in thy loins! So he went to his dwelling, but did not dare to approach his wife. And there appeared as if it were a white light shining upon his face.

Now he was the one who brought to the idols their food, which the devils would come to and eat. But they saw the angels there, and turned in hasty flight, so that the food remained as it was. So when

Another Story
of How
Abraham
Was Conceived

Terah went on the morn, he saw it still as it was, and thought that the idols were displeased at him. Thereupon he remained in service upon them in order that they might become appeased. And because he was tardy in returning home, his wife came unto him. So while they were together in the idol temple, he was moved with desire, and set about to have intercourse with her, although she said, Art thou not ashamed to do this in the presence of thy gods! So he lay with her, and she became pregnant from him with Abraham.

Abraham's
Star

Then the idols were overthrown, and there appeared the star of Abraham, having two points, one of them in the east and the other in the west. So the people were amazed at it; and Nimrod saw it, and was perplexed. So when morning came, he asked the astrologers about it. And they said, This is a new star that hath risen, denoting a child newly born, of notable folk, whose affairs will be exalted; so that we fear for thee because of him! Then a voice spoke to him, saying, O enemy of Allah! this is a child which hath been conceived by his mother; and, by Allah! thy destruction will be by him!

His Mother's
Narrow Escape
from Nimrod

And when his mother had completed nine months, she said to her husband, I wish to go into the temple of the idols and ask them that they lighten for me the birth. And he gave her permission, but he detained her until the night, for fear that the people know of her pregnancy. Then, when she entered the temple of the idols, they were overthrown from their pedestals. And so she started forth in fright— and behold, Nimrod came, with some people, having candles and torches! And Nimrod said, Who is this? She said, The wife of thy servant Terah. So then, when he wanted to say, Seize her! he said, Let her go free! So she came to her house in a panic, and the time of giving birth arrived. Then an angel from Allah came to her, and said, Fear not; but arise and deliver what is within thee! And she followed, until he caused her to enter the cave in which had been born Idrīs and Noah.

It is said further: When she entered the cave she found there every thing needful. And Allah made light for her the delivery. And she brought forth on the night of Friday, which was the night of the Tenth of Moharram.[3] And when the child came forth, Gabriel took him and cut his cord, and gave the *adhān* in his ears, and clothed him in a white garment. Then the angel took her back to her house; and she in returning moved lightly, as if she had not given birth. And the angel said, Conceal the matter, and all that thou hast seen! So she entered her house; and Terah came, and saw her sprightly and light. So she said to him, What was within me was not a child, but only wind, which hath passed forth from me. So he rejoiced over that; and Allah cast forgetfulness over Nimrod concerning Abraham.

Abraham Born and Concealed in a Cave, Where Were Born Idrīs and Noah

Then, on the third day, his mother went forth to the cave—and saw wild animals persistently remaining at the door. She fearfully imagined that he had perished; but she entered, and saw him on a couch of fine silk, conscious and awake. She was amazed, and she knew that he had a God Who was sufficient for him, and Who could protect him! So he returned to her dwelling, and reported the matter to Terah. And he forbade her from returning to the cave. But she would go to him secretly every three days, to look upon him, and return, until he had completed two years. And Gabriel brought him food from Paradise, and fed him and gave him to drink. Then, when four years had passed, an angel brought him a robe from Paradise, and gave him to drink of the draught of Unity; and said to him, Go forth, now, victorious! And he went forth, as accounts say, at the time of sunset.

The Child Abraham Divinely Cared for

Ath-Tha'labi says, on authority of Ibn Ishāq: Nimrod sent to every expectant woman a guardian who would sit by—except for the mother of Abraham. And the soothsayers said to Nimrod: The child about whom we told thee hath been conceived this night! So Nimrod gave orders for slaughter of the children. And when the time drew near for the birth of Abraham, and the flow began for her, she went forth in flight, afraid that someone might see her, and her child be killed. So she placed him in a dry stream-bed, then wrapped him in a piece of cloth, and placed him in a concealed spot. Then she returned, and informed her husband that she had borne a child and had placed him in such and such a spot. So his father went and took him from that place, and dug a cave for him near the dry stream-bed, and concealed him in it, closing up the door with a stone for fear of wild beasts. And his mother went constantly to him, and suckled him. It is said also: And whenever the mother of Abraham came to him, she found him sucking from one finger water, and from another finger milk, and from another finger honey, and from another finger cheese, and from another finger butter.

Another Story of Abraham's Birth and Divine Care

And may the blessings and peace of Allah be upon him and his descendants and his seed, forever!

CHAPTER THIRD

His Going Forth from the Cave; His Remonstrance with His People; His Being Thrown into the Fire; with an Account of the Tower (of Nimrod)

Abraham's
Early Search
for Truth

The people of learning say: When Abraham came to childhood, still in the cave, he said to his mother, Who is my lord? And she said, I am. And he said, And who is thy lord? And she said, Thy father. And he said, And who is my father's lord?—And she said, Hush!

Then she returned to her husband, and said, What thinkest thou! The child about whom it was said he would change the religion of the people of the land is thy son! Then she told him of what he had said. Thereupon the father went to him. And Abraham said, O father, who is my lord? And he said, Thy mother. And he said, Who is my mother's lord? And he said, I am. And he said, And who is thy lord? And he said, Nimrod. And he said, And who is the lord of Nimrod—and he gave him a slap, and said to him, Hush!

Now that is what is meant by the word of Allah: "And we indeed brought Abraham guidance beforehand, and were cognizant of him." (Sūrah 21. 52.)

Al-Baghawi says in his commentary, from Muhammad ibn Ishāq: Āzar had asked the mother of Abraham concerning her pregnancy, and what occurred; and she had said, I bore a man-child, and it died. And he believed her, and was silent. And a day to Abraham in his infancy was as a month, and a month as a year. And when he had remained in the cave only fifteen months, he said to his mother, Bring me forth. And she brought him forth at the time of evening. Then he looked about and mused upon the creation of the heavens and the earth. And he said, Verily, He who created me and sustained and fed me, and gave me to drink, He is my Lord; and there will be no other beside Him! Thereupon, he looked into the heavens and saw a star, and said, That is my lord! Then he followed it with his glance, watching—until it set. But when it went down he said, I love not the things that pass away.[9] Then he saw the moon, as it was rising, and said, This is my lord! And he followed it with his glance, until it also set. Then arose the sun, likewise—and so on.

Then he returned to his father, Āzar, who had made upright his way and knew his Lord, and was free of the idolatry of his people, except that he had not summoned them (to Allah). And he informed him that he was his son. Also the mother of Abraham told him that he was his son, and informed him of what she had done concerning him. And he rejoiced over that exceedingly. And it is said by some that he was in the cave seven years, and by others thirteen years, and by still others seventeen years. *His Showing to His Father*

Al-Baghawi continues: It is said that when Abraham came to his youth he said to his parents, Bring me forth! And they brought him forth from the cave, and walked about with him at the time of the setting of the sun. And Abraham looked about at the camels and the horses and the sheep, and asked his father what they were. And he told him, Camels—horses—sheep. And he remarked, These must needs have a Lord and Creator. Then he looked, and beheld the star Jupiter (al-Mushtari) which had risen, or, as others say, Venus (az-Zuhrah) — for the night was at the last of the month, when the rising of the moon was delayed, so that he saw the star before the moon was up. *Another Account of His Precocity*

And that is the meaning of His saying (Great and Glorious is He!), "And when the night cast its veil upon him (that is, 'entered'), he saw a star, and said, This is my lord." [10] Now people differ about his having said that. Some construe it literally, saying that Abraham was a seeker of the way unto the Divine Unity until Allah came to him and brought to him His guidance; so that that did not injure him, being in the status of a seeker. And also, he said it in the condition of childhood, before the mission of remonstrating with his people had come to him. So it was not disbelief! *Abraham Cleared of Disbelief*

He (al-Baghawi) writes also: Now when Abraham returned to his father, and had so passed through his childhood that the executioners would not be after him, Āzar fondly took him unto himself. Thereafter, Āzar began making images, and giving them to Abraham to sell them. So Abraham would go with them, and call out, Who will buy "what cannot hurt him or help him"! [11] And no one would buy. And when they proved worthless, he took them to the river and doused *Abraham Makes Sport of the Idols* their heads in, saying, Drink! thus ridiculing his people and the error they were following.

So his scoffing became known abroad among his people, and the people of his town; and they argued with him about his religion. And he said to them, "Do ye argue with me about Allah, when He hath guided me unto the Divine Unity and Truth! I fear not what ye set up as false gods!" And that was because they had said to him, Have a care of the images, for we fear lest they touch thee with harm, like insanity or derangement, because of thine affront to them. But he said to them, "I fear not what ye falsely set up as gods; unless my lord will anything; for my Lord hath knowledge equal to any circumstance (that is, His knowledge encompasses everything); and do ye not call it to mind?"

He Declares the Truth

Ath-Tha'labi says in his *Book of Brides* (*Kitāb al-'Arā'is*[12]): Then Abraham summoned his father Āzar to his religion, saying to him, "O father, why dost thou serve what cannot hear or see, and cannot avail thee anything!" (As the verse goes.) But his father refused to accede to that to which Abraham called him. Thereafter Abraham strove with his people, in his free innocence of what they were worshiping; and he manifested his religion, saying, "Do ye indeed behold what ye are worshiping, ye and your fathers of old? Verily, they are enemies to me, except only the Lord of the Worlds!" And they said, And what dost thou worship? And he said, I worship the Lord of the Worlds! They said, Our lord is Nimrod. He said, Nay! "He Who created me and guides me, Who feeds me and gives me to drink, and, when I am sick, heals me . . ." (and so on, as the verses go).[13]

Abraham Calls His Father and His People to the Faith

So that was bruited among the people until it reached Nimrod. And he summoned him and said, O Abraham, what thinkest thou—the angel which sent thee, and to whose worship and the mentioning of whose name thou dost invoke us, and whose rank is mighty—what is he? And Abraham said to him, "He is my Lord, Who maketh alive and causeth to die!" Nimrod said, "I make alive and cause to die."[14] Abraham said, How dost thou make alive and cause to die? He said, I take two men who have been adjudged worthy of death, and I kill one of them—and thus I cause to die—and I pardon the other, and let him go—and thus I make to live.

Abraham before Nimrod

Al-Baghawi says: There is a difference of opinion on these specu-
lations. Muqātil says: When Abraham broke the idols, Nimrod
imprisoned him, and then brought him forth to burn him in the fire.
And he said to him, Who is thy lord to whom thou dost summon us?
And he said, "My Lord maketh alive and causeth to die." But others
say that this was after he had been cast into the fire. And that because:
The people in the time of Nimrod suffered drouth, and were obtaining
their food from him. And when there came to him a man in quest of
food, he would ask him, Who is thy lord? And if he said, Thou art, *Abraham*
he would sell him the food. So Abraham came among the rest, and *Divinely Fed*
Nimrod said to him, Who is thy lord? And Abraham said, "My Lord
is He Who maketh alive and causeth to die!" Then he sought from
him the necessary provisions, but he would not give him a thing. So
Abraham, in returning, passed by a dune of reddish-white sand, and
took some of it to please the heart of his family when he should come
to them. So when he came to his people, he placed aside his travelling
outfit, and slept. Then his wife arose and went to it and opened it—
and behold! the most excellent food one ever saw! So she prepared
some of it for him, and brought it to him. And he said, Whence came
this? And she said, From the food which thou didst bring. And he
recognized that Allah had fed him, and he gave Him thanks and praise.

Allah said: "When Abraham said, My Lord is He Who maketh
alive and causeth to die . . ." (And this is an answer to a question
the point of which is unrecorded.) Nimrod had said to him, Who is
thy lord? And Abraham said, "My Lord is He Who maketh alive and *Nimrod Seeks*
causeth to die." And Nimrod said, "I make alive and cause to die." *to Show*
His Power
And most of the commentators say: Then Nimrod summoned two
men, and killed one of them and let the other live, and professed the
turning aside from execution as making to live.

Then Abraham went on to further argument, not weakening; and
indeed his contention was binding, for he meant by making alive the
raising of the dead. And so he said, Then make alive him whom thou
hast killed, if thou be truthful! Then he went on to argument more *Abraham*
revealing than the former, and said, " Verily, Allah bringeth the sun *Silences Him*
from the east; and now, bring it, thou, from the west! And speechless
was he who was an unbeliever!" (That is, he was perplexed and
bewildered, and his argument was cut off.)

Ath-Tha'labi says: When Abraham wished to portray to his people the weakness and impotence of what they were worshiping instead of Allah, in a way making his argument more binding upon them, he set to seeking a good occasion. And so he secretly bided his time, until there came one of their festivals. As-Suddi says: They had a festival every year, for which they would go forth (from the city) and gather together; and then when they returned from the festival they would enter unto their idols and worship them, and then return to their homes. So when that festival came, the father of Abraham said, O Abraham, if thou wouldst only go forth with us unto our festival, our religion would please thee! And he went forth with them. But as he came along the way, he threw himself down and sat, and said, I am ill! And as he lay there they passed on. And when they passed on, he called out to the last of them,

Abraham's Scheme

"The weakest of the people have remained behind. Verily, I will use wiles with your idols after ye have turned your backs and gone on!"[15]

And they heard him. But Mujāhid and Qatādah say that Abraham only said that in secret, so that no one heard him but one man; and he was the one who reported it against him (later).

Then Abraham returned to the house of the gods. This was in a great court, and facing the door of the court was a large image, with smaller ones beside it. Now they had brought food and placed it before the gods, saying, When we return, the gods will have blessed our food, and we shall eat it. So when Abraham looked upon them, and upon

Abraham the Idol Smasher

the food before them, he said to them by way of satire, Will ye not eat? And when not one of them answered him, he said, What is the matter with you, that ye do not speak! And he rushed upon them with blows by his right arm, and began smashing them with a pick-axe which he was carrying, until there remained only the largest of the idols, on the neck of which he hung the pick-axe — and went forth. And that is what is meant by His word: "And he made them into bits, all but the largest of them, to which they mayhap might return."[16] Others say he hung the pick-axe to its hand.

Now there were seventy-two idols, some of gold, some of silver, and some of iron, lead, copper, and wood. And the largest was of gold, crowned with gems, and with two radiant rubies in its eyes.

Then, as the account goes on, when the people returned from their festival unto the house of their gods, and saw their idols all in fragments, they said, "Who hath done this to our gods! Verily, he is one of the wrongdoers!" (That is, of the criminals.) And they said (that is, they who had heard the words of Abraham, "By Allah, I will use wiles with your idols after ye have turned your backs," as he spoke of them with insult and reviling): He who is called Abraham—we think he is the one who hath done this! *Abraham Accused*

So the matter reached Nimrod the mighty one, and the nobles of his people. And they brought him before the leaders of the people; for Nimrod said, "Bring him out in public (that is, exposed) before the people; perhaps they may witness" against him that he is the one who hath done this. (For they disliked to take him without proof.) Thus say al-Hasan and Qatādah and as-Suddi. But Muhammad ibn Ishāq says: (It means) perhaps they will bear witness, or propose his punishment and what is to be done with him.

And when they brought him, they said, "Hast thou done this to our gods, O Abraham?" Abraham said, "Nay; the biggest of them did it." He was angered that these smaller ones ye worshiped along with him, while he was larger than they; so he smashed them! *His Ironical Self-defense*

Now Abraham meant that in the way of offering remonstrance with them. And that is meaning of His word: "Then ask them, if they can speak"—until they were in confusion at what he had accomplished against them.

Al-Qutubi says: The real meaning of the words, "Nay, the biggest of them did it; but ask ye them, if they can speak," is in the stated condition. For the power of speech is made a condition corollary to the power of action. That is, the sense is, If they have any power. Thus he manifested their inability to speak (or to act). And implied therein is (Abraham's saying), I did it myself.

From al-Kisa'i it is related: He stopped when he said, "(He) did it — ." So he says the meaning is, He did it whoever did it. But the former opinion is more trustworthy, because of the following:

It is recorded by Abu Hureirah that the Prophet said: Abraham told only three untruths, two of them in the service of Allah: His saying, I am ill; and his saying, This the biggest of them did it; and his saying of Sarah, This is my sister. And this is not in the realm of real

Abraham
Cleared of
the Guilt
of Falsehood

lying which condemns the perpetrator as altogether blameworthy. For he only uttered the untruth in this way by innuendo. And this is only equivocation for a lawful religious purpose, as it is found in the traditions that equivocation is free from lying. Some say that his words about Sarah, She is my sister, meant, in a religious sense. These interpretations clear Abraham of lying. And it is possible that Allah gave him permission for the purpose of righteousness, and for reproof and remonstrance with them; just as he permitted Joseph to order his officer to say to his brethren, "O ye of the caravan! Ye are thieves!" —when they had not stolen.[16a]

His Attack
upon Idolatry

So when the time came for Abraham to present his remonstrance, he said to them: "Do ye indeed serve instead of Allah other things which do not avail you one whit (if ye serve them), or injure you (if ye leave off their service)? Shame upon you (that is, villification, offense upon you), and upon what ye serve instead of Allah! Do ye not sensibly understand?" (That is, have ye no sense by which ye might know this.)

The Cry to
Burn Him

Then when he had made his argument binding upon them, and they were unable to answer, they said, "Burn him, and help your gods, if ye are men who act!" (That is, if ye are helpers for them.) Ibn 'Omar says that he who said, Burn him! was a man of the Kurds, whose name is said to have been Heizan. And Allah caused the earth to swallow him up, and he is sunk therein until the Resurrection Day. Others say that Nimrod said it.

How Abraham
Was Cast into
the Fire

Then when Nimrod gathered his people for the burning of Abraham, they bound him in a house, and built a building like an enclosure. Muqātil says they made to it a surrounding wall of stone, the height of which in the sky was thirty cubits, and the width of which was twenty. And they filled it with wood, and kindled a fire, and cast him into it. Others say that they built a furnace in a town called Kūtha, then gathered unto it large pieces of firewood of various kinds of wood, for a long time. So that when a man became ill, he would say, If Allah will pardon (and heal) me, I will indeed gather wood for (the burning of) Abraham! And a woman would vow, among the vows which she made, that if she obtained her request she would gather wood for the fire to burn Abraham. And a man would put it into his will that wood should be bought and thrown on. And a woman would spin, and buy wood with her spinning, and cast it on, thus seeking merit in the way of her religion.

Ibn Ishāq says that they were gathering the firewood for a month. And when they had gathered what they wished, they set fire to all The Fire Set sides of the firewood, and the fire blazed up and became so hot that if a bird passed over it was consumed because of its vehemence. And they kept it burning for seven days.

Accounts say that they did not know how to cast him into it. But The Catapult Iblīs[17] came and taught them the art of building a catapult (man-janīq). So they built one. Then they stood Abraham up and took him up to the top of the enclosure, then bound him and placed him in the catapult, bound and manacled. And the heavens and the earth, and all the angels therein—and all creation except men and jinn—cried out Creation Seeks to Aid Him with one voice, O our Lord! Abraham Thy Friend is being cast into the fire; and there is no one in the earth beside him who worships Thee! Permit us to aid him! But Allah the Mighty and Glorious said, He is indeed my friend, than whom there is no other; and I am his God, than Whom there is no other! So if he seeks aid of any of you, or makes a plea for it, then aid him; for I have given him permission. But if he calls only upon Me, I am aware of him, and I am his protector—so interfere not between us!

And when they were ready to throw him into the fire, there came to him the Guardian of the waters, and said, If thou wilt, I will quench Abraham Relies upon Allah Alone the fire! And there came to him the Guardian of the winds, and said to him, If thou wilt, I will blow away the fire with the wind! But Abraham said, I have no need of you; " Allah is my sufficiency, and He is the best to trust in! "

It is related on authority of Ubayy ibn Ka'b that Abraham said when they bound him to cast him into the fire: " There is no god but Thee! Praised be Thou, Lord of the worlds! Theee do I extol, and Thine is the Kingdom, Thou without peer! " Then they threw him into the fire, by means of the catapult. And Gabriel came near to him, and said, O Abraham, hast thou any need? And he said, As concerns thee, nay! Gabriel said, Then ask of Allah! And Abraham said, His awareness of my condition suffices me for request!

Ka'b al-Ahbār says: Every creature then began to extinguish the fire for him, except the big lizard, which was blowing the fire up.

Transgression of the Big Lizard

Ath-Tha'labi says: And because of that, the Prophet commanded that it be killed; and he named it the "transgressor" (fūwsīq). Al-Bukhāri relates on authority of Sa'īd ibn al-Musayyib, on authority of Umm Shureik, that the Apostle of Allah commanded that the big lizard be killed; for, he said, it kept blowing up the fire on Abraham.

Why the She-Mule Bears No Offspring

An-Nawawi relates in the *Tahdhīb al-Asmā' wa-'l-Lughāt*, on authority of 'Ali ibn Abu Tālib: The she-mule used to bear offspring. But she was the fastest of the animals in bringing firewood for the fire to burn Abraham; and he prayed against her, and Allah made her bearing of offspring to cease.

And Allah the Exalted said: "We said, O fire, be cool and healthful for Abraham!"[18] And Ibn 'Abbās says, If He had not said "healthful," Abraham would have died from its coldness. And indeed it is known from the records that there remained in the earth, then, no fire that was not put out, and not a fire was used in the world on that day. And if He had not said, 'for Abraham,' fire would have remained cold forever!

Gabriel Brings Him Comfort in the Fire

As-Suddi says: Then the angels took Abraham by his arms and sat him upon the ground—and lo! a spring of sweet water, and narcissus! Ka'b al-Ahbār says: The fire did not burn anything about Abraham, but his bonds. It is said that Abraham was in that place for seven days. Al-Minhāl ibn 'Omar says: Abraham said, There was never a day more pleasant to me than the days in which I was in the fire! Ibn Yassār says: And Allah sent the angel of shade in the likeness of Abraham, and he sat in the fire beside Abraham, keeping him company. Accounts say also: Allah sent Gabriel with a silken robe from Paradise, and a carpet; and he dressed him in the robe and sat him upon the carpet, sitting by him in conversation. And Gabriel said, O Abraham! verily, thy Lord said, Know ye not that the fire cannot hurt my beloved ones!

Nimrod, Amazed, Calls Him Forth

Then Nimrod came to see about matters, and looked down upon Abraham from a castle of his; and he saw him sitting in a garden, and the angel seated beside him, with the fire burning the firewood all around him. And he called out to him, O Abraham! great is thy God Who hath sent His power to change thee from the condition thou wert in unto that which I now see! O Abraham, art thou able to come forth from it? He said, Yea! He said, Dost thou fear that if thou standest in it, it will harm thee? He said, Nay! He said, Then arise and come forth from it! So Abraham arose and walked in the fire, until he came forth from it.

And when he came out to him, Nimrod said to him, O Abraham, who is the man whom I saw with thee, in thy likeness, seated at thy side? He said, That is the angel of the shades which my Lord sent unto me to keep me company in the fire. And Nimrod said, O Abraham, verily, I shall present to thy God an offering, because of what I have seen of His power and might, regarding what He hath done for thee when thou hadst refused to worship any but Him, alone! Verily, I shall sacrifice to Him four thousand kine! And Abraham said to him, What if He will not accept it from thee, because of thy present religion, until thou leavest it for mine? And he said, I cannot forsake my kingdom; but I will nevertheless sacrifice. So he made the sacrifice. And thereafter he desisted from Abraham, and Allah caused him to refrain from him.

Nimrod Impressed But Will Not Be Converted

Shu'eib al-Jabbā'i says: Abraham was cast into the fire when he was sixteen years old. And His word, "And we made them to be the losers," means that they lost their endeavors and expenditures, and their desires were not attained. Others say its meaning is that Allah sent upon Nimrod and his people gnats, which ate up their flesh and drank their blood; and one of them entered into his brain, and consumed it.

Nimrod Defeated by Gnats

Says Zeid ibn Aslam: Allah sent to that mighty king (that is, Nimrod) an angel commanding belief in Him. And he refused. Then He summoned him a second time; and he refused. Then He summoned him a third time; and he refused. So He said, I shall collect my troops; and do thou collect thine. So Nimrod gathered his troops and armies at the time of sunrise—and Allah sent upon them a company of gnats, so many that the face of the sun could not be seen. And He gave them power over them, and they ate their flesh and their blood, leaving them bare bones. And one of them entered the nostril of King Nimrod, and it remained in his nostril four hundred years, during which time Allah punished him. And he kept striking his head with an iron bar all that time, until Allah destroyed him.

Ath-Tha'labi says: When Abraham confronted him with the claims of his Lord, Nimrod said, If what thou sayest is true, I shall not stop until I know what is in the heavens! So he built a lofty tower in Babel, the ascent of it continuing unto the Heavens, on which he thought to look into the matter of Abraham's god. Ibn 'Abbās says: The height of the tower in the Heavens was five thousand cubits. Muqātil and Ka'b al-Ahbār say its height was two parasangs.[19]

Nimrod's
Impious
Ascent into
the Heavens

Thereafter, he made a plan for use of four eagles, young ones which he fed with meat and bread until they had become large and were grown and powerful. Then he sat in an enclosed carriage, with him a lad, and he was bearing bow and arrows. And he had made to the carriage two doors, one above and one below. Then he tied the gondola to the feet of the eagles, and tied meat on a stick above the gondola. Then he released the eagles—and they flew, trying to get at the meat as food, until they were far distant in the air. Then Nimrod said to his servant, Open the upper door, and see what about the heavens, whether we have drawn near to them! So the servant opened the upper door, and looked; and behold, the heaven was just as it was. Then he said, Open the lower door, and look at the earth, to see how it is! And (when he had done so), he said, I see the earth like a white sea, and the mountains like smoke![20]

So the eagles flew on, and ascended until the wind ceased between them and the two fliers. And he said to his servant, Open the upper door, and look! And he opened the upper door; and behold, the heaven was as it had been! Then he opened the lower door, and behold, the earth was dark and shadowed! And a voice cried, O thou impious one! whither goest thou? And 'Akramah says: Then he commanded his servant to shoot forth an arrow; and it returned to him besmeared

The Marvel of
Blood from
the Sky

with blood. And he said, I have sufficiently attended to the business of the god of the heavens!

Now there is disagreement about the arrow — as to the blood of what it was besmeared with. 'Akramah says: It was a fish in the sky, which offered itself in protection of Allah the Exalted, from a sea suspended in the firmament. Some say the arrow struck a bird, and was besmeared with the blood of it.

Thereafter, Nimrod ordered his servant that he strike the staff and reverse the meat—which he did. And the eagles descended with the gondola; and the mountains heard the whistling of the gondola and

The Descent

the eagles, and trembled, thinking that somewhat amiss had happened in the Heavens, and that the Hour had come! In this connection is His word: "Even if it had been their scheme to make the mountains cease from him . . ."[21]

Then, indeed, Allah sent a wind upon the tower of Nimrod, and cast the top of it into the sea, and threw upon them its wreckage, so that their houses were destroyed, and a feverish trembling siezed upon Nimrod. And the tongues of mankind were confused when the tower of Nimrod fell, because of the terror, and they talked in seventy-three languages. For which reason it was named Babel, because of the confusion of tongues there. And in this connection is His word: "And he cast upon them the roof from above them."[22]

The Tower Destroyed, and Tongues Confused

Muhammad ibn Ishāq says: There responded to Abraham's call some of the men of his people when they saw the deed of Allah in making the fire cool to him, despite the fear of Nimrod and the crowds. And there believed in him Lot, who was the son of his brother—Lot, son of Haran, son of Terah (for Haran was the brother of Abraham). And there believed in him Sarah, daughter of the king of Harrān, or, as it is said, the daughter of his paternal uncle Haran the elder. We shall explain that in discussing his wives.

Some Believe, Including Lot and Sarah

Ibn Ishāq says: And there went forth with him Lot and Sarah; as Allah saith: "And Lot believed in him, and said, Verily, I am making a journey forth unto my Lord!"[23] So he went forth and settled in Harrān, and remained there as long as Allah willed that he should stay; then he went forth further until he came to Egypt. Then he came out of Egypt and returned to Syria, and settled in Shebah, in the land of Palestine. This is a village of Syria. And Lot settled in the (later) overturned Cities of the Plains, which are distant from Shebah by a journey of a day and a night. And Allah sent him as a prophet, as His word says: "And we brought by rescue him and Lot unto a land in which we have blessed the worlds"—meaning Syria.[24]

Abraham and Lot's Migration or 'Hijrah' to Palestine

And it is blest in that most of the prophets were sent from it, and it is the Holy Land, the land of the Resurrection and the Judgment Assembly. In it Jesus Son of Mary shall descend, and in it Allah shall slay Anti-Christ. And it is a land of fertility, having many trees and rivers and fruits, which give sustenance to the poor and the rich. Ubayy ibn Ka'b says: All sweet water springs from a source beneath the Rock which is in Jerusalem; then it separates to flow unto all the world.

The Blessedness of Syria-Palestine

Chapter Fourth

On His Migration to Canaan

At-Tabari says in his history: When Allah rescued Abraham His Friend from Nimrod the Mighty One, some of the men of his people heeded him, when they saw what Allah had done for him, despite their fear of Nimrod and the crowds. And there believed in him Lot and Haran (who was the brother of Abraham and the father of Lot), and Sarah, who was the daughter of the king of Harrān, or as say others the daughter of his (Abraham's) paternal uncle. And she had reproached her people for their religion, and Abraham had married her on condition that he not make her jealous.

Abraham and His Faithful Company

Thereafter, Abraham and those with him, his companions who were following his way, decided upon leaving their people. And they said to their people: "Verily we are free of you and of what ye worship instead of Allah! We consider you as unbelievers, and enmity and hate have risen between us and you forever, till ye believe in Allah alone!"

Their Leave-taking

Ath-Thaʻlabi says in the *Kitāb al-ʻArāʼis*: And Abraham married his cousin Sarah, and took her forth with him in his migration for the sake of his religion, and for safety in the worship of his Lord, until he settled in Harrān. And he remained there as long as Allah willed; then he left there, removing to another place, until he came to a city called Baʻlabakk. And there was there one of the pharaohs of olden time.[25] Now Sarah was one of the most beautiful of women; and her goodliness and beauty were described to him. So the giant sent for Abraham, and he came to him. And he said, What of this woman and her relationship to thee? And he said, She is my sister. For he feared that if he said, She is my wife, he would kill him. Then he said to him, Adorn her and send her to me, that I may see her. So Abraham returned to Sarah, and said to her, Verily, this giant asked me concerning thee, and I said to him that thou wert my sister. Now, do not make me a liar before him! For thou art my sister before Allah; and there is not in this country a true believer (Muslim) other than myself and thee! Then Sarah went to the giant, and Abraham remained constant in prayer.

Their Removal from Harrān; Trouble from " Pharaoh " of Baalbek

And when she entered unto him, and he saw her, his desire was aroused toward her. And he sought to touch her with his hand, but Allah caused his hand to wither, to his breast. And when pharaoh saw that, he respected her more than ever, and said, Ask of thy god, that he turn his anger from me; for by Allah, I shall not harm thee! And Sarah said, O Allah, if he be truthful, then restore his hand! And some of the accounts, with trustworthy links of evidence, say that he did that three times, trying to touch her with his hand; and his hand withered. And when he saw that, he returned her to Abraham. Thereupon Abraham ceased his prayers, and said, How went the matter? And she said, Allah the Mighty and Glorious was sufficient for the schemes of the profligate one!

Sarah Saved from Him

Al-Bukhāri gives an account of Abu Hureirah to the same point. And in some reports it is said that Allah raised the veil between Abraham and Sarah, so that he could see her from the time she went forth from him until she returned to him—as a divine honor to them, and setting at rest the heart of Abraham.

At-Tabari says: When the matter of pharaoh and Sarah turned out as it did, he summoned some of his chamberlains and said, Verily, ye have brought me not a human but a demon! Take her forth, and give her " Āgar " (Hagar). And she went forth, having been given Hagar. And (he continues) she came with her; and when Abraham perceived her coming, he turned aside from his prayer, and said, How went the matter? And she said, Sufficient is Allah for the wiles of the unbelieving, profligate one! Now take from me Āgar. (Or, as others say, Hagar.) [26]

Sarah Given Hagar

Ibn Ishāq says: Hagar was a maid-servant of goodly mien and beauty. And Sarah presented her to Abraham, saying, Behold, I find her an obedient woman; so take her, and perhaps Allah will give thee from her a son. For Sarah had been denied children, and had despaired of them. And Abraham had prayed Allah to give him a worthy successor, and the prayer had long gone unanswered, until the age of Abraham had advanced, and Sarah was still barren. Then Abraham lay with Hagar, and she bore Ishmael. And Sarah was thereupon very sad, in that she had no child, as is told in the account to come in its place, if Allah will.

Hagar, Given to Abraham, Bears to Him Ishmael

Reports say that then Abraham went forth from that country, for he dreaded the king who was there, and eschewed evil from him.

So he settled in Shebah of the land of Palestine. And he dug there a well, and made there a place of worship. And the water of that well was living and clear; and his flocks would come to it for drink. But after Abraham had remained in Shebah for some time, the people did him an injury, and he left, and settled in a district of the land of Palestine between Ramleh and Aelia, in a town called Qat, or Qut.

Abu 'l-Ma'āli al-Mushrif ibn al-Murajja, the Jerusalem traditionist, says in an account from Ka'b al-Ahbār: Abraham came forth from Kūthārabba and settled in Syria, in the district of Palestine, in a place which is known today as Wādy as-Sab'a. And he was a young man, without much property; and he remained there until his substance had increased, and he was old. Then the place became straightened for the people because of his substance and wealth. And they said to him, Move away from us; for thou dost injure us by reason of thy sub-

stance, O pious sheikh! (For they were accustomed to call him ash-Sheikh as-Sālih.) And he said to them, Yea! And when he was busy about moving, they said one to another, He came to us poor, and he hath gathered with us all this substance; and if we would only say to him, Give us a share of thy substance, and take a share—! So they said that to him. And he said, Ye speak truth; I came to you when I was young—so return to me my youth, and take what ye will of my substance! So he rebutted them, and moved away.

Then when the time came for the flocks to go down to water, the people came to draw—and behold, the wells had dried up! And they said one to another, Overtake ash-Sheikh as-Sālih, and ask him to

return to his place! For if he does not return, we shall perish, as will all our wealth! So they overtook him, and found him in a place which is known as al-Mughār. (For they said, Ghāra 'l-mā'! — "The water hath disappeared!"—And for that reason the place was named al-Mughār.) And they asked him to return; but he said, I am not going to return! But he gave them *seven* ewes from his flock, and said, Stand a ewe at every well, and the water will return. (So for that reason it was named Wādy as-Sab'a — "Valley of the Seven" — because he gave them seven ewes.) And they did thus, and the water returned.[27]

Ath-Tha'labi says that he gave them seven goats from his flock, and said, Take them with you, and go; and when ye take them down to the well to water, the water will become a source of living and clear water, as it was; so drink! But do not let a menstruant woman come near it. So they went forth with the goats; and when they placed them at the wells, the water appeared. And they continued to drink from it. And it remained thus—until a menstruant woman came and (touched it as she) got water, and it sank down, as it is today.

And Abraham moved on, and settled in al-Lajjūn,[28] and remained there as long as Allah willed. Then Allah revealed to him that he should settle in Mamre. So he took his journey thither. And there descended unto him in Mamre Gabriel and Michael, who were seeking out the people of Lot. And Abraham went out to slay a calf; but it got away from him, and did not stop until entered the cave of Habrūn (i. e., Hebron). And a voice called out, O Abraham! greet with a blessing the bones of thy father Adam, and all the prophets! And that deeply impressed him. And thereafter he slew the calf, and offered it to them (Gabriel and Michael). And then took place in connection with Abraham that which Allah relates in His Book.

And then he went with them on their way, to near the dwellings of the people of Lot. And they said to him, Sit thou here! And he sat. And he heard the voice of the Cock in the Sky; and he said, This is the voice of the *established truth* (al-Haqq al-Yaqīn); for the destruction of this people hath been determined. So he named that place the Mosque of al-Yaqīn.[29] And it is well known, about a parasang from the city of our lord Abraham. Then he returned, to seek from Ephron the cave; and he bought it from him, as we shall explain in the chapter on the subject of the cave, if Allah will.

Marginal note: How the Water Again Sank Down

Marginal note: The Visit of the Angels; and How the Cave of the Prophets Was Discovered

CHAPTER FIFTH

Account of the Birth of Ishmael, and His Migration with His Father Abraham; and the Story of Zamzam

The author of the *Jāmi'u 'l-Usūl* says: He was Ishmael son of Abraham al-Khalīl, and he was the eldest of his sons and the father of the Arabs, and a prophet of the Lord of the Worlds; and the Apostle of Allah was one of his sons. And his mother was Hagar, the handmaid of Abraham, who is said to have been a Copt. Abraham took him to

Marginal note: Biographical Notes on Ishmael, Father of the Arabs

Mecca when he was a suckling child, or as others say when he was two years old, or as others when he was fourteen. He was born before his brother Isaac by fourteen years. He died when he was a hundred and thirty-seven years old, or as others say a hundred and thirty years old. And he was buried in al-Hijr by the grave of his mother Hagar. And when his father Abraham died his age was eighty-nine years.

Ibn 'Abbās says: Ishmael was born to Abraham when he was ninety-nine years old. And there intervened between his death and the birth of the Prophet about two thousand and six hundred years—although the Jews deduct from that about four hundred years. And he was the sacrificed one, according to one view. And he was called *A'rāq ath-Tharā* [30] — "Veins of the Rich Earth." And he built the Ka'bah with his father Abraham.

Ibn 'Abbās on Ishmael

Mention has already been made of his mother Hagar, and of how that giant gave her as a servant to Sarah, and how she gave her to Abraham, saying, Take her; and perhaps Allah will give thee a son from her. For Sarah had been denied children, and had despaired of them. And Abraham had besought Allah to give him a pious successor, and his prayer had been unanswered until Abraham was aged, and Sarah was still barren. So Abraham lay with Hagar, and she bore to him Ishmael. And Sarah was thereupon very sad, because she had no children.

Ath-Tha'labi says: Sarah conceived Isaac at the time when Hagar had conceived Ishmael; and they bore them at the same time. And they grew up to boyhood; and while they were one day vying with each other, and Abraham was watching over their contest, Ishmael won. And Abraham sat him in his lap, and sat Isaac at his side. Sarah was watching this, and became angry. And she said, Thou didst place the son of the servant woman in thy lap, but *my* son at thy side! And thou didst swear to me that thou wouldst not vex me with jealousy! So the jealousy peculiar to women took hold upon her, and she swore that she would indeed cut a piece out of her, and would alter her neck, and would fill her hands with her blood. But Abraham said, Take her and circumcise her; and it will become a practice after thee, and thou wilt be quit of thine oath. So she did thus; and it became a practice for women.[31]

Sarah Jealous over Isaac

Then Ishmael and Isaac fought one day, as boys are wont; and

Sarah became angry with Hagar, and said, Thou shalt not live in the same town with me, ever! And so she bade Abraham to put her away. And Allah sent a revelation to Abraham that he should bring Hagar and her son to Mecca. So he took them; and the place of the Shrine at that time was covered with hawthorn and thorny acacias and mimosas.[32] And around it were a people called the Amalekites. And the site of the House (of Allah) was then a reddish clay hill. So Abraham said to Gabriel, Is it here thou commandest that I place them? He said, Yea! So he took his way with them to the place of the Stone, and made them to dismount there. And he commanded Hagar the mother of Ishmael to make there a trellis-shed; and she did that. Then Abraham engaged in private prayer, and said, "O Lord, I verily have caused to dwell one of my seed in a vale without vegetation, in the place of Thy Holy House! . . ." (As the verse says.)[33] *(Abraham Takes Hagar and Ishmael to the Site of Mecca)*

In the *Sahīh* of al-Bukhāri there is a long tradition, on authority of Ibn 'Abbās, giving the story of Ishmael and his mother and of Zamzam, to this effect:

Abraham took Ishmael and his mother Hagar, who was suckling him, from Syria to Mecca, and placed them under a *dauhah* (which is a large tree); and she had only a waterskin with water in it. And there was at that time no one in Mecca, and no water there. And he placed by Hagar a vessel containing dates — and he turned to leave. And the mother of Ishmael called out to him, O Abraham, where goest thou? Thou hast placed us in this valley where there is no companion, and nothing else! And she said that repeatedly; but he did not turn back to her. So she said, Did Allah command thee this? He said, Yea! She said, Then Allah will not cause us to perish! Then she returned to her place. And Abraham went on until he came to turn in the way, where they could not see him; and he faced the (place of the) Shrine, then prayed with this prayer, lifting up his hands and saying, "O Lord, verily I have placed my seed in a vale without vegetation. . . ." (As the verse says.) *(How Hagar and Ishmael Were Left; and Her Faith)*

Then the mother of Ishmael began suckling him, and drinking from that water, until, after it was finished, she thirsted — and Ishmael thirsted. So she looked upon him, as he writhed; and she went away, dreading to see him. And she found as-Safā, the nearest mountain in the district surrounding her; and she ascended it—as we shall give the tradition concerning this in its entire substance afterward, if Alllah will. *(Their Distress)*

Ath-Tha'labi says in the *Kitāb al-'Arā'is*: When she thirsted, and the child thirsted, she looked about at the mountains to see which of them was nearest; and she ascended as-Safā, and listened to find whether she heard any voice or saw anything. But she heard no voice, and saw no one. Then she heard the sounds of beasts around Ishmael, and she came to him in anxious haste. Then she heard a sound toward al-Marwah,[34] and she approached it until she had climbed it; but she saw nothing.

And according to one account she did that seven times. But at-Tabari says: Nay; she climbed as-Safā, praying unto Allah for help for Ishmael; then she ascended al-Marwah, and did the same; then she heard the noises of beasts in the valley about Ishmael, where she had left him. And she came to him in anxious haste—and found him taking up water with his hand from a spring, which had issued forth from beneath his hand, and drinking it. And she made a dam, and poured the water into her waterskin, storing it up for Ishmael. And if she had not done that, Zamzam would not have ceased being a clear spring, forever.

Their Salvation

Mujāhid says: We have always heard that Gabriel dug Zamzam with his heel, for Ishmael, when he was perishing with thirst. And the Apostle of Allah said, The mother of Ishmael—if she had not so done hastily, Zamzam would be a clear spring!

Al-Bukhāri gives an account from Ibn 'Abbās as follows: When there took place what transpired between Abraham and the people among whom he lived, he went forth with Ishmael and his mother, with them a waterskin containing water. And the mother of Ishmael went on drinking from the waterskin and giving her milk to her child—until they came to (the site of) Mecca. And he placed her under a tree—and then turned back. And the mother of Ishmael followed him until they reached a certain place, and she called out from behind him, O Abraham! to whom art thou leaving us? He said, To Allah! She said, I am content with Allah. So she returned, and continued drinking from the waterskin and giving her milk to her child, until the water was exhausted. Then she said, Perhaps if I went and looked about, I might find someone . . . So she went, and ascended as-Safā, and looked about to see whether she might perceive anyone; but she saw no one. And when she reached the valley, she hasted until she came

Another Account of the Same

to al-Marwah, and did the same there, hastily. Then she said, I must go and see what he is doing (meaning the child)! So she went; and he was in the same condition, and had begun the hiccoughing of death. And she was inconsolable. And she said, Perhaps if I went and looked about, I might perceive someone. So she went and ascended as-Safā, and looked, but beheld no one, — until she had done this fully seven times. Then she said, I must go and see what he is doing! — And behold, a voice! And she said, Help! if there be any goodness with thee! And behold, it was Gabriel! And he said, Do thus with his heel! And he touched with his heel the earth—and the water poured forth! And the mother of Ishmael was astounded, and she began digging. (And Abu 'l-Qāsim [i. e., Mohammed himself][35] says, If she had only let it be, the water would have been clear!) Then she resumed drinking from the water, and giving her milk to the child.

Thereafter there passed some people of the Jurham along the bed of the valley, and they beheld some birds, about which they wondered. For they said, Birds do not appear except around water! So they sent their scouts, who looked about, and found the water, and came back to them and informed them. So they came to Hagar, and said, O Umm Ismā'īl! permittest thou that we be with thee? (Or, That we dwell with thee?) and she allowed them. So her son came to manhood, and married a wife from them. *The Well Attracts Settlers* / *Ishmael Marries Among Them*

And al-Bukhāri relates from Ibn 'Abbās also, in another connection: The first woman to adopt the trailing skirt aforetime was the mother of Ishmael, who adopted it to efface her tracks from Sarah. Abraham brought her and her son Ishmael, when she was suckling him, and placed them at the site of the House, under a tree, over Zamzam, on the place of the Mosque. And there was no one in Mecca at that time and no water. And he placed them there, and set down by them a vessel with dates, and poured water therein. Then Abraham took the trail to leave them. And the mother of Ishmael followed him, and said, O Abraham, Where goest thou, leaving us in this valley in which there is no human or anything! And she said that to him repeatedly, but he went on without turning to her. So she said, Did Allah command thee to do this, He said, Yea! And she said, Then He will not forsake us! And Abraham went on until, when he was at the turn, where they could not see him, he turned his face toward the *Origin of Woman's Trailing Skirt* / *Another Account of Hagar and Ishmael in Mecca* (place of the) House, then prayed this prayer: "O Lord! verily, I have caused my seed to dwell in this valley, without vegetation, by Thy Sacred House! O Our Lord, may they stand here in prayer; and make the hearts of some folk love them, and feed them with fruits so that they may be thankful!"

Then the mother of Ishmael began suckling Ishmael and drinking from that water, until what was in the vessel was exhausted; and she thirsted, and her son thirsted. And she began looking upon him writhing, or, as accounts say, kicking. And she went away, not liking to look upon him. And she found as-Safā, the nearest mountain in the land adjoining, and went upon it. Then she turned toward the valley to see whether she beheld anyone—and she beheld no one. And she came down from as-Safā. Then she raised the tips of her arms, and hastened with the haste of a person exerting himself, until she passed through the valley. Then she came to al-Marwah, and got upon it, and looked to see whether she beheld any one, and she did not behold anyone. And she did that seven times.

Origin of the Pilgrimage Custom

According to Ibn 'Abbās, the Prophet said, For that reason the people (on Pilgrimage) hasten between them (the two mountains).

And when she had ascended al-Marwah, she heard a sound, and said, Silence! (Meaning herself.) Then she heard it again; and she said, I have heard thee! If there is any help with thee—! And behold, Gabriel was there at the place of Zamzam; and he scraped it with his heel (or, with his wing) until water appeared. And she began damming it up, and catching it with her hand, thus, and putting it by handfuls into her vessel. And Ibn 'Abbās says: The Prophet said, Allah have mercy on the mother of Ishmael! If she had only left Zamzam, or if she had not caught up the water with her hands, Zamzam would be a clear spring!

So then she drank, and suckled her child. And the Angel said to her, Fear not being forsaken; for here is the (place of the) House of Allah, which this child will build up, with his father; and verily, Allah doth not forsake His people!

And the House was elevated above the ground like a hill, the seils (waterfloods) [36] passing to the right and the left of it.

So they remained thus until there came by a company of the Jurham, or people of a tribe who approach by such a way; and they encamped at the lower part of Mecca. And they beheld a bird circling; and they said, Verily, this bird is circling about for water. We have carefully observed this valley, and there is no water in it. So they sent a scout or two—and behold, water! So they returned and informed them about the water; and they approached. And the mother of Ishmael was at the water. And they said, Wilt thou allow us to settle near thee? And she said, Yea; but ye shall have no right in the water. They said, Yea. 'Abdullah ibn 'Abbās says: Now the Prophet said, The mother of Ishmael was jesting in that, for she was desirous of human association. So they sent word to their people, and they settled with them, until, verily, there was a number of households of them. And the child grew to his youth, and learned Arabic from them, and was acceptable and pleasing to them when he became a young man. And when he reached maturity, they gave him a wife from among them. And the mother of Ishmael died.

Thereafter Abraham, when Ishmael had married, came to look over his inheritor, and he did not find Ishmael at home. And he inquired of his wife, who said, He hath gone out seeking game for us. Then he asked her about their life and welfare. And she said, We are in evil case, in distress and extremity! So she complained to him. And he said, When thy husband cometh, give him my peace, and say to him that he change the threshold of his door. So when Ishmael came, it was as if he sensed someone had been there. So he said, Hath anyone come to you? She said, There came to us an old man of such and such likeness, and asked me about thee, and I told him; and he asked me the manner of our living, and I told him, Verily, we are in distress and extremity. He said, Did he give thee any command? She said, Yea; he commanded me to give thee his peace, and he said, Change the threshold of thy door.[37] He said, That was my father; and he hath commanded me to separate from thee—so go, with thy people! So he divorced her. And he married another woman of them. So Abraham remained away from them as long as Allah willed; then he came to them. And he did not find Ishmael at home. So he entered unto his wife, and asked her of him; and she said, He hath gone forth seeking game for us. And he said, How are ye? and asked her of their living and welfare. And she said, We have plenty and do well—and she gave praise to Allah. And he said, What is your food? And she said, Meat.

Abraham's Visit to Mecca

A Proper Wife

He said, What is your drink? She said, Water. He said, O Allah, bless them in meat and water!

(And the Prophet said: They had no cereal grain at that time, or else he would have invoked blessing for them upon it. And they would not permit anyone not a Meccan to settle with them unless they were pleased with him.)

He (Abraham) said: When thy husband cometh, give him my peace, and tell him to make firm the threshold of his door.

Whom
Ishmael
Keeps

So when Ishmael came, he said, Did anyone come? She said, Yea; there came to us an old man of goodly countenance (and she praised him); and he asked me of thee; and I informed him that we were well off; and he asked me of our living, and I informed him that we were well off. He said, And did he give thee any counsel? She said, Yea; he gave thee his peace, and directs thee to make firm the threshold of thy door. He said, That was my father; and thou art the threshold, and he commands me to cling to thee!

Abraham
Returns and
Greets His
Son Ishmael

Then he remained away from them as long as Allah willed; then he came after that, and Ishmael was dressing an arrow under a great tree near Zamzam. And when he saw him, he arose before him; and they performed what father and son and son and father are accustomed to do. Then he said, O Ishmael, Allah hath given me a command! And he said, Then perform what Allah hath commanded thee. He said, And wilt thou aid me? He said, I will aid thee. He said, Then verily, Allah hath commanded me that I build here a Shrine. (And he indicated a hillock rising above its surroundings.)

And thereupon, as the account says, they raised the pillars of the House. And Ishmael began bringing stones, and Abraham was building, until, when the House was built up, he brought this Stone [that is, the sacred Black Stone in the corner of the Ka'bah kissed by the faithful on Pilgrimage], and he set it in place in it. And he (Abraham) stood at the House, as he was building, and Ishmael was bringing him stones; and they said, "O our Lord! accept from us! Verily, Thou art hearing and knowing!"

CHAPTER SIXTH

On the Beginning of the Building of the Ka'bah, and Description of It, from Its Building unto This Our Time

On His Word, "And when Abraham and Ishmael raised the pillars of the House . . ."[38] al-Baghawi says: Those who have handed down traditions relate that Allah created the place of the House before the world, by two thousand years; and it was a white hill, upon the water, and the world was spread out below it. And when Allah sent down Adam to the earth, he was desolate, and he complained to Allah; and Allah sent down to him from the Frequented House a Ruby of the rubies of Paradise, with two doors of green emerald, one door on the east and one door on the west. And He placed it on the site of the Temple; and He said, O Adam! verily, I have brought down for thee a House around which thou shalt perform the circuit as is done around My Throne; and thou shalt pray near it, as is done at My Throne. And Allah sent down the Black Stone. And it was formerly white, but became black from the touch of menstrous women in the Jāhilīyyah.[39] And Adam took his way from the land of Hind unto Mecca, walking, and Allah granted unto him an angel to direct him to the Temple; and he made the Pilgrimage to the Temple, and performed the rites. And when he finished, the angels met him, and said, Thy pilgrimage is accepted, O Adam! We have made pilgrimage to this House before thee by two thousand years. And Ibn 'Abbās says: Adam made forty pilgrimages from Hind to Mecca, on his feet.

The Heavenly Origin of the Temple and the Black Stone

And so it remained until the days of the Flood; and Allah raised it up to the Fourth Heaven, and there entered it every day seventy thousand angels, the same ones not returning. And He sent Gabriel to bring the Black Stone to Jabal Abu Qubeis, thus preserving it from the Flood. And the place of the Temple was empty until the time of Abraham.

The Ka'bah Saved from the Flood

Then Allah commanded Abraham, after there were born to him Ishmael and Isaac as his sons, that he should build a House in which His Name should be repeated. And he asked Allah to make clear to him the location. And Allah sent the Shekinah to guide him to the

Abraham Guided by the Shekinah

place of the House. And this was a strong wind, with two heads resembling serpents. And he ordered Abraham to build where the Shekinah should settle down. And Abraham followed it until they came to Mecca, and the Shekinah encircled the place of the House, as a leather shield encloses.

That is the account of 'Ali and al-Hasan. Ibn 'Abbās says: Allah, praised be He! sent a cloud of the size of the Ka'bah, and it began to move, and Abraham walked in its shadow, until it came to Mecca, and stood over the place of the House. And a voice from it called, that Abraham should build according to the limits of its shadow, not not increasing or diminishing.

Other accounts say that Allah sent Gabriel to show him the place of the House. And that is the meaning of His word: "And behold! we prepared for Abraham the place of the House . . ." And Abraham and Ishmael built the House, and Abraham was building, and Ishmael was bringing him stones. And that is the meaning of His word: "And when Abraham and Ishmael raised the pillars of the House . . ." (Meaning its foundations, and the singular of qawā'id is qā'idah.) Al-Kisā'i says it means he 'raised' the House. Ibn 'Abbās says: The House was built only with materials from five mountains, Mount Sinai, Mount Olivet, and Lebanon (which is a mountain in Syria), Jūdi (which is a mountain in al-Jazīrah), and its foundations were built from Hirā' (which is a mountain in Mecca). And when Abraham had finished to the point of the Black Stone, he said to Ishmael, Bring me a good stone which shall be a sign to mankind. And he brought him a stone; but he said, bring me a better than this. So Ishmael went along hunting, and Abu Qubeis cried out, O Abraham! I have for thee a deposit laid in trust; so take it! So he took the Black Stone and set it in its place.

And at-Tirmidhi and an-Nasā'i relate on authority of Ibn 'Abbās the following: The Apostle of Allah said, The Black Stone descended from Paradise; and it was more brightly white than leban, and only the sins of the sons of Adam blackened it. And at-Tirmidhi relates also from Ibn 'Abbās: The Apostle of Allah said with regard to the Stone: By Allah, Allah will indeed send it on the Day of Judgment, having two eyes to observe with and a tongue to talk with, and it will give witness for those who have kissed it in true belief!

How Abraham and Ishmael Builded

The Black Stone

And it is said that Allah built in the Heavens a House, the Frequented House, named Surāh; and He commanded the Angels that they build the Ka'bah in the earth as a counterpart to it, according to its size and likeness; and the first (human) to build up the Ka'bah was Adam. But it disappeared at the time of the Flood. Then Allah manifested it to Abraham so that he might build it (anew).

Ath-Tha'labi relates on authority of Meimūn ibn Mihrān, from Ibn 'Abbās; The Prophet of Allah said: The House before the fall of Adam was one of the rubies of Paradise, having two doors of green emerald, an eastern door and a western; and in it were lamps from Heaven. And it was the Frequented House in the Heavens, which seventy thousand Angels entered every day, not returning to it until the Day of Judgment. That was the counterpart of the Sacred Ka'bah which Allah sent down to the place of the Ka'bah. And it was like the celestial sphere in the night of its thundering (as it descended). And He sent down the Black Stone, which shone as if it were a pearl for whiteness. And Adam took it and clasped it to his breast to keep it in his company. Then Allah made His covenant with the sons of Adam, and set the stone as witness.

Then He sent down to Adam the Staff, and said, O Adam! walk on! And he walked (and he was at that time in the land of Hind). And he continued thus as long as Allah willed. Then he longed for the House. And it was said to him, Wilt thou go on pilgrimage, O Adam? And he approached it walking. And the spot of every step of Adam became a village, and everything between them desert, until he came to Mecca. And the Angels met him, saying, Thy pilgrimage is acceptable, O Adam! Verily, we have made pilgrimage to this House before thee by two thousand years! He said, And what were ye wont to say around it? They said, We said, Praise be to Allah, and thanks be to Allah, and There is no God but Allah, and Allah is Great! So Adam when he made the circuit of the House said these same words. And Adam circuited the House seven weeks by night and five by day. And he said, O Lord! grant to this House of my seed inhabitors who will dwell by it! And Allah revealed to him, Verily, I shall cause to inhabit it of thy seed a prophet by the name of Abraham; whom I shall take as my Friend, and I shall place its building up in his hands, and shall teach him its ordinances and ceremonies.

Adam's
Pilgrimage

And when he finished building it, he called, O ye people! Verily, Allah hath built a House; so make pilgrimage to it! And there heard him all people from the east to the west. And whoever made pilgrimage to this House would say, Behold, here am I, O Allah! Behold, here am I!

And 'Abdullah ibn az-Zubeir said: After he had finished the Ka'bah, Abraham turned toward the south, and gave summons to the Pilgrimage, and there answered, Labbeika![40] Then he faced the north, and there answered, Labbeika! Then he faced the east, and there answered, Labbeika! Labbeika! Then he faced the west, and there answered, Labbeika! Labbeika!

Abraham
Summons
Mankind

Later History
of the Ka'bah

And the House continued in the form in which Abraham built it until thirty-five years after the birth of our Prophet Mohammed—which was five years before his Mission—when the Koreish demolished the Ka'bah. Then they rebuilt it, and the Ka'bah continued in the form in which the Koreish built it until the time of 'Abdullah ibn az-Zubeir; and, it being demolished, he changed its form to stone. Thus (he rebuilt it and) it remained in the form in which Ibn az-Zubeir built it until the year 54 of the Hijrah, when al-Hajjāj ibn Yūsuf ath-Thaqafi killed him. And al-Hajjāj demolished it, and then restored it to its original form, as witnessed by old men of the Koreish.[41] And it is today in the form in which al-Hajjāj built it — and Allah Most High knoweth best!

CHAPTER SEVENTH

The Story of the Sacrificing of Ishmael, and an Account of the Disagreement on the Matter

Muslim scholars differ about the identity of the youth whom Abraham was commanded to sacrifice. The two people of Scripture agree upon the fact that it was Isaac; and a company of the Companions and the Followers say the same, as we shall make clear in the story of Isaac, if Allah will.

Isaac or
Ishmael
Sacrificed?

But a company of the Muslim scholars say it was Ishmael. And this is the view 'Abdullah ibn 'Omar, and the statement of Sa'īd ibn al-Museyyib, and ash-Sha'bi, and al-Hasan al-Basri, and Mujāhid, and ar-Rabī' ibn Anas, and Muhammad ibn Ka'b al-Qarzi, and al-Kalbi. And it is the tradition followed by 'Attā' ibn Abu Ribāh, and Yūsuf ibn Māhik, on authority of Ibn 'Abbās, that the sacrificed one was Ishmael. And both the views are cited in traditions from the Prophet.

Now whoever says that the sacrificed one was Isaac is resting his argument upon the Divine word, "And we gave him good news of a patient son. And when he reached the time of trial," [42] He commanded him to sacrifice the one about whom he had given him the good news. And there is not in the Koran any statement of His having given him good news of any child but Isaac.

And whoever says it was Ishmael argues from the fact that Allah mentions the annunciation of Isaac after the completion of the story of the sacrificed one, saying thereupon, "And we gave him the annunciation of Isaac, a prophet" [43] — which indicates that the sacrificed one was other than he. And again, Allah says in the Sūrah of Hūd, "And we gave him the good news of Isaac, and after Isaac Jacob." [44] So, just as he announced to him Isaac, he announced to him his son Jacob; and how could He order him to sacrifice Isaac, when he had promised him a grandson through him!

Al-Qarzi says: 'Omar ibn 'Abdullah ibn al-'Azīz asked a man who was a Jewish scholar, and who had become a good Muslim, Which of the two sons of Abraham was commanded to be sacrificed? And he said, Ishmael. Then he said, O Prince of the Believers, verily the Jews know that, but they are envious of you Arabs in that it was your father who was commanded to be sacrificed; and they assert it was their father Isaac. And one of the proofs is that the horns of the goat were hung up in the Ka'bah by the hands of Ishmael, until the House was burned, and the horns burned also, in the days of Ibn az-Zubeir and al-Hajjāj. *A Converted Jew Says: Ishmael*

And ash-Sha'bi says: I saw the two horns of the goat hanging up in the Ka'bah. And from Ibn 'Abbās: By Him in whose hand is my life, in the beginning of Islam the head of the goat was hung up on the gutter of the Ka'bah, with its horns, and it had become *wahisha*, that is, it had dried up. And al-Asma'i says: I asked Abu 'Amr ibn al-'Alā' about the one who was sacrificed, whether it was Isaac or Ishmael; and he says, O Asma'i! where tend thy senses! When was *The Goat's Head* *The Question Again*

Isaac in Mecca? Only Ishmael was in Mecca, and he was the one who built the House, with his father.

Ath-Tha'labi, from as-Sanālihi, says: We were in the presence of Mu'āwiyah, and the question was mentioned, whether it was Ishmael or Isaac who was sacrificed. And he said, Ye do well to be perplexed. I was in the presence of the Apostle of Allah, and there came to him a man, who said, O son of the two sacrificed ones! And he laughed; and he (as-Sanālihi) said, O Prince of the Believers, who are the two sacrificed ones? And he said, Verily, 'Abd al-Mutallib when he was digging the well Zamzam made a vow, that if Allah would prosper the matter he would sacrifice one of his sons. And the arrow came out for 'Abdullah. But his kindred prevented him, and said, Redeem thy son with a hundred camels. And the second was Ishmael.

The Story of the Sacrifice

As for the story of the sacrificed one. Al-Baghawi reports that as-Suddi says: When Abraham prayed and said, "O Lord, give to me one of the pious"[45] (as an heir and son), and He gave him the good news of him, he said, He shall be a sacrifice to Allah. And when he became a lad, and reached the time of trial, He said to him, Fulfill now thy vow! This was the reason why Allah commanded him to sacrifice his son.

They Go Forth to the Mountain

So he said to Isaac, Come, let us go and make a sacrifice to Allah! So he took a knife and rope, and went with him to the mountains. And the youth said, O father, where is thine offering? And he said, "O my son, verily I have seen in a dream that I should sacrifice thee; and now, see what thou thinkest. And he said, O Father, do what thou art commanded . . ."[46]

Abraham's Vision and Command

Muhammad ibn Ishāq says: When Abraham used to visit Hagar and Ishmael, he was borne upon al-Burāq,[47] leaving in early morn from Syria and going to Mecca, and leaving in the evening from Mecca, and spending the night with his people in Syria. And so it went, until Ishmael "came to the time of trial"; and he was cleaving to him, and begging him, because of what he hoped from him in worshiping his Lord, in making great His glory, he was commanded in a dream that he should sacrifice him. And the manner was thus; He saw, the Night of Heeding, as if one were speaking and saying to him, Allah commandeth thee to sacrifice this thy son! And when the morning came, he reflected in his mind, that is he meditated, from morn to eve, Is this dream from Allah or from Satan? (And for this reason it was named the Night of Heeding.) But when the evening came, he saw it in a dream a second time. And when the morning came, he *knew* that was from Allah. (And for this reason it was named the Day of 'Arafah.)

Muqātil says that Abraham saw that three nights in succession. And when the matter was established, he announced it to his son, saying, "O son, verily I have seen it in a dream that I am to sacrifice thee! Now see what thou dost counsel." (And he only directed him thus to know his patience about the will of Allah, and his resolution in His obedience.)

Ibn Ishāq and others say: When Abraham had been commanded thus, he said, O son, get the rope and the knife; we go to yonder brush for wood! And when Abraham was apart with his son in the brush, he told him of the divine command. And he said, "O father, do what thou art commanded; thou wilt find me, if Allah will, of the patient ones!" And when they had made themselves resigned and submissive, and had humbled themselves to the will of Allah (Qatādah says that Abraham submitted himself, and the boy submitted himself), and then he laid him down, *tallahu li'l-jabīn*. (That is, he flung him down on the ground.) Ibn 'Abbās says: He flung him down on his side. Their Resignment

And all the accounts say: And his son, whom he was going to sacrifice, said to him, O father, make firm the bonds, so that I not struggle; and keep clear from me thy garments, lest any of my blood be sprinkled upon them, and my reward be lessened—and my mother see it and be saddened! And whet thy knife, and make swift the passing of the knife over my neck, so that it may be easier for me; for verily, death is severe! And when thou comest to my mother, give her my greeting; and if thou thinkest well to take back my coat to my mother, then do so, and perhaps it may be something of a consolation to her; Abraham said to him, Most helpful art thou, O my son, in what Allah hath commanded! And Abraham did what his son told him. Then he approached him and kissed him on the forehead—and he had bound him—and he was weeping, and his son was weeping; then he got ready the knife. The Youth's Submission

It is told that he drew the knife across his neck but could not cut; then he whetted it two or three times with a rock — all to no avail. As-Suddi says that Allah had set a band of brass about his neck.

Accounts go on: And the son said, O father, turn my face aside, for when thou lookest on my face, thou pitiest me, and thy compassion restrains thee, coming between thee and the command of Allah; and I will not look upon the knife, and fear! So Abraham did that. Then he placed the knife upon his neck, but the knife was averted.

Release!

Then a voice called, O Abraham! Desist! Thou hast fulfilled the vision!"

And Abu Hureirah says, on authority of Ka'b al-Ahbār and Ibn Ishāq, from those he follows: [48] When Abraham was shown the vision of sacrificing his son, Satan said, If I do not cause the family of Abraham to rebel this time, I shall never do so! So Satan took on the form of man, and came to the mother of the youth, and said to her,

Satan's Wiles

Dost thou know where Abraham has gone with thy son? She said, He hath taken him to get wood from yonder brush. He said, Nay, by Allah! he hath taken him to sacrifice him! She said, Nay indeed; he hath tender regard for him, and loveth him too strongly for that! He said, But he asserts that Allah hath commanded him thus. She said, Then, if Allah hath so commanded him, he doth well to obey his Lord! So Satan went forth from her, and overtook the boy, walking in the steps of his father And he said to him, O youth! Knowest thou where thy father is taking thee? He said, To get wood for our folk from this brush. He said, By Allah, he intends only to sacrifice thee! He said, Why? He said, He asserts that his Lord hath commanded him thus. He said, Then let him do what his Lord hath commanded him; and to hear is to obey! And when the son was forfended from him, he approached Abraham, and said to him, Where goest thou, O sheikh? He said, I go to yonder brush for certain needs. He said, By Allah, I think Satan hath come to thee in thy dream and hath commanded thee to sacrifice this thy son! Then Abraham recognized him, and said, Away from me, thou enemy of Allah! for by Allah, I shall certainly execute the will of my Lord! So Satan turned back in anger, having not accomplished anything of his design with Abraham and his family. And they were forfended from him by the help of Allah.

Abu Tufeil says on authority of Ibn 'Abbās: When Abraham was commanded to sacrifice his son, Satan appeared to him in this thicket and raced with him, and Abraham outstripped him. Then he went to the stone of the end of the course, and Satan appeared to him; and he pelted him with seven pebbles, until he withdrew. [49] Then he overtook him at the largest stone, and he pelted him with seven pebbles, until he withdrew. Then Abraham passed on to fulfill the will of Allah.

Allah says: "When they submitted themselves, and he cast him on to the ground, and we called unto him, O Abraham! Thou hast fulfilled the vision! Verily, we thus reward the doers of good!"[50] And the meaning is: Verily, as we have freed him from sacrificing his son, we have rewarded him for his merit in obedience. Muqātil says: Allah rewarded him for his meritorious obedience by freeing him from sacrificing his son. And (in explanation of): "Verily, this was indeed a manifest *balā*'," a clear testing in that He tested him in the sacrificing of his son, Muqātil says: *Balā*' here means divine favor, in that he substituted for him the goat. And: "And we summoned him to a mighty sacrifice" (means that) Abraham looked about, and behold Gabriel was there with a goat horned, and white and black. And he said, This is the redemption of thy son; so sacrifice it in his stead! And Gabriel and the goat and Abraham and his son all said, God is great! So Abraham took the goat and brought it to the slaughtering place of Mina, and sacrificed it. And most of the commentators say that the sacrifice was a goat which had pastured in Paradise forty autumns. The Redemption The Goat from Paradise

It is related on authority of Sa'īd ibn Jubeir, from Ibn 'Abbās: The goat which Abraham sacrificed was the one which Abel son of Adam had sacrificed.[51] And Sa'īd ibn Jubeir says, It was rightfully called "mighty." And Mujāhid says: He called it "mighty" because it was (divinely) prepared. Al-Husein ibn al-Fadīl says: Because it was from Allah. Others say: Mighty in size; others: mighty in its reward. Al-Husein says: Ishmael was redeemed by a mountain goat which was sent down to him from Mt. Thabīr.

And: "We left record of him among those after" means we left for him among those after him praise, with goodliness. "Peace upon Abraham! Thus we reward the doers of good; verily, he is of our believing servants; and we have announced to him Isaac, a prophet of the pious ones."

And those who assert that Isaac was the sacrificed one say that He gave news, after that event, of Isaac, a prophet as a reward for his obedience. And those who say the sacrificed one was Isaac say that He gave news to Abraham concerning the fact that Isaac was to be a prophet. 'Akramah in his account, on authority of Ibn 'Abbās, says: He gave him good news twice, when he (Isaac) was born and when he became a prophet.

And: "We blessed him" means Abraham, in his sons. And as for Isaac, most of the Prophets are of his seed — may the blessings and peace of Allah be upon them all!

CHAPTER EIGHTH

The Story of Isaac, and Record of the Disagreement upon Whether He Was the One Sacrificed

He was Isaac son of Abraham, Friend of the Merciful, the prophet, son of a prophet, father of the prophets. And his mother was Sarah the wife of Abraham. The author of *Jāmi'u 'l-Usūl* says he was born fourteen years after Ishmael, and was the sacrificed one, according to one view, which is held by the two people of Scriptures, the Jews and the Christians. His descendants include the Romans and Greeks and the Armenians and the related peoples, and the Israelites. Isaac lived a hundred and eighty years, and died in the Holy Land; and he was buried beside his father Abraham.

Isaac's History

At-Tabari says: Abraham was cast into the fire when he was sixteen years old; and Isaac was sacrificed when he was seven. Sarah bore him when she was ninety years old. The scene of his offering was two miles distant from Jerusalem. And when Sarah learned what was intended for Isaac, she concealed herself for two days, and died on the third. Others say that Sarah died when she was a hundred and twenty-seven years old.

And the scholars of the Muslims differ about the youth whom Abraham was commanded to sacrifice, despite the agreement of the people of the two Scriptures that it was Isaac, as was mentioned above. This is the view of some of the Companions, 'Omar, 'Ali, Ibn Mas'ūd, and al-'Abbās; and of the Followers and their followers, Ka'b al-Ahbār, Sa'īd ibn Jubeir, Qatādah, Masrūq, 'Akramah, 'Atā', Muqātil, as-Zuhri, and as-Suddi. And this is the account given by 'Akramah and Sa'īd ibn al-Jubeir on authority of Ibn 'Abbās; and they say this was the story as it was current in Syria. And it is related from Sa'īd ibn Jubeir:

Abraham saw the sacrifice of Isaac in his sleep, and he travelled with him a journey of a month on one morn, until it brought him to the moment of sacrificing him in Mina. And when Allah commanded him to sacrifice (instead) the ram, he sacrificed it—and travelled (back) with him the journey of a month in one evening, the ways and the mountains being folded smoothly for him.

The hāfiz ibn 'Asākir says on authority of Zeid ibn Aslam, from 'Abdullah ibn 'Ubeid ibn 'Umeir, from his father: Moses said, O Lord, Thou hast remembered Abraham and Isaac and Jacob in what Thou hast bestowed upon them. He said, Abraham did not waver from Me, but chose Me; Isaac offered himself to Me—and that is better than anything else; and Jacob tried and tempted Me not at all, but increased in good intentions toward Me.

Ath-Tha'labi says on authority of Anas ibn Mālik: The Prophet of Allah said, Isaac will intercede for me afterward, and will say, O Lord! Thou didst give the truth to Thy prophet, and I did offer myself in sacrifice! He will not enter the Fire, who doth not make to Thee a partner! And Allah will say, By my might and glory and power! he will not enter the Fire, who doth not make to me a partner!

CHAPTER NINTH

How Abraham was Given the Annunciation of Isaac: and the Story of Abraham and the Angels

Ath-Tha'labi says: Abraham was wont to be hospitable to whoever came unto him; and Allah gave him abundance, and made him prosperous in food and property and servants. And when Allah purposed the destruction of the people of Lot, He commanded His messenger angels to reveal it to Abraham, and to announce to him and to Sarah the birth of Isaac, and after Isaac, Jacob. And that is the meaning of His word: "And Our messengers came to Abraham with the annunciation—." [52] Al-Baghawi says, By the messengers is meant the angels; and there is disagreement about the number of them. Ibn 'Abbās and 'Atā' say there were three, Gabriel and Michael and Israfel. Ad-Dahhāk says there were nine. Muqātil says there were twelve. Muhammad ibn Ka'b says it was Gabriel, and with him were seven. As-Suddi says

The Angels Visit Abraham

there were eleven angels in the form of young men with shining faces; and they came with the annunciation of Isaac and Jacob, or as others say, concerning the destruction of the people among whom was dwelling Lot. Ath-Tha'labi says: When they came to Abraham, guests had been withheld from him for fifteen days, until the matter distressed him; for Abraham was wont not to eat unless with a guest, whenever possible. So when he saw them in the form of men, he rejoiced over them, and he supposed them guests the like of whom for goodliness and beauty he had never entertained. So he said, No one shall serve these folk but myself! And he went forth to his people, and brought a calf, fat and roasted (and it was roasted on stones). And al-Baghawi says that Qatādah reports that the greater part of Abraham's wealth was in cattle.

And when he saw that their hands did not touch it (that is, the calf), he thought strange of them, and conceived fear of them. (Qatādah says that this was because when a guest came to them, and would not eat of their food, they suspected that he did not come with good intention, but that he came for evil.) But they said, Fear not, O Abraham! verily, we are the Angels of Allah, Who hath sent us unto the people of Lot. And his wife Sarah, daughter of Haran son of Nahor (and she was the cousin of Abraham) was standing behind the dividing-curtain listening to their speech. Or as others say, she was standing to serve the Messengers, and Abraham was seated with them. And she laughed![53] Mujāhid and 'Akramah say that *dahakat* here is in the sense of menstruating; but the majority believe that it means, as ordinarily, to laugh. There is disagreement over the cause of her laughing. Some say she laughed when fear ceased from her and from Abraham, when they said, Fear not! As-Suddi says, It was because when Abraham offered them the food and they did not eat, and Abraham was afraid, thinking them robbers.

So he said to them, Why do ye not eat? They said, We will not eat the food except by paying its price. Abraham said, It indeed hath a price! They said, And what is its price? He said: That ye mention the name of Allah at the beginning of it, and that ye thank Him after it! And Gabriel looked at Michael and said, Worthy was this man that his Lord should take him as His Friend!

And when Abraham and Sarah beheld their hands, not touching it

Abraham and
Sarah's Fear

(the food), Sarah laughed, and said, How strange of our guests! We indeed served them ourselves in honor to them, and they eat not of our food! But Qatādah says that she laughed because of the heedless- *Sarah Laughs* ness of the people of Lot, and the near approach to them of punishment. Muqātil and al-Kalbi say that she laughed at Abraham's fearing three, when he was among his servants and household. Others say that she laughed over the annunciation.

And Ibn 'Abbās and Wahb say that she laughed with wonder that she should have a child in her old age and the age of her husband. According to this opinion, the verse would be the former and the latter parts of a syllogism, the virtual meaning of which is: "His wife was standing, and we gave her the news of Isaac, and after Isaac, Jacob. And she laughed, and said, Woe is me! Shall I bear when I am old?"

As for His Word, "And we gave her news of Isaac, and after Isaac, Jacob," (that is, that after Isaac should come Jacob, in the meaning of the child of her child; for she was given the news that she should live to see the child of her child. And when she was given the news of a child) she *sakkat* her face — that is, she struck her face in wonder. And she said, Woe is me! the voice of lamentation! (Which is an expression men use when they see something because of which they are surprised; and the original form of it is *ya weilata*!) Shall I bear when I am old! (And she was ninety years old according to the report of *The Promise* Ibn Ishāq. But Mujāhid says ninety-nine.) And this my lord and *Made Sure* husband! (They were so called because they were become old, and they were distressed by the fact. And the age of Abraham was a hundred and twenty years, according to the view of Ibn Ishāq, though Mujāhid says a hundred. And there intervened between the annunciation and the birth a year.) Verily, this is a marvellous thing! (They said), that is the angels, Do ye wonder at the command of Allah? Verily, when Allah wishes a thing—! May the mercy of Allah and His blessing be upon you, and upon the people of this family! (i. e., the family of Abraham.) Verily, he is *hamīd* and *majīd*! (And *hamīd* means praised; and *majīd* means *noble*).

"And when there departed from Abraham the *rau'* (fear), and there came to him the annunciation of Isaac and Jacob, he contented with Us (most Interpreters say the meaning is, He contended with Our messengers).[54] And the matter of his contention was that he said to the angels: What think Ye! if there be in the cities of Lot fifty believers—will Ye destroy them? They said, Nay. And if forty? They said, Nay. Or thirty? They said, Nay. Until he came to five; and they said, Nay. He said, What think Ye—if there is one Muslim will ye destroy the city? They said, We know well who is there, that we may bring him forth safely with his family, except for his wife, who was one of those remaining behind. Verily, Abraham is forbearing and penitent." [55] And we shall set forth the remainder of the story in the comment on Lot, if Allah will.

The sheikh and hāfiz Abu Muhammad Mahmūd al-Muqaddasi says in his book which he edited on *The Merits of Jerusalem and Syria*: Abraham did not die until Isaac was sent unto the land of Syria, and Jacob was sent as prophet to the land of Canaan, and Ishmael to (the tribe of) Jurham, and Lot to Sodom. And they were prophets of the covenant of Abraham.

CHAPTER TENTH

The Story of Jacob, and the Extent of His Life, and His Death

He was Jacob, son of Isaac, son of Abraham, a Prophet, son of a Prophet, son of the son of a Prophet, and father of the Prophets. He was the one who was named Israel, about which it is said the meaning was the *true friend*, or the *choice*, of Allah. He was the father of the tribes, and he was the brother of Esau.

Some say, He was named Jacob because of the following: He and Esau were twins, and when he came forth from the belly of his mother he took hold of the *heel* of his brother Esau.[56] But that is speculation, because *Isaac* is derived from Arabic, but Jacob is a *foreign* name.

The author of the *Jāmi'u 'l-Usūl* says: He (Jacob) lived a hundred and seven and forty years, and died in Egypt. And he had commanded at death that he be carried to the Holy Land and buried beside his father and grandfather. So Joseph his son took him and buried him there.

Al-Baghawi says: When death approached Jacob, he gathered his sons, and his sons' sons, and said, My time hath come! Now, what will ye worship after my death? [57] That is the circumstance of His word: " Were ye witnesses when death approached Jacob (or when Jacob came near to his death)." Some say: This verse was revealed when some people said to the Prophet, Knowest thou not that Jacob, when he died, gave commands to his sons in Hebrew? And according to this view, these addressed would be the Jews. Al-Kalbi says: When Jacob entered Egypt, he beheld them worshiping idols and animals. So he gathered his sons, and expressed his fear of that for them, and said, What will ye worship after I am gone? (And 'Atā' says that Allah never takes away the life of a prophet until He hath let him choose between death and life. And when He gave Jacob the choice, He said, Wait Thou upon me until I make inquiry of my sons and give them commands. And He did that. And he collected his sons, and the sons of his sons, and said to them, My time hath come! Now, what will ye worship after me?) And they said, " We shall worship thy God, and the God of thy Fathers, Abraham, and Ishmael, and Isaac! " (Now Ishmael was their uncle, and the Arabs called their uncle " father," just as they called their aunt " mother.")

Now the story of Jacob and his son Joseph is well known.

CHAPTER ELEVENTH

The Story of Joseph, and a Description of Him, and the Extent of His Life, and His Death [58]

He was Joseph the Trustworthy, the son of Jacob, son of Isaac, son of Abraham. And he was a prophet of Allah, son of a prophet of Allah, son of the prophet of Allah, Abraham, who was also Allah's Friend. And Allah mentions his story in the Koran in extensiveness and detail, to great length. The chapter by his name is devoted to his story, except for what was added to it. And trustworthy and notable traditions there are of his virtues; one of them is that given by Ibn 'Amr: The Prophet of Allah said, Verily, a noble person, son of a noble person, son of a noble person, was Joseph—son of Jacob, son of Isaac, son of Abraham. Al-Bukhāri relates this. And another on authority of Abu Hureirah: The prophet of Allah was asked, Who is the noblest of mankind? He said, He who is most pious toward Allah! They said, It is not of this we ask thee. So he said, The most noble was Joseph,

Joseph—Noble and Pious

a prophet of Allah, son of a prophet of Allah, son of prophet of Allah, son of the Friend of Allah. Al-Bukhāri relates this also.

And on authority of Anas is this in connection with the tradition of the Night-Journey: He (Mohammed) said, Then I was taken up to the Third Heaven, and a door was opened unto us — and behold, I was near Joseph! And he had been given the best station; and he welcomed me, and invoked blessings upon me.

Seen by the
Prophet in
Paradise

And on authority of Abu Saʿīd al-Hudhri it is said: The Apostle of Allah said, The night I was taken on the Night-Journey, to the Heavens, I passed along and saw Joseph. And I said, O Gabriel! Who is this? And he said, This is Joseph. And they (the hearers) said, And how didst thou find him, O Apostle of Allah? He said, Like the moon on the night of its being full!

In his *Book of Brides*, Abu Ishāq ath-Thaʿlabi mentions this in his account of Joseph: As Joseph went along the streets of Egypt, the light of his face shone upon the walls. And Kaʿb al-Ahbār says: Verily, Allah likened for Adam his descendants like to the number of the raindrops, and He showed him the prophets, one by one; and he showed him in the seventh rank Joseph, crowned with a crown of dignity, decorated with the vestments of nobility, clothed with the cloak of honor, upon him a waist of glory, and in his hand the sceptre of a king, on his right seventy thousand angels, and behind him the nations of the prophets, with shouts of holiness and praise to God, before him the tree of happiness, changing with him from place to place, wherever he went. And when Adam saw him, he said, My Lord, who is this noble one whom Thou hast clothed with the cloak of honor, and raised to very high rank? He said, O Adam, this is thy son, who shall be envied for what I have given him; I have granted him two-thirds of the goodliness of thy offspring! Then Adam clasped Joseph to his breast (or as it were, kissed his forehead), and said, O son! Thou shalt not *regret* —for thou art *Joseph*.[59] And the first to call him Joseph was Adam. And he was like Adam the day Allah created him with His Hand, and breathed into him of His spirit. And He fashioned him before the event of his rebellion. And it has been said that He gave to Adam goodliness and beauty and glory the day He created him. And when he rebelled, He deprived him of such; then He restored to him a third of the beauty until He forgave him. And Allah granted the goodliness and

His Divinely
Given glory

Named
by Adam

beauty and light and glory which He had taken away from Adam, when he was guilty of wrong, to Joseph. And that was because Allah desired to show His servants that He was able to accomplish whatever He wished. Then Allah granted him the knowledge of interpreting visions, and he would give news of a matter which was seen in a dream before it came to pass.

An-Nawawi says in description of him: He was fair of hue, handsome of face, having curly hair, large eyes, evenness of form; thick of fore-arm and upper-arm and leg, thin of stomach, having a curved nose, and a small navel. And there was on his right cheek a black mole, and this mole adorned his face. Between his eyes there was another mole, which added to his beauty, so that he was like the moon on the night which it is full. The lashes of his eyes were like the forewing feathers of the eagle. And when he smiled, there could be seen a light from the displaying of his teeth. And when he spoke, there could be seen the brilliance of light shining from his mouth.

Description of Joseph

An-Nawawi says further: His grandfather Isaac was handsome, and the mother of Isaac, Sarah, was handsome, And so they say that Allah gave to Joseph beauty and purity of complexion, and clearness of skin, such as He gave to no other. They say also that Sarah inherited that beauty from her ancestor Eve, the wife of Adam.

Ath-Tha'labi relates from 'Abdullah ibn Mas'ūd, from the Prophet: Gabriel descended unto me, and said, O Mohammed, verily Allah saith, I have clothed the face of Joseph with beauty from My Throne, and I have clothed thy face with the light of My Throne! And someone asked some of the learned whether Joseph was more handsome, or Mohammed; and they said, Joseph was *one* of the most handsome of mankind—and Mohammed was the *most* handsome of them.

Ath-Tha'labi relates from the learned, from their accounts of those of past times: Jacob and his sons remained, after they went down to Joseph in Egypt, four and twenty years, in most prosperous welfare. The author of *Jāmi'u 'l-Usūl*: The length of his absence from his father was forty years — or as others say, eighty years. And ath-Tha'labi relates from Mujāhid: Joseph went forth from the presence of Jacob when he was six years old, having not shed his first teeth. And Allah brought them together when he was forty years old. And when death came to Jacob, he commanded them that they bear his noble body

Summary of the History of Joseph

to Jerusalem and bury him with his father and his grandfather. And
Joseph and his brothers and his soldiers took him, in his coffin.[60] And
the age of Jacob was a hundred and seven and forty years, as was
mentioned before in the story of him. And Joseph lived after Jacob
three and twenty years, and Joseph died when he was a hundred and
twenty years old. And he was buried in Egypt, in the Nile. Then
Moses carried him, in his time, to Syria, when the Sons of Israel went
forth from Egypt.[61] And there were between him and Moses four
hundred years.

Chapter Twelfth

The Story of Lot, and What Happened to His People, and the Place of His Tomb

He was Lot, a prophet and apostle of Allah, son of Haran, son of
Terah (who was Āzar). And Lot was the son of the brother of
Abraham al-Khalīl. Ath-Thaʻlabi says: He was named Lot because
love of him lūta—that is, it clove and stuck to—the heart of Abraham.
And Abraham loved him with a strong love. And the verses about
Lot are well known. He was one of the Prophets of Allah whom He
succored by destroying those who treated them as liars. His story is
told in the beloved Koran, in several places.

The History of Lot

An-Nawawi says, that ath-Thaʻlabi says, that Wahb ibn Munabbih
says: Lot went forth from the land of Babel, in Iraq, with his uncle,
Abraham, following him in his religion and being a migrating pilgrim
with him, to Syria. And with them was Sarah, the wife of Abraham.
And there went forth with them Āzar, the father of Abraham, differing
from Abraham in his religion and persisting in his unbelief. And so
they came to Harrān; and Āzar died.[62] And Abraham and Lot and
Sarah passed on to Syria, until they went to Egypt; and then they
returned to Syria. And Abraham settled in Palestine, and Lot settled
in Jordan.

Migrates with Abraham

And Allah commissioned him (Lot) unto the people of Sodom,
and others there, for they were unbelievers, practising abominations,
as Allah records concerning the people of Lot, "practising abominations such as had not been done by any one before them of all creation."[63] Ath-Thaʻlabi says that ʻUmar ibn Dīnār says: There is no

record of men having dealings with men until the people of Lot, Sent as Prophet to Sodom according to His word: "Do ye indeed come unto men, and cut the ways and practice toward the one who summons you what is disapproved by Allah!" And their cutting of the way, according to what the interpreters mention, and their practising of abominations were upon whoever came down to their city. And as to their offering reprehensible conduct to the one who summoned them, the interpreters say: It was that they would sit beside the way, and sling stones at those who passed by, and act foolishly where they sat. And ath-Thaʻlabi relates on authority of Abu Sālih, from Umm Hāni, who said: I asked the Prophet of Allah about this verse; and he said, They used to sit by the way, and pelt whoever passed by them, and scoff at him; and this was the blameworthy action they would do.

Now Lot would try to make them desist, and would summon them to the worship of Allah, and would threaten them with hurt for what they were doing, and for their neglect of repentance — from which is painful punishment. But his chiding and warning them only increased their procrastination and their insolence, and their hastening unto the retribution of Allah, and their denying him (as a prophet), and His Call for Divine Aid their treating him as a liar. But they said, "Bring us the grievous punishment, if thou be one of the truthful" — until Lot asked his Lord that He aid him against them, saying: "O lord, aid me against this corrupted people!"

And Allah answered his prayer and sent Gabriel and Michael and The Angel Came Israfel to destroy them and to give the annunciation to Abraham. So they approached, walking, in the form of men, beardless and handsome; and they came unto Abraham. And he entertained them, and they gave him the annunciation of the birth of Isaac and Jacob, as was mentioned before in the story of Isaac.

And when they had finished that, they informed Abraham that Allah had sent them to destroy the people of Lot. And Abraham discussed and plead with them about it, as Allah says: "And when fear left Abraham, and the annunciation came to him, he contended with Us about the people of Lot." And his contending with them, according to the account of Ibn ʻAbbās, was that they said, Verily, we shall Abraham Intreating destroy the people of this town; indeed, the people of it are unjust! And Abraham said to them, Will ye destroy a town in which are four hundred believers? They said, Nay! He said, Will ye destroy a town in which are two hundred believers? They said, Nay! He said, Will ye destroy a town in which are forty believers? They said, Nay. He said, Will ye destroy a town in which are fourteen believers? They said, Nay.

Now Abraham was counting for them fourteen believers including the wife of Lot, and so he ceased from them, and his soul was quieted.

It is related from Sa'īd ibn Jubeir, from Ibn 'Abbās: When Abraham knew the situation of the people of Lot, he said to the Messengers, verily, Lot is there (out of anxiety for him)! But the Messengers said to him, "We know well who is there, that we may bring him forth to safety with his family, except for his wife, who was one of those who turn back; verily, Abraham is kind, compassionate, penitent!"

Al-Baghawi says that Ibn al-Jureij says: There were in the cities of Lot four thousand thousand. And the Messengers thereupon said to Abraham, "Leave off this!" (That is, leave off this talk, and lay aside contention.) Verily, the command and punishment and judgment of thy Lord have come, and they have come to them; there descendeth upon them a punishment not to be averted or escaped.

The Angel Came to Lot

And when Our Messengers (meaning those angels) came to Lot in the form of young men, beardless and goodly of face, Lot was grieved by their coming, and was distressed because of them. And that was because Lot, when he saw the goodliness of their faces and the goodness of their smell, was anxious for them because of his people, who might direct their abominations toward them; and he knew that they would have to be protected from them. And he said, "This day is difficult!" (That is, intense, as if evil and calamity were both put together on it!)

He Witnesses Against His People

Al-Baghawi and Qatādah and as-Suddi say: The angels went forth from Abraham toward the town of Lot, and they came to Lot at midday, when he was in a piece of ground of his, working there; or as others say, he was getting firewood. And Allah had said, Do not destroy them until Lot hath witnessed against them four times. And they asked hospitality of Lot, and he went along with them. And when they had walked an hour, he said, What have ye been informed of the affairs of this town? They said, And what about it? He said, I witness by Allah that it is the most evil town in the land for its deeds! And he said that four times. And Gabriel said to the angels, Wait until he comes to his folk.

It is related also that the angels came to the house of Lot, and found him in his house. And none knew that but the household of Lot; but his wife went out and told her people, saying, In the house of Lot are men whose like I have never seen! "And there came to him his people in haste." [64] And Lot said to them, when they made for his guests, thinking they were young men, "O people! these my daughters are more suitable for you!" (meaning, for sexual intercourse) ; and he offered his womenfolk for the sake of his guests. And in that time the giving in marriage of a Muslim woman to an unbeliever was allowed, just as the Prophet married a girl to 'Utbah ibn Abu Lahab and to al-'Āsī ibn ar-Rabī' before the revelation, and they were both of them unbelievers. [65]

Attempted Violence

Al-Hasan ibn al-Mufaddil says: He offered his daughters to them on condition that they accept Islam. Mujāhid and Sa'īd ibn Jubeir say: His expression, "my daughters," meant their (own) women, including them in his own because every prophet is the father of his people.

And Lot continued: "Fear Allah, and do not grieve me concerning my guests," and do not do evil to me, and do not shame me! "Is there not among you an upright man?" (Ibn Ishāq says, He was giving command for kindliness, and forbidding what is reprehensible.) But "they said: We know well, O Lot, the claim we have to your daughters" (that is, we are not seeking wives; we have right to them for marriage. And some say the meaning is, We have no need or desire of them.) "But verily, thou knowest what we wish" from the men who have come to you!

And Lot said to them, then, "If I only had power against you, or could take refuge in a Mighty Support!" That is, if there could be added to me defending associates, verily we would fight you and free ourselves from you: Al-Baghawi reports on authority of al-A'raj that the Prophet said, Allah will forgive the sins of Lot, because he took refuge in a Mighty Support!

Al-Baghawi says that Ibn 'Abbās and the interpreters say: Lot fastened the door, the angels being with him in his house, and he discussing and adjuring them (the disturbers) through the door, and they striving to scale the walls. And when the angels saw what had come upon Lot by reason of Them, they said, O Lot! verily, thy Support is indeed mighty! "We are messengers of thy Lord. They shall not touch you." So open the door, and let us get at them! So he opened the door; and they entered.

And Gabriel asked permission of His Lord to punish them, and He gave leave. And he arose in the form which he really is, and spread his wings. And he had on a sash of strung pearls, being clear of forehead, **Punishment to the Wicked** and his head smooth like coral, and like the snow for whiteness; and his feet were green-like. And he smote their faces with his wing, and put out their eyes, so that they suddenly did not know their way, and could not guide themselves to their houses. And they turned away, saying, Help! Help! In the house of Lot are the most powerful magicians in the world! And they began to say, O Lot, just wait till the morn and thou wilt see what thou wilt receive from us tomorrow!— thus threatening him.

But Lot said to them (the angels), When is the set time for their destruction? They said, At the dawn. He said, I wish it more quickly than that! If ye would destroy them now—! But they said, Is not the dawn quite near? Then they said, O Lot, "Go thou with thy family **Lot Flees Forth** in a certain portion of the night. And none of you will turn about but thy wife"; she will turn back and will perish.

Now Lot brought her forth with him, and he forbade those who followed him, as they were travelling by night, to turn back, except his wife. And as for her, when she heard of this manner of divine punishment, she turned about, and cried, O ye people! And stones struck her and killed her.

"And when the event of Our punishment came, we turned them upside down," as Allah saith in the Koran. And that was because **The Evil Cities Overthrown** Gabriel inserted his wings under the towns of the people of Lot (and they became) the *overthrown* ones. They were five cities. And all the cities were raised aloft until the people of Heaven heard the crowing of the cocks and the barking of the dogs. And not a vessel of theirs was upset, and not a sleeper awakened. Then they were overturned, and set upside down, "and we rained upon them stones of clay." Al-Hasan says: The substance of the stones was clay, made exceedingly hard. And Qatādah and 'Akramah say: The stones had upon them red lines, like the Venus shell. Al-Hasan and as-Suddi say: There were sealed upon them things like seals. And some say there was written upon each stone the name of him it was supposed to strike. And as it is related, the stones would pursue those of them who were away from home, and those travelling, wherever they were in the land. And it is related by ath-Tha'labi from Muqātil ibn Suleimān, that the latter said: I said to Mujāhid, O Abu 'l-Hajjāj! did there survive any of the people of Lot? He said, Nay—except for one man, a merchant. He remained forty days in Mecca, and there came toward him a stone to strike him in the Haram. But there arose the Angels of the Haram in his behalf, and they said to the stone: Return whence thou camest! For verily the man is in the protection of Allah! So the stone went forth and remained stationary outside the Haram for the forty days, between Heaven and the earth, until the man finished his business. And then when he went forth the stone struck him, outside the Haram! [66]

The Punishment Inescapable

It is reported from Abu Sa'īd al-Hudhri: The ones who were guilty of such things among the people of Lot were only thirty odd men— not totalling forty; and Allah destroyed them altogether. And the Prophet said: Thou art commanded kindness, and forbidden what is wrong, for punishment will prevail on all of you!

As for his tomb. The learned and moderate Hanafite sheikh Abu 'Uqbah 'Abdullah ibn Muhammad al-Marwari says: I read in some of the lives of the Prophets that Lot was buried in a town named Kafar-Barīk, about a parasang distant from the Mosque of al-Khalīl— and likewise his two daughters.[67] And verily in the western part of the Cave under the old mosque are (buried) sixty prophets, of them twenty apostles. And the tomb of Lot has been wont to be visited and sought out from olden time, as information about it has been handed down from generation to generation of the people of the region. And they are commonly agreed about the facts, as we mentioned concerning the tomb of Abraham.

Lot's Tomb Near Hebron

Abu 'Abdullah Muhammad ibn Ahmad al-Bannā', of Jerusalem, says in the *Kitāb al-Badī' fi Tafdīl Mamlakat al-Islām*: A parasang from Habra is small mount which overlooks the lake of Sughār and the location of the cities of Lot. Moreover, there is a mosque which Abu Bekr as-Sabbāhi built, containing the site of the sleeping-place of Abraham, sunken in the rocks about a cubit. About it, it is said that Abraham, when he saw the towns of Lot picked up in the air, said, 'I witness that this is the certain truth.' And the author says: I have not seen (the works of) anyone of the historians who had cleared up the circumstances of the death of Lot or of his age. And I concur.

CHAPTER THIRTEENTH

Record of the Sons of Our Lord al-Khalīl, and His Wives, and the Wives of His Sons, and Their Children

Our Lord Ishmael was the eldest of the sons of Abraham. And Abraham took him to remove him to Mecca, and made him to dwell there. And when Ishmael grew up, and reached the age of marriage, he wedded a wife of the Jurham. And there took place concerning her the circumstances already mentioned, in the account of him. Then he divorced her by command of his father. Then he married another woman whose name was as-Seyyidah, daughter of Buddād ibn 'Umeir, of the Jurham tribe. And she was she to whom it was said, Tell thy husband when he comes, I approve of the threshhold of thy door!

As-Seyyidah bore to Ishmael twelve sons: Thābit, Qīdār, Adabīl, Mīshā, Damā, Māsh, Azar, Humeisa', Qetūra, Qabsā, Tamyā, and Qidmān. And of Qīdār and Thābit Allah propagated all the Arabs. And Ishmael, as said before, lived a hundred and seven and thirty years. And the mother of Ismael was Hagar the Copt. And she it was whom the giant gave to Sarah and whom Sarah gave to Abraham. She died before Sarah, in Mecca, and was buried in al-Hijr. She it was for whose sake the Prophet bade leniency for the Egyptians. As as-Suddi recounts on authority of Ka'b ibn al-Mālik of the Ansār: The Prophet of Allah said, When ye conquer Egypt, then I bid you good to her people. For verily they possess the statute of protection, and of kinship. And Ibn Ishāq says: I asked az-Zuhri about the kinship which the Apostle of Allah mentioned. And he said, It is through Hagar, the mother of Ishmael; for she was of them.

As for Isaac, he was the second of his sons, and he was blind.[68] He married Rebecca, daughter of Bethuel. And she bore to him Esau and Jacob, after sixty years of his life had passed. And Isaac lived a hundred and eighty years, as stated above in the account of him. His mother was Sarah, daughter of Haran, the first cousin of Abraham,

Résumé of the History of Ishmael

Of Isaac

although others say otherwise. She died when she was a hundred and
seventeen years old (or as others say, a hundred and twenty-seven)
in Syria, in the town of the giants, in the land of Canaan. And she was
buried in the field of Hebron, which Abraham bought. Ath-Tha'labi
says: Some of the learned regard three women as having possessed
prophethood, Sarah, and the mother of Moses, and Miriam. But the
majority are of the opinion that they were merely upright women.
Those who speak of their prophethood argue from the fact that the
Angels brought to Sarah the annunciation of Isaac; and in His word,
"And we revealed unto the mother of Moses that she should suckle
him"; [69] and that the Angel came to Miriam and gave her the
annunciation of Jesus.

And when Sarah died, Abraham married in her stead a woman of
the Canaanites who was named Qeturah, the daughter of Yaqtūr.
And she bore to him six children: Yoqshān, Zimrān, Midan, Midyān, *Abraham's Other Wives*
Yishbaq, and Shūkh. Then he married another woman of the Arabs, *and Children*
whose name was Hajjūn, daughter of Uhyab. And she bore to him
five sons: Keisān, Serug, Umbam, Lūtān, and Nāfis. And all the sons
of Abraham were thirteen, including Ishmael and Isaac.[70]

And Ishmael was the eldest of his sons, and he settled in the district of the Hejāz, and Isaac in the land of Syria. And the rest of his
sons separated in the earth. And they said, O Abraham! O our father!
thou hast kept Isaac with thee, and Ishmael in thy vicinity; but thou
hast commanded us that we dwell in strange and savage regions! And
he said, That have I commanded you! Then he taught them some of
the names of God, and they were wont to fear Him and seek His aid.

(This chapter is very lengthy—although we have sought to be brief.
And Allah knoweth!)

Chapter Fourteenth

Account of the Death of Abraham

The biographers say: When Allah wished to take away the life of
his Friend, Allah sent to him the Angel of Death in the form of a
decrepit old man. And (as ath-Tha'labi quotes from as-Suddi, with

his links in the chain of tradition) Abraham was richly endowed with food, and he was wont to feed people. And while he was feeding people, lo! a very old man, walking in the heat. And he sent unto him his ass, and mounted him upon it, so that, when he came to him, he gave him food. And the old man set to taking a morsel and (seeking to) place it in his mouth; but he would put it in his eye or his ear. Then, when he put it in his mouth and it entered his belly, it would come out his posteriors.

Now Abraham had asked of his Lord that He not take away his soul until he himself should ask for death. So he said to the old man, when he saw his condition, O thou sheikh! what aileth thee that thou doest thus? And he said, O Abraham! extreme age. And he said, How old art thou? And when he answered, he was two years above the age of Abraham. And Abraham said, Indeed, there are only two years difference between us! Now when I reach that age, shall I become like thee? He said, Yea! So Abraham said, O Lord! Take me away unto Thyself before that! And the old man arose, and took away his soul; for he was the Angel of Death.

The hāfiz Abu 'l-Qāsim ibn 'Asākir says: 'Abdullah ibn Ribāh has given us the tradition on authority of Ka'b as follows: Abraham was wont to receive guests and show mercy to the poor and the wayfarer. But as it came to pass that guests slackened, he was disturbed about the matter. So Abraham went forth to the way, and sought a guest. And there passed by the Angel of Death in the form of a man. And he prayed peace upon Abraham, and Abraham returned his greeting. Then Abraham asked him, Who art thou? And he said, A wayfarer. And he said, I sat here only for sake of such as thou; come with me! So he went with him to his dwelling. But Isaac saw him and recognized him, and wept. And when Sarah saw Isaac weeping, she wept because he was weeping. Then the Angel of Death rose (to depart). And when they wept, Abraham was angered, and said, Ye wept before my guest so that he departed! And Isaac said, O father! blame me not! verily, I saw the Angel of Death with thee, and I perceive that thy time of death, O father, hath come! So arrange the inheritance of thy family. And he gave him his last commands.

Now Abraham was (afterward) in a house in which he devoted himself to worship, and into which he let no one enter but himself;

and whenever he went forth he would lock it. So Abraham came to open his house in which he was wont to worship—and behold, a man seated there! And he said to him, Who art thou? And who hath admitted thee? He said, By the permission of the Lord of the house I entered. Abraham said, The Lord of the house hath the first right to it. Then Abraham faced in the direction of the House (in Mecca) and prayed as he was wont. So the Angel of Death arose and ascended. *Abraham's Piety* And he was asked, What sawest thou? He said, O Lord! I have come to thee from the presence of a servant of Thine than whom there is none better in the earth! He hath not left a creature of Thy creation whom he hath not summoned to his religion or his bounty!

Then Abraham tarried as long as Allah willed. Then he opened the door of his house in which he worshiped, and behold, a man seated. And Abraham said to him, Who art thou? And he said, I am the Angel of Death. Abraham said, If thou art truthful, then show me a sign so that I may know thou art the Angel of Death! The Angel of Death said to him, Turn aside thy face, O Abraham! And Abraham turned aside his face. Then he said, Face me and behold! So Abraham turned; and he showed him the form in which he took the souls of the faithful, and (Abraham) saw such a light and glory as no one knows but Allah. Then he said, Turn away thy face, O Abraham! And he turned away. Then he said, Face me and behold! So Abraham faced him; and he showed him the form in which he would take away the souls of the unbelievers—and Abraham trembled greatly with fear, so that his muscles quivered, and his belly cleaved to the ground, and his spirit almost left him!

So the Angel of Death ascended. And it was said to him (by Allah), Deal gently with him (that is, in taking the spirit of Abraham). So he came to him again, when Abraham was in his vineyard, in the form of a very old man, nothing remaining of him. So Abraham looked and beheld him, and had pity upon him, and took a basket and cut him some grapes in it. Then he brought it and placed it before him, and said, Eat thou! Then the Angel of Death set to making an appearance *Abraham's Release in Death* of eating, so he began chewing, and letting the saliva run down on his beard and his breast. So Abraham marvelled, and said, The years have not left of thee anything! How many years have come upon thee? And he counted, and said, There have come to me so and so many—

(like the days of Abraham!). So Abraham said, I myself have reached this age; and I must expect to be like this! O Lord, take me unto Thyself! So Abraham willingly surrendered himself, and the Angel of Death took away his spirit at that moment.

In an account on authority of the hāfiz Abu 'l-Qāsim al-Makki, of Jerusalem: The Angel of Death said, O Abraham! verily I am commanded to take thy spirit! He said, give me respite, O Angel of Death, until Isaac cometh! So he gave him respite. And when he (later) came unto him, they (Abraham and Isaac) kissed each other. And the Angel of Death had pity on them, and he returned unto his Lord and said, O Lord, I have seen that Thy Friend is very anxious about death! He said, O Angel of Death, then go to my Friend in his sleep, and take him thus! So he came to him in his sleep and took him thus.

An-Nawawi reports from Ka'b al-Ahbar and others: The circumstance of the death of Abraham was as follows. There came to him the

Other Stories of Abraham's Death

Angel of Death in the form of a very old man; and he received him hospitably. And when he was eating, he let his food and his drivel flow down upon his beard and his breast. And Abraham said to him, O servant of Allah, what is this! He said, I have reached the age the possessor of which is thus. He said, and how old art thou? He said, Two hundred years. And Abraham at that time was two hundred years old; and he loathed living on lest he come to this condition. So he died, without ever having been ill.

It is recounted also, on authority of Abu 's-Sakan al-Hijri: Abraham and David and Solomon died suddenly. And likewise (all) the pious

His Burial Place

ones; for this is a lightening (of death) to the believers. Said an-Nawawi: I say that it is an easement and a mercy which are the right of those who fear Him. And in Allah is the victory! And so Abraham died when he had reached the age of two hundred years— with some lack of agreement about the matter, as was said above. And he was buried in the Holy Land, in the field of Habrūn, as will come in the chapter concerning that, If Allah will.

CHAPTER FIFTEENTH

*Account of the Cave in Which Are the Noble Tombs, and Which of
the Prophets Are in It; and a Description of Them and of Their
Tombs; and the Purchasing of the Cave*

The scholars say: When Abraham went forth from Kūthā, he
settled in Syria in the district of Palestine, in a place which is known
today as Wādy as-Sab‘a.[71] Then there took place with him and his
people what took place. Then he settled in al-Lajjūn, and remained
there as long as Allah willed. Then Allah revealed to him that he
should settle in Mamrā. So he made his journey.

And there descended unto him Gabriel and Michael in Mamrā,
who were on the way to the people of Lot. And Abraham went out to
slay the calf; but it escaped from him, and ceased not until it entered
the Cave of Habrūn. And a voice called, O Abraham! pray peace upon
the bones of thy father Adam and upon all the Prophets! And that
deeply impressed Abraham.

Then he slew the calf, and offered it to them. Then there took
place in connection with him what Allah recounts in His Book. And
Abraham went along with them to the neighborhood of the dwellings
of Lot. And they said, Sit here. So he sat. And (when, after the cities
were overturned) he heard the crowing of the cock in the Heavens,
he said, This word (of the Angels) was the established truth (al-
Yaqīn)! For he was sure of the destruction of the people. So that place
was named Masjid al-Yaqīn.[72]

Then Abraham returned and besought of ‘Afrūn the Cave; and he
bought it from him for four hundred dirhams, every dirham having
the value of five, the total being a hundred dirhams in royal coinage.
So the burial place came to be his, and for whoever died of his people.
And there has preceded the extended story (on this subject) in the
fourth chapter, regarding his migration.

Purchase
of the Cave
in Habrūn

The hāfiz ibn ‘Asākir relates on authority of Ka‘b al-Ahbār: The
first one who died and was buried in Habrā was Sarah, whom Abraham
buried. When she died, Abraham went forth seeking a place for her
burial. And he was hopeful of finding a place in the vicinity of Mamrā.
So he went to ‘Afrūn, who was the king of that locality, with his resi-

dence in Habrā. So Abraham said to him, Sell thou me a place where
I may bury whoever dies of my people. And 'Afrūn said to him, I give
thee permission to bury where thou desirest in my land. Abraham said
to him, Verily, I like it not, except by purchase price! So he said
(again), O Sheikh Sālih! Bury wherever thou wishest! But he refused.
Now he was asking of him the Cave. So he said, I will sell it to thee
for four hundred dirhams, every dirham five, altogether a hundred,
royal coinage. He purposed to make the price excessive, in order that
he not find (the money). So he held to what he had said. So Abraham
went forth from his presence. And behold, Gabriel! who said, Verily,

Abraham
Divinely
Aided

Allah hath heard what this giant hath said to thee. Now (take) these
dirhams and pay them to him. So Abraham entered, and paid the
dirhams to him. And he said, O Abraham! whence (came) this to
thee? And he said, from my God, and my Creator, and my Sustainer!
So he took the dirhams from him.

And he bore Sarah to the Cave, and buried her there. And thereafter Abraham died, and was buried by her side. Then Rebecca, the

Burials
There

wife of Isaac, died and was buried there. Then Isaac died and was
buried there opposite his wife. Then Jacob died, and was buried near
the door of the Cave. Then Leah his wife died, and was buried beside
Jacob.

Then the sons of Jacob, and Esau and his brethren, made agreement and said, Let us leave the door of the Cave open, so that whoever
of us dies we may bury him. Then they quarreled; and one of the
brethren of Esau (or, as one account says, one of the sons of Jacob)
lifted his hand and smote Esau a blow, so that his head fell into the
Cave. And they bore off his body, and buried it without the head,
while the head remained in the Cave. Then they walled up the Cave,
and made in it grave-stones for the graves in every spot, and they
wrote upon them, This is the tomb of Abraham; This is the tomb of
Sarah; This is the tomb of Isaac; This is the Tomb of Rebecca; This is

The Tomb
Inscriptions

the tomb of Jacob; This is the tomb of his wife Leah. And all who
passed along there passed by it, and no one found it; until the Greeks
came after that, and opened up a door to it, and entered, and built a
church there. Then Allah revealed Islam afterward, and the Muslims
came to rule those districts.

In another account of his on authority of 'Abd al-Mun'im, from his father, from Wahb ibn Munabbih, it is said: I found, upon the tomb of Abraham, an inscription made in the stone:

> For the foolish one, hopes may grow;
> He dies whose fate wills it so;
> No scheming avails him now.

And someone of wisdom and fortitude has added:

> With him only his deeds shall go.[73]

The hāfiz ibn ʿAsākir says, Abu Hudheifah Ishāq ibn Bishr al-Qureishi says: It was reported to me by ash-Sharafi ibn Qattā'i on authority of a sheikh of the learned that Noah, when he embarked on the ark, took with him Adam in a coffin of *sāj* wood, and commanded his son not to move the coffin. And when he should see a bull at his door, pulling an ox-cart, he should place the coffin upon it. Then he should follow his steps, and wherever the bull should stop, he should bury the coffin in that place. But Shem, the son of Noah, supposed money was in the coffin, and he opened it—and behold, Adam, sixty cubits in length,[74] in a white shroud! And he repented his action and he immediately left it and he waited for the bull. And one day, behold the bull, and it stopped at his door, pulling the ox-cart. So he loaded the coffin upon it, and he walked along behind it, until it stopped at Jerusalem; and he buried him there. So the tombs of Noah, Shem son of Noah, Abraham, Sarah, Isaac, and Jacob are in Jerusalem.

The Tomb of Adam

In (the Land of) Jerusalem

And it is said that Abraham bought that place with two qantars of gold.

It is reported also, on authority of ʿAbdullah ibn Farrās: The body of Adam and his legs are there (in Hebron), and his head is near the Rock (in Jerusalem). Or his head is here and his legs near the Rock. It is reported from Nāfiʿ, from Ibn ʿAmr, that the feet of Adam are at the Rock, and his head at the Mosque of Abraham. And on the Resurrection Day, Allah will set him upon his legs, and will gather to him all his seed. And Allah will say, O Adam! unto thee I assemble thy seed; and all of them are assembled to do thee honor! It is reported from Abu 'l-Walīd ibn Hammād: I heard Hamīd ibn Zanjaweih, or someone else, say: The tomb of Adam (stretches) all along from Jerusalem unto the Mosque of Abraham. Ibn ʿAsākir says: Abu Hudheifah

says that 'Ammār ibn as-Sāji and Muqātil ibn Suleimān told him that
in the Mosque of the Haram (in Mecca), between Zamzam and the
Column, are the tombs of seventy Prophets, of them Hūd, Sālih, and
Ishmael. And the tombs of Abraham, Adam, Isaac, Jacob, and Joseph
are in (the land of) Jerusalem.

Muhammad ibn Bakrān ibn Muhammad al-Khatīb, the mosque-
preacher of the Shrine of Abraham, gives this story: [75]

How an
Ancient
Inscription
Was Read
I heard Muhammad ibn Ahmad an-Nahawi say: I went with the
Qādi Abu 'Amr 'Uthmān ibn Ja'far ibn Shādhān to the tomb of
Abraham. And we remained there three days. And when it was now
the fourth day, (the qādi) came to the graffiti facing the tomb of
Rebecca the wife of Isaac, and ordered them to be washed, so that the
writing appeared. And he recommended to me that I make a copy-
likeness of what was on the stone in a note-book we had with us.
Then he returned to Ramleh, and summoned people of every tongue
that they might read it for him.

But there was none among them who could read it. They agreed,
however, that it was in the ancient language of the Greeks, and they
did not know whether anyone survived who could read it, except a
sheikh in Aleppo. So he had him to come, and when he was there, he
had me to present with him. And, lo, he was an aged sheikh. And the
sheikh who had personally come from Aleppo dictated (the translation)
to me, as follows:

In the Name of My God, and the God of the Conquering Throne!
the Guider, the Mighty, the Valiant! The marker which adjoins
this inscription (indicates) the grave of Rebecca, the wife of Isaac;
and the one over against it is the tomb of Isaac; and the larger marker
which is over against it is the tomb of Abraham al-Khalil; and the
marker facing that from the east is the tomb of his wife Sarah; and
the farther marker adjoining the tomb of Abraham is the tomb of
Jacob; and the marker adjoining that on the east is the tomb of Illīya
(Leah) the wife of Jacob. May the blessings and peace of Allah be
upon them all! And Esau wrote this by his own hand.

Muhammad ibn Bakrān al-Khatīb says: I saw in another copy
that the inscription on the inscribed stone to the east as mentioned,
was (over) the head of Adam. And this is a translation of it: In the
Divine Name, God of the Powerful Throne, the Conquering, the

Mighty, the Valiant! The marker which adjoins this inscription is the tomb of Rebecca, wife of Isaac; and the marker which adjoins it from the west is the tomb of Isaac; and the large marker which faces it is the tomb of Abraham; and the marker which is by its side to the east is the tomb of his wife Sarah; and the farthest marker coming next to the tomb of Abraham, is the tomb of Jacob; and the marker which adjoins that to the east is the tomb of Illīya wife of Jacob— and may the blessing and peace of Allah be upon them all! and His Mercy and Blessings! For justification is by His grace! *Another Account*

Thus in the two accounts on authority of Muhammad ibn Bakrān the name of the wife of Jacob is (given as) Illīya. In some books her name is Līyya. The well-known form is Līqā. But Allah knoweth best. And the qādi mentioned in the first report is Abu 'Amr 'Uthmān ibn Ja'far ibn Shādhān, a qadi of excellent ability, well known and famous —although the writer shows doubt about the name of his father. Now I believe him to be 'Uthmān ibn Muhammad ibn Shādhān, who was qādi in Ramleh from about the year three hundred and twenty and following in the days of ar-Rādi-bi-'llāh. He is cited for traditions which he heard from several, and several scholars have given traditions through him.

The hāfiz Ibn 'Asākir says: I have read in some of the books of the traditionists, and have made an extract from them, as follows: Muhammad ibn Bakrān ibn Muhammad al-Khatīb, preacher in the Mosque of Abraham, says: I heard Muhammad ibn Ahmad ibn 'Ali ibn Ja'far al-Anbāri say: I heard Abu Bakr al-Ashkāfi say: It is certain with me that the tomb of Abraham is in the place where it is (recognized to be) at present, by that which I saw and viewed. That was because I had expended upon the caretakers and upon the shrine considerable donations, to the amount of about four thousand dinars, hoping for the reward of Allah, and seeking that I might know the certitude of the question. And so I had gained influence over their hearts by means of what I had done for them of kindness and generosity and favors and gifts and benefits, all for the purpose that I might arrive at certitude for the uncertainty in my breast. *A Personal Report of Visiting the Tombs*

So I said to them one day, when all of them had gathered unto me, I ask of you that ye bring me to the door of the Cave in order that I may descend unto the Prophets, that I may behold them. And they said, We had heeded thee in that matter, for thou hast compelling right with us; but it is not possible at this time, for travellers unto us are many. But (abide patiently) until winter enters. So when the month of Kānūn ath-Thāni [76] began, I went unto them. And they said, Remain with us until the snow falls; and I remained, until snow fell, and travellers were hindered from them.

The Descent

Then they came to that part of the rock between the tomb of Abraham al-Khalīl and the tomb of Isaac, and removed the flat stone. And there descended in my presence a man of them named Sa'lūk, a truthful man, of good character. So he descended, and I descended with him, I behind him. We went down two and seventy steps, and behold, on my right a very large bier of black stone, and upon it an old man lying on his back, with thin, long beard, having on a robe of green. And Sa'lūk said to me, This is Isaac. Then we went a short

He Beholds the Patriarchs

way, and behold a bier larger than that one, upon it an old man lying upon his back, having grey hairs which had overtaken all the hair between his shoulders, with a white head and beard and eyebrows and lashes, having below this grey head a green robe which enveloped his body and the greater part of the bier; and the wind was gently blowing his grey hairs to right and left. So Sa'lūk said to me, This is Abraham al-Khalīl! Thereupon I fell upon my face and called out unto Allah (with thanks) for the success He had vouchsafed to me!

Then we went further, and behold a narrow bier, upon it an old man with very brown skin, and thick bearded, having upon him a green robe which covered him. And Sa'lūk said to me, This is Jacob the Prophet.

Then we inclined to the left that we might look upon the Haram.

But Abu Bakr al-Ashkāfi indicated to me that the story was finished. So I arose from his presence immediately the time of his giving me the story was over, and went at once to the Mosque of Abraham. And I came there, and asked about Sa'lūk. And I was told, He is coming now. So when he came, I met him, and sat down by him, and I told him part of the story. And he looked at me in a manner denying the story which he heard from me. So I showed signs of kindness to him, and set myself free of blameworthiness inasmuch as Abu Bakr al-Ashkāfi was my uncle. So he thereupon became friendly to me.

So I said, O Sa'lūk; by Allah! When ye turned toward the Haram, what happened, and what saw ye? He said to me, Did not Abu Bakr tell thee? But I said, I desire to hear about it from thee also! So he said, We heard from the direction of the Haram a voice saying, Turn away! the Haram! may Allah have mercy upon you! So we fell down in a faint. Then after a time we came to, and arose — after we had despaired of life, and the group had despaired of us!

The Warning Voice

The sheikh said, And the sheikh Abu Bakr al-Ashkāfi lived after he told me this story only a few days—and likewise Sa'lūk.

He says further: I read (the following) in the book of Abu 'l-Fath Muhammad ibn Ismā'īl al-Farghāni, a notable among students of the Koran and science and tradition, who used to be in Cairo, whom I never met, but about whom many had told me, and whose writings I had copied, as well as an oral report by the hāfiz Abu Bakr ibn Ahmad ibn 'Amr ibn Jābir of Ramleh:

The Tombs Certified by a Noted Traditionist

He was asked about the tomb of Abraham al-Khalīl, and its authenticity. And he said, I have not seen any of the scholars of the learned people whom I have met who did not certify that this is the tomb of Abraham al-Khalīl and Isaac and Jacob and their wives. And they say that no one disparages that except those who are heretics. And he said further, This is a matter handed down from one generation to another, and about which I have no doubt. And he mentions the fact that Mālik ibn Anas says that such handing down is more trustworthy than a tradition; because error often occurs in case of traditions, but it does not occur in case of such handing down of information.

He was asked again about the tomb of Abraham and its authenticity, and he told the following story: It is related by al-Hasan ibn 'Abd al-Wāhid ibn Rizq ar-Rāzi that Abu Zar'ah, qādi of Palestine, went to the Mosque of Abraham, and we came to greet him. And he had seated himself near the tomb of Sarah, at the time of prayer. And there came an old man whom he asked, O sheikh! which of these is the tomb of Abraham? And he pointed out to him the tomb of Abraham, and passed on. Then there came a youth, whom he addressed, and who said the same, pointing it out to him, and passing on. Then there came a child, whom he addressed, and who indicated it to him likewise. So Abu Zar'ah said, I witness that this is the tomb of Abraham! There is no doubt of it. It has been directly handed down from generation to generation. And as Mālik ibn Anas says, such handing down is more trustworthy than traditions, because error often enters into traditions, but error does not enter such handing down. And no one disparages that except a heretic and innovator.

Then he arose and went inside and prayed the noon prayer, and then entered again on the morrow.

Abu 'Abdullah Muhammad ibn Ahmad ibn Bakr, the architect, of Jerusalem, writes in his book, *al-Badī' fī Tafḍīl Mamlakat al-Islām*: Habrā is the town of al-Khalīl; in it is a mighty fortress which is said to be of the construction of the jinn, of mighty, chiseled stones, in its center a dome of stones of Islamic workmanship, over the tomb of Abraham. The tomb of Isaac is in the forepart in the covered structure, and the tomb of Jacob in the rear; and next to each of the prophets is his wife. The enclosure was made into a mosque, and there were built around it the lodgings of the pilgrims, and it is connected with the Cave, on every side. They have a small aqueduct of healthful water. Around this town to the extent of half a stage on every side are villages and gardens of grapes and apples, the greater part of which is transported to Egypt. And in this town are a perpetual hospice, a cook, a baker, and organized servants, who provide lentils with oil to all of the poor who come and this is distributed to the rich if they accept.[77]

Report of Another Author of Palestine

Al-Hauqali records in his book, *al-Masālik wa 'l-Mamālik*:[78] To the south of Bethlehem is a small city, as it were a town, known as Masjid Ibrāhīm al-Khalīl. And in its mosque, where the Friday services are held, are the tombs of Abraham al-Khalīl, and Isaac, and Jacob, in rows, the tomb of the wife of each adjoining him. It is a holy place, much visited. It is in between mountains thick with forests; and the trees of these mountains, and the other mountains of all Palestine, are olives, figs, grapes, and other fruits.

From al-Hauqali the Geographer

The sheikh 'Imād ad-Dīn ibn Kathīr records in his history: Isaac, when he died, was a hundred and eighty years old; and his sons Esau and Jacob buried him by his father Abraham al-Khalīl in the cave which Abraham had bought (as was related above), in the town of Habrūn, which is in the land of Canaan, where Abraham formerly dwelt. And his death occurred after the arrival of Jacob with his children.

From Ibn Kathīr the Historian

Chapter Sixteenth

How Solomon Son of David Built the Enclosure around the Cave, by Revelation of Allah; and an Account of Solomon

The ḥāfiz ibn 'Asākir records on authority of Ka'b al-Ahbār: When Solomon finished building the Temple of Jerusalem, Allah sent unto him a revelation, Build at the tomb of My Friend a building, that he may be known by it! So Solomon went forth, and built at a place called ar-Rāmah. But Allah revealed to him, This is not the place; but behold the light extending from Heaven to earth! So he beheld, and lo, light was over one of the vales of Ḥabrūn, and he knew that that was the intended place! So he built the enclosure over the vale.

Another Account of the Death and Burial of the Patriarchs

And he relates on authority of the ḥāfiz Makki of Jerusalem, from Makhūl, from Ka'b al-Ahbār: The first person who died and was buried in Ḥabrā was Sarah, the wife of Abraham. Now when she died, Abraham went forth to seek a place to bury her. And he approached Ephron, who differed in his religion and whose dwelling place was the neighborhood of Ḥabrā, and purchased from him the place for fifty dirhams. And the dirham of that era was worth five present dirhams. So Sarah was buried there. Then Abraham died, and was buried beside her. Then Rebecca the wife of Isaac died and was buried there. Then Isaac died and was buried beside her. Then Jacob died and was buried in that place. Then his wife Leah died and was buried with them.

And the place remained as it was until the time of Solomon. And when Allah sent him (as a prophet), He revealed unto him, O son of David, build upon the tomb of My friend an enclosure that it may remain to those who come after thee, in order that it may be known! So Solomon went forth and the Tribes of Israel from Jerusalem until they came to the land of Canaan. And they sought about, but did not find the place. So they returned to Jerusalem. Then Allah sent him a revelation: Solomon, thou hast left off My command! He said, O Lord, the appointed place has eluded me! And Allah revealed to him: Travel along, and thou shalt see a light from the Heavens to the earth; and that is the place of the tomb of Abraham, My Friend.

and of the Work of Solomon

So Solomon set out a second time, and sought; and he commanded the jinn, and they built over the place which is called ar-Rāmah. But Allah revealed to him, Verily, this is not the place; but when thou seest the light in the highest clouds of the Heavens—. So Solomon set forth, and beheld the light from the highest clouds of the Heavens unto the earth. And he built over that place the enclosure.

As for Solomon, he was a prophet of Allah, son of the Prophet of Allah David, the son of Jesse, son of Ghawīl, son of Ghābir, son of Salmon, son of Takhshūn, son of 'Ammi, son of Bārib, son of Rām, son of Khadrūn, son of Fārid, son of Judah, son of Jacob, son of Isaac, son of Abraham the Friend of the Merciful. No one ever attained such a kingdom as his. For, indeed, Allah gave him power over men and jinn and birds and animals and the winds. An-Nawawi says in his *Tahdhīb al-Asmā'*: Ath-Tha'labi says in the *Kitāb al-'Arā'is*: In connection with His Word, " And Solomon was heir of David," he was so in his prophethood and wisdom and judgment instead of the other sons of David. David had twelve sons. And Solomon was the king of Syria unto Istakhr. And it is said that he was the king of the earth.

Ibn 'Abbās relates that there ruled the earth two believers, Solomon and Dhu 'l-Qarnein, and two unbelievers, Nimrod and Nebuchadnezzar —as was mentioned above.

Description of Solomon

Ka'b al-Ahbār and Wahb ibn Munabbih says: Solomon was fair, corpulent, comely, pleasant, beautiful, modest, humble; he wore white garments; he would sit down with the poor, and would say, A poor man sits with the poor! His father was wont to advise with him in many matters despite his youthful years, because of the fulness of his intellect and knowledge. And when he was king, Solomon had great power, and it never forsook him. The wind used to carry him and his army and their mounts over the fields, and the standing grain would not be disturbed.

And of His Place in History

Muhammad ibn Ka'b al-Qarzi says: The report has reached us that the army of Solomon was a hundred parasangs long, twenty-five for the men, and the same for the jinn, the birds, and the animals. And Allah granted him that which He hath granted no one else of the two worlds; and he was the heir of his father David in the kingship and prophethood. He established the law of Moses, until Jesus was sent and it was abrogated. And there were between him and the Hijrah about a thousand and eight hundred years, although the Jews say a thousand and three hundred and sixty-two years. It is said that between his death and the birth of the Prophet there were a thousand and seven hundred years, although the Jews say less by three hundred years. He lived somewhat over fifty years. The author of the *Jāmi'u 'l-Usūl* says: An-Nawawi says, The historians say that the lifetime of Solomon was three and fifty years, and he became king when he was thirteen years old; and he began building (the Temple of) Jerusalem four years after the start of his reign. And according to the certification of the Muslim authorities, there have been from the time he built the enclosure over our Lord Khalīl ar-Rahmān, unto our present era, two thousand and six hundred and fourteen years. And the author of the *Jāmi'u 'l-Usūl* says also: There were between David and Moses five hundred and ninety years, or as some say, seventy-nine. And he (David) lived a hundred years, and gave his dying commands to Solomon.

CHAPTER SEVENTEENTH

On Visions of the Places of the Pious Ones and Saints, Agreeing with What Has Preceded of the Accounts of the Prophets and Descriptions of Their Tombs

The hāfiz Ibn 'Asākir relates on authority of the hāfiz Abu Bakr ibn Ahmad ibn 'Amr ibn Jābir of Ramleh the following: I went a certain year, along with Ibn al-Murajjā and a company of learned and pious men unto the Mosque of Abraham, which was in care of Abu Zeinūr. There was there an imām called Abu Hāmid, who told us:

I saw a vision the night of the middle of the month Sha'bān. I had engaged in prayer, and sat by the minbar, and gone to sleep.[79] And I saw, as he who has a vision sees, one who came to me and said, Dost thou wish to see the people? And I said, Yea! So he took me by the hand to the back of the enclosure near the tomb of Jacob. And he raised up a stone—and lo, a light like the daylight! And he entered, and I entered. And behold, the tombs all in a row, upon them white coverings, and also above. So he removed (the covering) from the tomb of Jacob; and lo, it was the form of an old man, with a very white beard, resting upon his side, with his face toward the qiblah. And he (the guide of the vision) said, This is the Prophet of Allah,

Account of a Vision of the Tombs

Jacob. Then he replaced the covering, and passed on until he came to the tomb of Abraham, in the center. And there was over him a covering of white. This he raised, and behold, an old man with a whitened head and beard and eye-brows, as if his face were the moon. And he said, This is Abraham. And he replaced the covering.

And he passed along, and I with him, toward the tomb of Isaac. And I said within myself. Oh, that so and so were with me so that he might behold them as I do! And he turned unto me, from before me, and said, Verily, that such an one cannot behold these, because he is a contentious person, and the contentious cannot see them.

And then I awoke, and did not reach the tomb of Isaac. And I was grieved because I did not see Isaac. Abu Bakr ibn Jābir said, Abu Hāmid told us, And I have been asking Allah for forty years that He would allow me to behold them (again) as I beheld them.[80]

And Abu 'l-Hams ar-Rāzi said, This story was told me by Abu Hāmid ibn Muhammad ibn al-Mu'tasim and company of the learned in biography. And this is substantially what Abu Bakr told him.

Another Vision of the Tombs

It is also related on authority of the aforementioned Abu Hāmid, who was imām of the Mosque of Abraham for a long time: I saw in a dream, as if the Cave, over which is the structure of the mosque, was open; and a man took me by the hand, and said to me, these are Abraham and Isaac, and Jacob, on their biers, with the wife of each of them beside him.

And it is related from 'Abdullah ibn Muhammad an-Najjār, the trustworthy and pious sheikh: I saw, in such dreams as a sleeper sees, as if I had set out for the Mosque of Abraham. And when I came to where I could overlook the mosque, I saw a light shining on its walls, upon each of its two pinnacles beating rays of shining light. And I descended and entered the Mosque; and lo, a couch with a cover spread upon it; and behold, Abraham al-Khalīl seated upon it, with a white beard, a hooked nose, and a fair face, on his cheeks as it were two roses.

Greeted by Abraham

And I approached him, and greeted him. And he clasped me to his breast; and I thought secretly within myself, This is the Friend of Allah who embraces me! And he knew what was in my secret thought, and said, Marvel not from this; verily, Allah hath saints who visit me, and I go to meet them in the way.

The same man above says: There told me the sheikh Abu 'l-Hasan

Mūsa ibn al-Husein ibn Muhmmad ad-Dauri, saying: There told me
a man of the folk of the Mosque of Abraham, saying, There told me a
pious man who was among us, that one night when he slept he saw
al-Khalīl, and asked him that he ask Allah to make possible for him
the Pilgrimage and visitation of the Tomb of the Prophet. And al-
Khalīl said to him, Bide with us until the night of Friday; for every
Friday night the Prophet Mohammed cometh to visit me.

Friday Visits
of the Prophet
to Abraham

The author says, If I were to include the matters related by servants
of the shrine (and indeed, it is of shining and noble and purifying
light!), the chapter would be over long. And Allah Exalted and Praised
knoweth!

Chapter Eighteenth

*On the Tomb of Joseph the Trustworthy, and How His Coffin Was
Borne from Egypt, and Its Burial near His Fathers*

The hāfiz ibn 'Asākir relates in his history, on authority of Ibn
'Abbās: Allah revealed unto Moses that he should bear Joseph unto
Jerusalem unto his fathers.[81] And he knew not where he was (buried).
So he asked the Children of Israel, but none of them knew. But an old
man, three hundred years of age, told him, O Prophet of Allah, there
knoweth of the grave of Joseph only my mother. And he said to him,
Come with me unto thy mother! And the man arose and entered his
dwelling, and brought him a basket in which was his mother. And
Moses said to her, Hast thou knowledge about the grave of Joseph?
She said, Yea; and I will guide thee on condition that thou pray to
Allah to return unto me my youth as it were of seventeen years, and
add to my time of life as much as hath passed! And Moses prayed for
her. And he said, How long hast thou lived? She said, I am nine hundred years old, and I shall live a thousand and eight hundred years.
So she then showed him the grave of Joseph. And it was in the center
of the Nile in Egypt. And Moses brought it forth, and he was in a
coffin of marble. And he bore it on a chariot of iron unto Jerusalem,
and buried him in the vale behind the enclosure adjacent to the tomb
of Jacob and near his ancestors Abraham and Isaac.

How Joseph's
Coffin Was
Found

Joseph
Buried in
Hebron

It is related on authority of 'Ali: The Apostle of Allah was accustomed when he was asked anything and wished to comply, to say, Yea;

and if he did not wish to grant it, to remain silent; and he never said Nay to anything. So there came to him a bedouin, and made a request, and he remained silent. Then he asked again, and he remained silent. Then he asked again and the Prophet said to him in an upbraiding manner, Ask what thou wishest, O bedouin, and we shall grant it. So we (who are present) said, Now he will ask him for Paradise! But he said, I ask of thee a riding camel. And the Prophet said to him, That is thine. He said, And a saddle for her. And he said, That is thine. And he added, Ask on! He said, And a bridle. He said, That is thine.

How the
Prophet
Told This
Story

And we wondered at that. And the Prophet said, To the bedouin be what he hath asked. Then the Prophet said, What a difference between the request of this bedouin and that of the old woman of the Children of Israel! Then he continued:

Moses, when was commanded to go through the sea, and was halted—that is, at the place where the pack animals had been driven—turned back. And he said, O Lord, I have not the power! And He said, Verily, thou art near the tomb of Joseph; so bear his bones with thee. Now the tomb had become covered (and lost) in the ground. So Moses found he knew not where it was. And he asked, Knoweth any of you where it is. And they said, We know not anyone who knoweth but an old woman of such and such a tribe, who perhaps may have knowledge of where it is.

So Moses sent messengers to her, and they came to her. She said, What will ye? They said, Come thou to Moses! And when she came to him, he said, Dost thou know where is the tomb of Joseph? She said, Yea! He said, Then lead us unto it! She said, Nay—not until thou givest me what I ask! He said, That be to thee. She said, Then, verily, I ask thee that I may be with thee in thy station in which thou shalt be in Paradise! He said, Ask me just for Paradise! She said, Nay! Only that I be with thee!

Al-Karāshi says in his commentary: And she was a believer. And Moses began to dispute with her; but Allah revealed to him, Grant her that, O Moses; verily, it will not at all deprive thee! So he granted it to her; and she led him to the tomb of Joseph. And he took forth his bones, and crossed the sea.

We were told (by Ibn 'Asākir?): It is related by Ibrāhīm ibn

Ahmad al-Khalanji that on an occasion there appeared to him a maid-servant of al-Muqtadir, known as *al-'Ajūz* [i. e., "Old Woman"], who was living in Jerusalem, and was seeking to go to the place in which it was reported the tomb of Joseph was, and to build over it. And he continues: So there went forth with me workmen to uncover the place in the vale, which reports indicated was outside the enclosure, next to the tomb of his father Jacob. So he bought the vale from its owner, and set about uncovering it. And he went forth to the place about which it was reported there was a great stone, and ordered that it be broken through. And they broke a piece of it. And, as he says: I was with them in the excavation; and when they lifted up the piece of the stone, behold, there was Joseph, like the description of him as to goodliness and beauty! And the odor of the spot became like musk. Then there came a strong wind, and the workmen closed back the stone as it was. Then he built over it the dome which is over it at present, as an indication of the proof of the report. And the one who witnessed this was an honest man, and he was imām of the Mosque of Abraham.

An Account of Uncovering the Tomb of Joseph in Hebron

He says: I had leaned my head on the lowest step of the minbar, and had gone to sleep. And there came to me the voice of one unseen, saying, Come forth to the tomb of Joseph! And he indicated to me the vale and the place three times. And thereupon I went unto Jerusalem and found the old woman, the servant of al-Muqtadir bi'llāh; and she wrote to her protectors. And the matter resulted in discovery of the place and the construction of a building upon it. And this agrees with what was said before.[82]

Its Substantiation

Abu 'Abdullah Muhammad ibn Ahmad ibn Abu Bakr al-Bannā', of Jerusalem, says in the book, *al-Badī'a fī Tafdīl Mamlakat al-Islām*: I heard my uncle Abu 'l-Husein ibn Abu Bakr al-Bannā' say: The tomb of Joseph was flattened down, and people said it was the tomb of a certain one of the tribes—until there came a man of Khorasan, and told that he had seen in a dream as if one were saying to him, Go thou to Jerusalem and inform them that that is the tomb of Joseph! He continues: And the sultān ordered my father to send me forth; and I set out with them. And the workmen did not cease digging until they came upon the wood of a cart, in which decay had set in. And I saw our old women continually using the crumbled portion to cure opthalmia.

Another Account

It is related on authority of Ibn 'Abbās, in a long tradition: No one was granted his request about death before Joseph. For he said, "O Lord, Thou hast given me royalty, and hast taught me the interpretation of events. O Creator of Heaven and earth! Thou art my protector in this world and the Next! Bring me to mine end a Muslim, and join me with the pious ones!" (Meaning his fathers Abraham, Isaac, and Jacob.) So Allah brought him to his death as a good and acceptable man in Egypt. And he was buried in the Nile, in a coffin of marble.

Joseph's Prayer

That was for this reason: When he died, the people vied with each other, all wanting him to be buried in their neighborhood because of their blessing through him; and they discussed that until they in their heat were on the point of fighting. So they decided that he be buried in the Nile, and the water would flow over him and then touch all Egypt, so that all of them would share in his blessing. So they did that. And the matter remained thus until Moses bore him away and buried him beside his father Jacob and his ancestors.

Why Joseph Was Buried in the Nile

Chapter Nineteenth

On the Merit of Visiting the Tomb of Abraham al-Khalīl, and His Noble Sons; and the Reward and Recompense for So Doing

The hāfiz Makki ibn 'Abdullah al-Muqaddasi relates, with his authorities, from Qatādah, from Ibn Zarrārah, from Ibn Ubeyy Aufi, from Abu Hureirah: The Apostle of Allah said, When I was taken on the Night-Journey to Jerusalem, Gabriel carried me to the Tomb of Abraham. And he said, Descend here, and pray two rak'ahs, for indeed here is the tomb of thy father Abraham. Then he took me to Bethlehem, and said, Descend here and pray two rak'ahs, for verily here was born thy brother Jesus. Then he carried me to the Rock (of Jerusalem), and so on, according to the tradition.

Connection with the Night-Journey

And also from him, and from 'Abdullah ibn Salām, going back to the Prophet, it is related: (The Prophet) said, Whoever cannot make pilgrimage unto me let him make pilgrimage unto the tomb of Abraham al-Khalīl.

And in an account from Wahb ibn Munnabih, from him, he said: There will come to the people a time when the way (of pilgrimage) will be closed to them, And Allah will prevent them from the Pilgrimage. And whoever cannot attain it, let him make pilgrimage to my father Abraham; for verily he who visiteth him, it is as if he visited me!

In an account from 'Abdullah ibn Salām, it is said: Verily, a visit to the tomb of Abraham, and prayer there, is a Pilgrimage for the poor and an efficacious work for the wealthy.

In an account from Wahb ibn Munnabih from Ka'b al-Ahbār, he said: Make many pilgrimages unto the Tomb of the Prophet, and offer prayers there upon him and his Companions Abu Bakr and 'Omar, before ye be prevented from that, or disturbance and rebellion prevent your going. And whoever is prevented or obstructed from the Pilgrimage to my tomb, let him visit the Tomb of Abraham, and offer prayer upon him, and make manifold his petitions there, for verily, petitions there are granted, and no one makes entreaty through him to Allah about any matter without His unfailingly granting the answer sooner or later.

And in an account from Ka'b al-Ahbār, he said; If only there were known what is to be known of the great reward in visiting the Tomb of Abraham, the vale there would never be free of pilgrims! And no one makes entreaty through Abraham without Allah's giving him what he requests and adding to that an increase without his asking, by reason of the merit of Abraham.

And on authority of Wahb ibn Munnabih: Blessed is he who visits the Tomb of Abraham! Allah will forgive all his sins, though they be like Mt. Ohod.[83] From him also: When cometh the latter age, people will be obstructed from the Pilgrimage. And whoever cannot successfully make the pilgrimage he hath the Tomb of Abraham; for verily a visit to him is equivalent to the Pilgrimage. From him also: Whoever visits the Tomb of Abraham once, having no other purpose but this, he shall be gathered on the Day of Judgment safe from the great fear, and he shall be guarded from the ordeal of the tomb, and it will be incumbent upon Allah that He join him with Abraham.

On authority of Himām ibn Munnabih, from Ka'b al-Ahbār: Who visits Jerusalem, and directs his way unto the Tomb of Abraham for prayer there, and prays there five prayers, and then asks anything of Allah, He will grant it to him; and He will forgive all his sins. And whoever visits the Tomb of Abraham and Isaac and Jacob and Sarah and Rebecca and Leah, he will be granted for that visitation lasting merit and abundant food in his earthly life; and Allah will bring him, thus supplied, to the Dwellings of the Just, and he will not return to his home without Allah's forgiving him his sins; and he will not depart from this life before Abraham appears to him and gives him the good news that Allah hath forgiven him.

On authority of Ibn 'Abbās: When Allah wished to take the soul of his friend Abraham, He revealed to the world, Verily, I am burying in thee My Friend! And the earth was shaken with a great shaking, and its mountains were raised up, and there was set down from them the spot called Habra. And Allah said, O Habra! Thou art my brightness; thou art my brightness; thou art my holiness; in thee are the stores of my knowledge, and upon thee have I sent down my mercy and blessings. Unto thee shall I gather my servants of the children of My Friend. And blessed is he who toucheth his face to thee in prayer! I shall give him to drink of the presence of my holiness, and I shall keep him safe from the terror at my resurrection, and I shall make him to dwell in Paradise by my mercy. And blessed art thou, and blessed! I am burying in thee My Friend.

The hāfiz Ibn 'Asākir relates on authority of Ka'b al-Ahbār that he (the Prophet) said: There are four mountains, the mount of Hebron, and at-Tīn, and al-Jūdi, and Olivet, every one of which on the Day of Resurrection shall be of gleaming whiteness, shining between the Heavens and the earth, returning to Jerusalem to be set at her corners; and the Lord shall ascend upon them to judge between the people of Paradise and those of the Fire. And the Angels shall go around the Throne sounding the praises of their Lord. And He shall judge between them in truth. And they will say, "Praise be to Allah, Lord of the Worlds!"

The Mount of Hebron among the Sacred Mountains

The hāfiz Ibn 'Asākir says also: The pious sheikh Abu 'l-Hasan Mūsa ibn al-Husein ibn al-Duweiri, the merchant, tells me that a man of the people of Baalbek said: We visited the Tomb of Abraham al-Khalīl, and there was with us a stupid man of the people of Baalbek, whom we overheard, who had visited the Tomb of Abraham, and was

An Instance of Efficacy of Prayer There

weeping and saying, O my beloved Abraham, ask of thy Lord that he requite me of So and So, and So and So, and So and So! Verily, they have cause me hurt! And we laughed at him, and wondered. Then we returned after a while unto Jaffa, and there arrived a boat from Beirut, with a man in it of the people of Baalbek, who told us that the three men whom he had named had died!

Al-Baghawi relates on authority of 'Abdullah ibn 'Amr ibn al-'Āsi: I heard the Apostle of Allah say, Verily there shall be flight after flight and the best of the people shall go to the refuge of Abraham! May the prayers and peace of Allah be upon him, and his worthy, pure sons! Appointed for Refuge

CHAPTER TWENTIETH

Accounts of What Is Related by Reports of His Hospitality, and of What Merit and Noble Qualities of Character Allah Distinguished Him with

It is related by the hāfiz Ibn 'Asākir on authority of Ibn 'Abbās: Verily, Allah was bountiful unto Abraham in property and servants. And he made himself a guest-house with two doors, and the stranger entered through one of them and departed through the other. He placed in that house clothing for days of winter and clothing for days of summer, and a spread table having upon it food. And men would come and eat; and if there were one naked, he would be clothed. Then Abraham would renew things every time. Abraham the Paragon of Hospitality

He says further: I heard one of the scholars say: Abraham had made for himself a castle for hospitality, in which were four doors, one from every direction. So that whoever came from any direction would enter that door, not needing to go around unto another direction. Further I heard some of the learned scholars say that a great party of the noblest of the (pagan) people came to visit Abraham, and he entertained them in the most hospitable manner, and honored them in the noblest fashion, and continued his honors to them so long as they remained with him. Then when they were of the intention to depart, they said to each other, Verily this man hath honored us, and exceeded in honoring us, so that he hath embarrassed us. So come, let us inquire if he hath a need which we may discharge for him, or a Even to Pagans matter about which we may assist him, in requital for what he hath done to us in the way of noble deeds.

So they said to him, O Abraham! Thou hast honored us, and hast exceeded in honoring us! Now if there be need to thee, we will discharge it, or if any matter requiring aid, we will aid thee. Then he said to them, I have an important matter of need touching you, and I wish that ye discharge it for me! And they said, What is it? And he said, That ye bow once in worship to my God! But they said, There is no way we can do that! And the matter was difficult for them, and they were sorely perplexed! For they were polytheists. So he said to them. I have no further need touching you but this; and if ye will discharge it, (well), and if not, then I have no need in your regard.

So they said to each other, There will be no harm to us in this; so let us go and perform his need, and worship his god once—but we shall remain in our own religion, not changing from it! So they agreed upon that, and they said to Abraham:

We shall perform thy need. And he said, Then do so! So they faced the qiblah of Abraham, and all of them worshiped, and Abraham worshiped with them, and he praised Allah as he worshiped, saying O Allah, I have done what I could in making sound their outward actions, but I am not able to make them sound within! But Thou art able to make them whole within and without! There is no God but Thee!

And, as it is said, Allah made them whole, within and without, and lead them all to the truth Faith and the Unity of God. And they raised up their heads from their worship as true believers, believing in the One God! And Abraham rejoiced over that; for all of them became members of his faith, hanīfs and Muslims—praise be to Him Who is powerful over all things!

He says further: Muhammad ibn ʿAbd as-Salām ibn al-Husein tells me, on authority of certain sheikhs: There was a man of Damascus, noble, modest, of great integrity, who betook himself to visit our Lord Khalīl ar-Rahmān ever so often. And he would give back the guest-alms which it was the custom to bestow upon the pilgrims, and return them, and not accept them, and not eat anything of them. Then he came upon a time in sorrow, and set to seeking them (the, alms) until as it was said he would seek after what remained in the wooden bowls, and would take what was left over of the pieces and crumbs of

The Pagans
Saved
through
Him

Humility
Necessary
for Blessing
There

bread, and would eat them. So someone spoke to him about the matter. And he said: I saw Abraham al-Khalīl in a dream, and he said to me, Thou eatest not of our alms-provisions, and we will not accept thy pilgrimage! But if thou wilt eat, we will accept thy pilgrimage.

And it is related on authority of Saʿīd ibn al-Museyyib: Abraham was the first one to receive guests; and he was wont to walk a mile or twain in search of a guest; and he was the first to strike with the sword, and the first to smash idols. *Abraham's Distinctions*

And ath-Thaʿlabi relates: A tradition says that one said to the Prophet, O lord of humanity! And he said, That is Abraham! He used not to dine or sup unless with a guest. And he often walked two miles or more to find a guest. And his hospitality remaineth unto the Day of Resurrection. And he is the Blessed Tree—the blessings and peace of Allah be upon him and upon his children altogether!

Chapter Twenty-first

How He Was Graced by Divine Friendship and Love

As for his characteristic of love, it is what is ascribed to him by mankind in general, both believers and unbelievers. And that has been made clear in the Sacred Book, and the sacred Sunnah.[84] As for the Book, there is His word: "And Allah chose Abraham as his Friend."[85] And as for the Sunnah, it is contained in many famous traditions; among them the account given by the qādi ʿIyād in the *Kitāb ash-Shifāʾ*, on authority of Ibn ʿAbbās: He says, Some of the Companions of the Prophet were seated awaiting him, and when he came forth (from his apartment) and drew near to them, he heard them discussing, and overheard their conversation. And some of them were saying, How strange that Allah should take one of His creatures as His Friend! And another said, That is not more strange than that Moses should have been granted His inspired Word! And another said, And Jesus was the Word and the Spirit of Allah! And another said, And Adam—Allah chose him! *Abraham Distinguished by Allah Like Moses and Jesus*

So he came on out to them, and greeted them; and he said, I heard your speech and your wonder that Allah chose Abraham as a Friend, which was the case; and that Moses was the confidant of Allah, which was the case; and that Jesus was the Spirit of Allah, which was the case; and that Allah chose Adam, which was the case. But I am the beloved of Allah—without vaingloriying! And I shall be the bearer of the Banner of Praise on the Resurrection Day—and no vaingloriying! And I am the first interceder and the first by whom intercession is made—without vaingloriying! And I shall be the first to stir up the creatures intended for Paradise, and Allah shall open it for me, and cause me to enter in, with me the choice ones of the believers—and no vaingloriying! And I am the most noble of the former and latter generations—and no vaingloriying!

And there is certified in the two *Sahīhs*[86] a tradition of 'Abdullah ibn 'Amr ibn Mas'ūd, from the Apostle of Allah, that he said, O people! verily, Allah hath taken me as His Friend as he took Abraham!

The qādi 'Iyād says: There is difference of opinion about the meaning of the word *khillah* and its original etymology. Some say that a *khalīl munqata'* to Allah means one who is without interruption in his
devotion and love toward Him. And some say, *al-khalīl al-mukhtass* (or a khalīl is one who is especially and exclusively devoted); and more than one chooses this opinion. Some say the original meaning of *khillah* is the condition of being chosen as the best. And hence Abraham was named *khalīl* because he found in Him a friend and a helper; and the *khillah* of Allah toward him was that He helped him and made him leader to those who came after him.

It is said also that the original meaning of *khalīl* is one who is habitually needy, derived from *khalah* which means *need*. And hence Abraham was named by this because he directed his need exclusively to his Lord, and became attached to Him in his anxiety, not setting for himself any helper other than He. When Gabriel came when he was in the catapult to be cast into the fire, he said to him, Hast thou any need? And he said, From thee, nay!

And the professor and imām Abu Bakr ibn Faurak says: *Khillah* is sincerity of friendship which entails exclusive devotion and dissolves secrets. Some say that *khillah* is friendship, with the meaning of helpfulness, kindliness, honor, and friendly intercession. Now Allah has explained that in His Book where he says: "And the Jews and the Christians say, We are the children of Allah, and His beloved friends. Say, then why doth He punish you for your sins?" For it is granted to the beloved that he not be taken to task for his sins. So He speaks.

And *khillah* here is a relationship more strong than (that in) prophetic revelation. For in case of prophethood there may be enmity; as Allah says: "Verily, some of your wives and your children are enemies to you!"[87] But it is not reasonable that there should be enmity in case of *khillah*.

And indeed the designation of Abraham and Mohammed by the term *khillah* was either due to their exclusively devoting themselves unto Allah and their satisfying of their needs in Him, and separation from all beside Him, and doing away with intermediaries and means. Or it was a heightening of the peculiar relationship between Him and them, and doing away with formalities between them, and revelation to them of divine mysteries and hidden secrets, and knowledge. Or, His choosing them, and His wholly taking their hearts away from things other than Himself — until they were not concerned for love for anything else.

For this reason, some say that a *khalīl* is one who enlarges his heart to others than himself. And this, for those, is the meaning of his (the Prophet's) word: "If I were choosing a *khalīl*, I would take Abu Bakr as one. But brotherhood in Islam is better!"[88]

The learned masters differ as to which of them is of higher rank, *khillah* or *muhabbah*. Some set them as equal; for one could not be a "beloved" without being a *khalīl*, and one could not be a *khalīl* without being a "beloved." Howbeit, Abraham was distinguished by his (divine) relationship of *khillah*, and Mohammed by that of *muhabbah*.

Some say that the rank of *khillah* is higher — which is argued for by his (Mohammed's) saying: "If I were taking as a *khalīl* anyone other than my Lord . . ." but he did not. But he gave his love (*muhabbah*) to Fātimah and her two sons, and Usāmah, and others.

But the majority say that *muhabbah* is higher than *khillah*, because the rank of our Prophet, the *Habīb* is higher than that of Abraham, the *Khalīl*.

The original meaning of *muhabbah* is, inclination unto what is pleasing to one's beloved. But this is the right of one who deserves the inclination toward him, and the enjoyment of the friendly agreeability. And that is the degree of a created being. But as for the Creator (may He be exalted!), there are the circumstances of His freedom from temporal accidents, and His love toward His servant,

and His enabling him to enjoy happiness, divine protection, and success, and His providing the means of communion, and His granting
unto him of His mercy — the climax of which is removal of the veil
from his heart until he sees Him with his heart, and beholds Him with
his sight.

So it becomes as is said in the tradition: And when I love Him,
I become the hearing with which He hears, and His sight with which
He sees, and His tongue with which He speaks. One is not supposed
to understand from this anything other than exclusive devotion to
Allah, and separation unto Allah, and turning from everything but
Allah, and purity of heart toward Allah, and sincerity of actions toward
Allah. As 'Āyeshah relates: The creation of the Koran was by His
pleasure, insofar as He was pleased, and His anger in so far as He was
angered. And one of the poets has given expression to this, concerning
khillah:

> Thou art all suffused through my spirit;
> And thus was *khalīl* called *khalīl*.
> When I speak, it is thou, as men hear it;
> In my silence, thou the longing I feel.[89]

And Allah made him imām, as a model (for mankind), and he was
glorified with the rank of *khillah*, which is the highest of the degrees
of *muhabbah*. The cause for this was none other than the greatness of
his obedience to his Lord, as He describes him in His Word, "And

Why Abraham Was So Distinguished

Abraham is one who fulfilled."[90] And most of those in his train say
(in explanation), that is, in that he met all that he was commanded,
and fulfilled every one of the stages of service (to Allah); and he was
not diverted from any commandment, either high or mean, either
great or small. And it is recorded that Allah revealed unto Abraham:

—for His Utter Devotion

O Abraham, when thou didst devote thyself with thy hospitality to
strangers, and thy son to be offered, and thine own self to the fire,
and thy heart to the Merciful, We chose thee as a Friend!

It is related in the *Sahīh* of Muslim, on authority of Anas, that a
man said to the Prophet: O thou best of mankind! But he said. That

(But Mohammed Higher!)

is Abraham! But this is to be counted as humility, for indeed the
Prophet is noblest, according to his own saying, I am the lord of the
sons of Adam, and no vaingglorying.

The hāfiz Abu Na'īm relates on authority of 'Abdullah ibn 'Omar, saying: The Apostle of Allah said, O Gabriel, why did Allah take —for His Hospitality Abraham as a Friend? He said, For his providing food (to the hungry), O Mohammed!

The hāfiz Ibn ʿAsākir relates on authority of ʿAbdu 'r-Rahmān ibn Yazīd ibn Aslam, from his father, that the Apostle of Allah said: Verily, Allah sent Gabriel my Beloved unto Abraham, and said, O Abraham, verily, I take thee not as a Friend for that thou art the most devoted of servants to me, but I have exalted thee over the hearts of mankind; for I find not a heart more generous than thine; and for that I take thee as a Friend.

The hāfiz Abu Naʿīm relates on authority of Wahb ibn Manabbih, saying, I read in certain books which were sent down from Heaven, that Allah said to Abraham, Knowest thou why I take Thee as a —and Piety Friend? He said, Nay, O Lord! He said, For the way thou dost humble thyself before Me in prayer.

The hāfiz Ibn ʿAsākir related on authority of Wahb: When Allah took Abraham as Friend, the beating of his heart could be heard from a distance because of his fear of Allah. And from him on authority of Ibn ʿAbbās; At the time when Allah took Abraham as a Friend and Prophet, he had three hundred slaves, whom he freed — and they became Muslims. They had been fighting with him against rebels, as the first freed-men to fight for their emancipator.

And from him (Ibn ʿAsākir) on authority of Ibn ʿAbbās: The Apostle of Allah said, When Allah wished to take Abraham as a Friend, How the News Was Brought to Abraham He said so to the Angels. And the Angel of Death said, I will be the one to give him the news, as I shall be the one to take away his spirit! And, as he says, Allah so commissioned him. And he cites as evidence what is related by Ibn Abu Hātim on authority of ʿUbeid ibn ʿUmeir, to this effect:

Abraham was wont to show hospitality to guests. So he went forth one day seeking someone he might entertain, and found no one. So he returned to his house; and he found there a man, standing. And he said, O servant of Allah, who let thee enter my house without my permission? He said, I entered it by permission of its Lord! He said, And who art thou? He said, I am the Angel of Death. My Lord hath sent me to a certain servant of His to announce to him that He hath chosen him as a Friend! He said, And who is he! By Allah, if thou wilt tell me of him, if he were in the most distant part of the land, I would go to him; and afterward I would not cease being his neighbor until death parted us! He said, That servant is thyself! He said, I? He said, Yea! And for what cause hath my Lord chosen me as the Friend? Because, thou givest unto people and askest not of them!

And the traditions and accounts on that subject are many, and we have recorded sufficient and convincing on it—and Allah knoweth best!

CHAPTER TWENTY-SECOND

On the Traditions Handed Down Concerning His Being Clothed on the Day of Judgment

The imām Abu Bakr al-Beihaqi says: We are informed by Abu 'Abdullah the hāfiz, We are informed by Abu 'l-'Abbās al-Asamm (the Deaf), We are told by al-'Abbās ad-Dauri: We are told by Abu 'Āsim, on authority of Sufyān, on authority of 'Amr ibn Qeis, on authority of al-Minhāl, on authority of 'Abdullah ibn Hārith, from 'Ali ibn Abu Tālib, saying:

Abraham and Mohammed First

The first ones to be clothed (with heavenly garments) on the Day of Resurrection will be Abraham, in Coptic (fine Egyptian linen), and the Prophet, in striped sacredotal vestments—and he will be on the right hand of the Throne.[91]

It is reported to us by the two *Sahīhs*, on authority of Ibn 'Abbās, that the Prophet of Allah said: The first creature who will be clothed on the Day of Resurrection will be Abraham.

The Judgment Scene

It is reported by Ahmad ibn Hanbal in a long tradition, that the Apostle of Allah said: Verily, I shall assume the Praised Station on the Day of Resurrection! And a man of the Ansār said, And what is that Praised Station? He said, That means that when ye are brought forth barefoot, naked, and uncircumcised, the first who will be clothed is Abraham. And He will say, Clothe ye my Friend: And he will be brought two shining garments, and will put them on. Then he will sit facing the Throne. Then will be brought my garments, and I shall put them on, and shall take my stand at its right—a station not taken by any other—and the first and the last shall envy me over it!

The hāfiz Ibn 'Asākir relates from Talaq ibn Habīb, that his grandfather told him, saying: I heard the Apostle of Allah say:

Mankind will be assembled on the Day of Resurrection barefoot and naked and uncircumcised. The first clothed will be Abraham the Friend of Allah. Allah will say: Clothe ye Abraham My Friend, so that mankind may know today his merit over theirs. So he shall be clothed in striped sacred vestments—and then mankind will be clothed in their ranks and orders.

It is reported from him also, from al-Mu'tamir ibn Suleimān, that he heard Ismā'īl ibn Abu Khālid relating a tradition from Sa'īd ibn Jubeir, saying:

Mankind will be assembled on the Day of Resurrection barefoot, naked, and uncircumcised (or he used another word for it); and I was informed the first who will be provided with clothes will be Abraham.

The hāfiz Abu Na'īm relates on authority of Mujāhid, from 'Ubeid ibn 'Umeir, saying: Mankind shall be assembled on the day of Resurrection barefoot, naked, and uncircumcised. And Allah will say: I will not see My Friend naked! And He will clothe Abraham with a white robe—and he will be the first to be clothed.

And in the history by al-hāfiz Ibn 'Asākir, with his line of authority from 'Ubeid Allah ibn Anas, from his father, it is related:

The Prophet of Allah said: the first who will be clothed with the sacred vestments of Heaven will be I and Abraham and the Prophets.

And with a line of witnesses from 'Abdullah ibn Hārith, from 'Ali ibn Abu Tālib: The first to be clothed will be Abraham, the Friend of the Merciful, with two robes of Coptic stuff; then the Prophet will be clothed with sacred vestments of red. And he will be on the right of the Throne.

In another account, the first of the Creatures, Abraham, will be clothed in Coptic stuff; and Mohammed will be clothed in a striped garment—and he will be on the right of the Throne.

CHAPTER TWENTY-THIRD

A Description of His Palace in Heaven

The hāfiz Abu Bakr al-Bazzār relates with a line of witnesses from 'Akramah, from Abu Hureirah, this: The Apostle of Allah said: Verily, there is in Heaven a palace of pearl, in it no blemish or fault, which Allah hath set apart and prepared for His Friend, as his dwelling.

Abraham's Palace of Pearl

The hāfiz ibn ʻAsākir relates with his chain of reference from ʻAli ibn al-Husein al-Azdi, freed-man of Sālim ibn Thaubān: I heard ʻAli ibn Abu Tālib crying from the minbar in Kūfah: O ye people! Verily, in Heaven there are two pearls, one of them white and the other yellow. As for the white, it is the innermost parts of the Throne. And the Praised Station is of the white pearl, with seventy thousand rooms, its every house three miles in width; and its rooms, doors, and couches are as if they were one room. And its name is al-Wasīlah (Place of Favor and Honor). And it is for Mohammed and his people. And the yellow is like unto it—and it is for Abraham.

But this is an apocryphal tradition.

The same hāfiz relates with a line of reference from ʻAkramah, from Abu Hureirah: The Apostle of Allah said: Verily, in Heaven there is a mansion of white pearl, without defect or fault, which Allah hath prepared for His Friend Abraham, as his dwelling.

And in another account of his: Verily, in Heaven there is a mansion of pearl, without blemish or fault, which Allah hath set aside for His Friend Abraham, as his dwelling—the blessings and peace of Allah be upon him and his good and pure family, with true peace!

Chapter Twenty-fourth

How He Came to See Grey Hairs; and His Circumcision; and His Being Given Trousers

A Token
of Honor

In the *Muwatta'* of Mālik, on authority of Saʻīd ibn al-Museyyib it is related:

Abraham was the first to cut his moustaches, and the first to behold his grey hairs. And he said, O Lord, What is this? And Allah said, Dignity for thee, O Abraham! And he said, O Lord, increase me in dignity!

The Practical
Reason for
Greyness

The hāfiz Ibn ʻAsākir relates on authority of al-Asbagh ibn Nabā-nah: I heard ʻAli ibn Abu Tālib say: A man used to come to advanced age and not become grey. And so a man would come to a people among whom was a man and his family, and would say, which of you is the father? For he didn't know the father from the son. So Abraham said,

Lord, grant to me something by which I may be known! So his hair and his beard became white.

And the same hāfiz relates with his chain of authority, from al-Qāsim ibn Abu Umāmah: While Abraham was one day praying the prayer of morning, behold, he saw a hand extending from Heaven, with a white hair between two of its fingers. And it ceased not to draw near until it had approached the head of Abraham, and the grey hair joined itself to his head. Then it said, Make him hoary in honor! (Another reference says: Make hoary his cheek and make hoary his head!) And Allah revealed to him that he should purify himself, and he performed ablutions. Then Allah revealed to him that he should purify himself, and he bathed. Then Allah revealed to him that he should purify himself, and he became circumcised. And Abraham was the first one who became grey and who was circumcised. *His Purification*

And in another account by him: Abraham asked his Lord for a boon—and two thirds of his hair became white. And he said, What is this? And it was said to him, Respectability for thee in this world, and light in the next.

Abu Hātim ibn Hayyān relates, with his line of authority from Abu Hureirah, that the Prophet said: Abraham was circumcised when he was one hundred and twenty years old. And he lived after that for eighty years. And we are told in the *Sahīhs* of al-Bukhāri and Muslim on authority of Abu Hureirah: The Apostle of Allah said, Abraham was circumcised when he was eighty years old, in his foreskin. (And it is related that the word *qadūm* is spelt without or with a double "d." An-Nawawi says so.) And the hāfiz ibn 'Asākir relates in his history, from Abu Hureirah, that the Prophet said: Abraham bound his prepuce and took hold of it and stretched it out, and cut it with a piece of wood which he had, and it fell in his hands without pain or bleeding. And Ishmael was circumcised when he was thirteen years old and Isaac was circumcised when he was seven years old. *The Institution of Circumcision*

Muhammad ibn Ismā'īl al-Wāsiti says in his commentary in line with the accounts we have related, on authority of Yahyā ibn Sa'īd from Sa'īd ibn al-Museyyib, from Abu Hureirah:

Abraham was the first to be clothed with drawers, and the first to part his hair, and the first to shave himself, and the first to be circumcised in his foreskin (when he was a hundred and twenty years old.

And he lived after that, eighty years), and the first to invite guests, and the first to become grey.

Thus he relates from secondary sources, at variance with Ibn Hayyān.

The hāfiz Ibn ‘Asākir relates on authority of Muhammad ibn Bakrān, preacher of the mosque of Abraham al-Khalīl, with a line of evidence from Ibn ‘Abbās: Abraham was exceedingly modest, and with his modesty he was ashamed for the ground to see his nakedness (that is, his male organs). So he complained to Allah, and Allah commanded Gabriel about the matter; so Gabriel descended unto him with a piece of cloth from Heaven, and he fashioned that into a pair of drawers.

And he said to him, Give this over to Sarah (now her name was Yasārah),[92] so that she may sew it. And when Sarah had sewn it, Abraham put it on, and said, How excellent are these! I conceal myself in them, O Gabriel! And they are the best kind of covering to the believer!

So Abraham was the first to wear drawers and sandals, and the first to fight with the sword, and the first to divide the spoil, and the first to be circumcised in the place called the foreskin.

And the reason he was circumcised was: He was commanded to fight the Amalekites, so he fought them mightily, and many of both companies were slain. So Abraham did not know his own folk in order that he bury them. So he was ordered to institute circumcision, for this reason, so that it might be a symbol for the people of Islam. And he was thereupon circumcised, and he gave orders for circumcision of others of posterity. And he was the one who circumcised himself in the foreskin.

And in an account of his (Ibn ‘Asākir) on authority of Muqātil, from Abu ’l-Akhwas, from ‘Abdullah: The Apostle of Allah said: Verily, Allah revealed unto Abraham, Verily, thou art My Friend, and the dearest of the people of earth to Me. But now when thou bowest (to earth) to worship, thy nakedness toucheth the ground. So take for thyself a garment which will hide it.

So he called to Gabriel, O Gabriel! what name of garment is this which will cover it? He said, Drawers! Abraham said, And what are Drawers? Gabriel said, Call for cloth that I may cut it for thee. And, as the account says, Abraham was a cloth merchant. So he called for

The margin notes:

Abraham's Modesty

The Reason for Circumcision

The Reason for Underclothing

cloth and gave it to Gabriel. And Gabriel cut it into drawers, and Sarah sewed it. And when Abraham put it on, He said, I never wore a garment I liked better than this! So when I die, wash me beneath it and bury me with it on.

Chapter Twenty-fifth

Description of Him, and the Splendid Qualities Which Allah Gave Him; and His Rank; and an Account of the Sacred Books

We are told in the *Sahīh* of Muslim, on authority of Abu Hureirah: The Apostle of Allah said, when I was taken on the Night-Journey, and I saw Abraham, I was just like a son of his. *Mohammed's Similarity to Him*

And in the *Sahīh* of al-Bukhāri, on authority of Ibn 'Abbās: The last word of Abraham when he was cast into the fire was, My recompense is Allah, Who is the best of guardians!

In the two *Sahīhs* it is thus reported: The Apostle of Allah informed me about the Night-Journey, and his seeing the prophets in Heaven, and how he saw Abraham in the sixth Heaven (in one account in the *Sahīh*, in the seventh Heaven), with his back on a couch toward the Ancient House. *His Place in Paradise*

And in an account in the *Sahīh* of al-Bukhāri from Samrah ibn Jandab: The Apostle of Allah said, He (Gabriel) came and took me at night, and there came to us a man so tall I could hardly see his head for his length—and he was Abraham. *His Stature*

And Allah hath graciously bestowed upon us a connected and prepared account in relation to his Friend Abraham, as He hath graciously granted to us concerning the beloved Friend and Chosen One Mohammed. It is along that line that it is related by at-Tirmidhi on authority of 'Abdullah ibn Mas'ūd: The Apostle of Allah said, I met Abraham the night I was taken on the Night-Journey, and he said, O Mohammed, Greet thy people with peace from me, and tell them that Heaven is pleasant as to soil and its waters sweet, and that it is smooth land, and that its trees are proclaiming, Glory be to Allah! And praise unto Allah! And there is no God but Allah! And Allah is most great! At-Tirmidhi relates this, and says it is a sound tradition. *Abraham's Greeting and Message*

In an account from Ibn Wahb from Abu Ayyūb al-Ansāri, it is

reported he heard the Apostle of Allah saying, I was taken up to heaven, and I saw Abraham and he said, O Gabriel, Who is this with thee? He said, Mohammed. So he welcomed me and treated me graciously. Then he said: From thy people may the trees of Paradise increase; for its soil is goodly, and its land is extensive! And I said, and what are the trees of Paradise? He said, (The proclaiming of) "No might or power save in Allah!"

Abraham's Prophecy

Al-Beihaqi relates on authority of Ibn Mas'ūd in a tradition of the Night-Journey: Gabriel said to me, Betake thyself to thy father Abraham! So we went unto him, and greeted him, and he returned our greeting. And Abraham said, Who is this with thee, O Gabriel? He said, this is thy son Ahmad. He said, Welcome to the unlettered prophet,[93] who hath given an eloquent message, and watered his people! O My son, Thou shalt meet thy Lord tonight! And verily thy people are the last of nations, and the weakest of them; and if thy cause is able to stand and to become great among thy people, perform it!

Mohammed among the Prophets in Jerusalem

Thereupon we turned away and came over to the Mosque al-Aqsa. So I descended and tied up my steed (al-Burāq) in the ring which is in the door of the Mosque, where the prophets used to tie up theirs, and then I entered the Mosque. And I recognized the Prophets, some kneeling, some bowing down, and some standing (in prayer). Then there were brought to me two vessels, one with honey and one with milk; and I took the milk, and drank. And Gabriel struck me on my shoulders and said, Thou hast attained the true religion, by the Lord of Mohammed! Then I was assigned to lead prayers, and I acted as imām—and then we departed.

In an account from Ibn Jarīr on authority of Abu Hureirah or someone else (about whom Ibn Jarīr is uncertain), it is said: Then he met the souls of the prophets, and they were steadfastly praising their Lord. And Abraham said, Praise be to Allah Who hath chosen me as His Friend, and hath given me a mighty kingdom and hath made for me a devout nation, imitating me, and hath rescued me from the fire, and made it cool and wholesome for me!

Allah's Acceptance and Praise of Abraham

It is related by the hāfiz Abu 'l-Qāsim ibn 'Asākir, with his line of evidence from Abu Hureirah, from the Prophet: Allah revealed unto Abraham: O My Friend, most excellent is thy nature, and even though among infidels thou wouldst enter the door of the pure! For verily

My Mercy goeth before whoever is excellent of character, so that I may shelter him in the shadow of My Throne, and give him to drink of My Holy Presence, and draw him near unto Me on the day when he who hath rebelled against Me will not be near!

Ath-Thaʻlabi relates from Abu Idrīs al-Khaulāni, from Abu Dharr al-Ghaffāri: I said, O Apostle of Allah, how many books did Allah send down? He said, A hundred and four. He sent down to Adam ten documents, and unto Seth fifty, and unto Idrīs thirty, and unto Abraham ten; and Allah sent down (also) the Torah, and the Evangel, and the Psalms and the Guidance (the Koran).[94] *The Revealed Books*

I said: O Apostle of Allah, what were the documents of Abraham? He said, They were all similitudes. (For example:) O thou arrogant and conceited king, I sent thee not to gather the world, one part of it after another, but I sent thee to return (to me) the prayers of those in oppression! And verily I will not turn them back, though they be from an unbeliever! *Examples of the Books Revealed to Abraham*

And others are similitudes like this: There are incumbent upon the wise—the one whose evil inclinations cannot overcome his reason— of all the hours which he has, one hour in which he speaks to his Lord and gives up created (material) things, and one hour in which he settles accounts within himself as to what was before and after, and one hour in which he devotes himself to his needs of what is lawful of food and drink and other things. And it is incumbent upon the wise that he be watchful for his lifetime, addressing himself to his affairs, guarding his tongue. And whoever is aware that his words are (supposed to be) of that he knows, say, verily, his speech is of what concerns him!

CHAPTER TWENTY-SIXTH

On the Noble Characteristics with Which Allah Distinguished Him, and the Pleasing Precedents Which Were of No One before Him, and Which Became Sacred Law and Polite Usage to Those after Him

He was the Friend of the Merciful, and father of those who are hospitable to strangers. He was the imām of the believers in One God; the one who was given the tongue of truthfulness, by the estimate of all who were after him. For there is no nation but their tongue flows with his trustworthiness, and his merit, and his honor, and his respect. And that because of his petition, "Grant me a tongue of truthfulness among all who come after!" And he was tried by all kinds of affliction, and famous for his faithfulness.

And Allah saith: "And when Abraham was given by his Lord words (of command), he fulfilled them." [95] And it is said: Abraham is the one who remained faithful and he is the obedient nation, as is mentioned in His Word: "Verily, Abraham was an obedient nation . . ." [96] That is, he was instructing men in what was good. And there were gathered up in him the goodness and virtue of a whole nation. As one has said:

> And think it not strange of Allah.
> That He gather all the world into one!

He was the one to whom his divine guidance came before he reached maturity. He was the one to whom was granted the tongue of remonstrance unto Unity, and he summoned Creation unto the Truth with this tongue of remonstrance from his youth unto his age — as Allah saith: "And that is one remonstrance which We gave to Abraham against his people."

He was the first whom Allah named a Hanīf [97] and Muslim. And Allah absolved him from the calumnies of the Jews and the Nazarenes, and made him a sincere and a pious witness. And He said: "Abraham was not a Jew or a Christian, but he was a Hanif and a Muslim—and He was not a idolater, and he was the first of those we have named Muslims."

He was the first to shake hands and embrace and kiss between the eyes. And he was the first to wear sandals. And he is the guardian of the children of Muslims. He is the leader of the people of Paradise unto Paradise — the Abode of the Pious. He was the first to break idols. He was the one who built the Sacred House. He was the first to show hospitality to guests, the first to strike with the sword, the first to crumble and soak his bread in broth, the first to divide the spoil, the first to circumcise himself, and the first to become grey, and the first to begin wearing drawers, and the first to perform the rites of pilgrimage and of the Hajj. And the last was in connection with his prayer wherein he said: "And show us our proper rites, and forgive us"—and he was answered. [98]

He was the first to slaughter a sacrificial victim, and the first to be cast into the fire in the cause of Allah, and to have it become cool and wholesome for him. He was the first to have the dead raised to life by his request, when he said "Lord, show unto me how Thou canst restore to life my dead." [99] He was the one for whom was lifted the veil between himself and Sarah, so that he might see her wherever she was.

He was the first who will be clothed with garments of white on the Day of Resurrection. He is the one for whom there will be set up a minbar on the left of the Throne of the Merciful. He was the first to speak on pulpits, the first to cut his moustaches, the first to part his hair, the first to pare his nails, the first to pluck the hairs off the armpits, the first to shave the pubes, the first to clean the teeth with the miswāk,[100] the first to rinse out his mouth, the first to snuff water in his nostrils, the first to purify himself with water after excretion, the first to perform the ablutions for Friday-Devotions.

He was the first who migrated from his home for the sake of the religion of Allah, the first to raise his hands in prayer in every depressed place and height. He was the first to pray at the first of the day four rak'ahs, making this a duty for himself, for which Allah named him "Fulfiller of Duty."

As the account continues: Abraham was the one who fulfilled his duty. And he was the one who set up a shrine as the place for prayer to be taken as direction of prayer by the people — and it was made incumbent upon Mohammed. He is the best of the prophets, and his people are the most noble of peoples in the following of his religion. As Allah says: "And we revealed unto thee that thou shouldst follow the religion of Abraham, as a Hanīf." [101]

He was not of the idolaters: and He called him the penitent, kindly pitying; and someone has said: Mighty is He Who says that "Abraham was kind, compassionate, penitent." [102]

May the blessing and peace of Allah be upon him, and may his merit be increased, and honor toward him, also upon his seed the pious and pure, and upon all the prophets and of Apostles; and may He grant great Peace!

Notes on the Book of Arousing Souls

[1] This invocatory phrase, which begins nearly all the Sūrahs or chapters of the Koran, is used by Moslems in their prayers, as a grace before meals, and on many other occasions. It is called the " Basmala," and in Arabic is: *Bismi 'llāhi 'r-Rahmāni 'r-Rahīm*. For Companions, Helpers, Followers, see the glossary.

[2] The full title is: *Al-Jāmi'u 'l-Mustaqsa fī Fadā'ili 'l-Masjidi 'l-Aqsa*, or, *The Thorough Collection on the Merits of the Mosque al-Aqsa*. The title of the second work used by our author is to be translated: *The Merits of Jerusalem and Syria.* " Shām," the land to the *north*, or the land on the *left-hand* (as one faces the east), is used indiscriminately by Moslem writers for Syria proper, for Damascus, or for Syria including Palestine. (In fact, Palestine has been quite commonly called *Southern Syria*, or *Sūriya (tu) 'l-Janūbiyyah*.)

[3] An *isnād* is a chain of authorities by whom a tradition has been handed down, and through whom it is traced back to its source for critical consideration of its trustworthiness. The traditions of the Jewish rabbis were prefaced by much the same authorizing chain of reference. The contrastingly independent teaching method of Jesus led to the wonder of the multitudes, " for he taught them as one having (personal) authority, and not as their scribes." (Matthew 7. 28-29.)

[4] *Al-Aqsa* (the farthest mosque—from Mecca) is used at times to designate the mosque itself, in the southern end of the Temple area, and at times for the Temple area and its structures in general. The latter is the case in the famous verse, Sūrah 17. 1, which underlies the legend of the Prophet's Night-Journey to Jerusalem. Likewise, Jerusalem is used both for the Holy City and for the entire land of Palestine.

[5] The *Shekīnah*, in Arabic *as-Sakīnah*, is the glory of God which dwelt in the Temple. It is of course a concept borrowed from the Jews, who say that the Shekinah still dwells at the place of the Temple, especially in the Western Wall (or the " Wailing Wall ").

[6] " The Chosen Friend " of Allah. *Al-Khalīl* is used for Abraham himself, and for the town of Hebron (in which case it is short for *Madīnatu 'l-Khalīl*, or the *City of the Chosen Friend of Allah*). While using the common form of Abraham, instead of the Arabic *Ibrāhīm*, I have retained the characteristic *al-Khalīl*, untranslated.

[7] One of the great canonical works of *hadīth* or tradition, the author of which died in 257 after the Hijrah, 870 A. D. The other outstanding one is that of Muslim, who died in 262 A. H./ 875 A. D. Both are called *Sahīh*, " genuine," denoting that the authors sifted the great mass of sayings of and incidents about the Prophet, preserved the authentic, and rejected the spurious and fabricated. Such duplicate accounts as those in the two first paragraphs are found often in the two books here translated, and are very frequent in the works of the Koran commentators. This is proof of honest effort to give all the evidence. Abu Dharr was one of the Companions.

[8] The Ibn 'Asākir of our author is not the celebrated historian of Damascus, but the younger by that name. He lectured in Jerusalem during the year 596 A. H. (1190 A. D.), three years after the re-conquest of the Holy City from the Crusaders by Salāh ud-Dīn (Saladin), on the subject of " The Merits of the Holy City," the material of which, in his book, *Kitābu 'l-Uns fī Fadā'ili 'l-Quds*, has unfortunately been lost. About the second author from whom Ibn al-Firkāh al-Fazāri drew his work, Abu 'l-Ma'āli, it is known only that he

139

was one of the learned Moslems of Jerusalem, and that he was earlier than Ibn al-'Asākir. (See the introduction to my Arabic edition, cited above, p. vi.) Al-Farrā' was a ninth century teacher in Baghdad, tutor of the son of the Caliph al-Ma'mūn.

[9] An-Nasā'i was another of the most noted traditionists (d. 915 A. D.), his work being one of the three famous collections with the title *Sunan*, "customs" of the Prophet and incidents and anecdotes from his life. Al-Qazwīni (d. 1283) is a noted cosmographer, of Persian origin. (Excellent sources in English for the great men of Islamic learning and letters are: Reynold A. Nicholson (of Cambridge University), *A Literary History of the Arabs*, London, T. Fisher Unwin, 1907 (in the series, *Library of Literary History*); Philip K. Hitti (of Princeton University), *History of the Arabs*, London, Macmillan, 1937); and de Slane's translation of Ibn Khallikān's (d. 1282) great biographical dictionary (Paris, 1843-71). Notes upon individuals are restricted in the present volume to those of popular interest. Most of the rich sources of such information, anyway, are still available only to the specialist in Arabic, and too numerous citations would not suit the intended popular nature of the book.

[10] Ka'b al-Ahbār (or al-Hibr), and Wahb ibn Munabbih, both of whom are often cited by our author, were two early Jewish converts to Islam who furnished to Mohammedan writers much popular Biblical lore.

[11] The interesting idealizing process by which Islam makes all the Biblical worthies to be prophets paralleled that in popular Judaism, which considered Shem, for instance, to have been a priest. See Louis Ginzberg, *The Legends of the Jews*, Philadelphia, Jewish Publication Society, 1913, etc., I, 332; II, 35; V, 187. (This is a most important set for the Jewish background of Islam.)

[12] Written by Ibn Batīsh (d. 655/1257), one of the teachers of the noted biographer Ibn Khallikān, in explanation of the *Muhadhdhab* of Abu Ishāq ash-Shirāzi, who was a pupil of the famous historian and Koran commentator at-Tabari (838-923 A. D.).

[13] Al-Janad was a place in Yemen (the southwestern corner of Arabia, so important for early civilization of the peninsula), as I was led to recognize by a fortunate marginal note in one of the British Museum copies of *The Book of Arousing Souls*. An interesting observation on the mosque there is found in Yāqūt's geography (Wüstenfeld's edition, II, 127): "I saw the people making pilgrimage to it as they make pilgrimage to the Sacred House" (in Mecca).

[14] Servant of Mohammed, participant in the Arab conquest, and reputedly father of seventy-eight children. He is the source of many traditions, but is not to be confused with Mālik ibn Anas, noted religious legist of the eighth century, founder of the Mālikite school.

[15] Here the usually careful copyist of the Yale text made the slip of dotting the Arabic word so as to make it *house* instead of *daughter*, *beit* instead of *bint*!

[16] This is a popular combination of Solomon's vision at Gibeon at the time of his coronation (I Kings, 3. 1 f.; II Chron. I 1 f.), and his prayer at the dedication of the Temple (I Kings, chapters 8 f.; II Chron., chapters 6-7). Solomon is naturally glorified in both Jewish and Mohammedan popular literature.

[17] *Proofs of Prophethood.* The author was a noted teacher of the Shāfi'ite school who was born in Persia and died in 1066. This tradition is one of the most important bases of popular Mohammedan veneration for Palestine and Jerusalem. The legend of the Night-Journey, which probably developed from a mystic dream of the Prophet, has always been devoutly and literally believed by the common folk. Although educated Moslems interpret it metaphorically, its place in popular Islam is unshakeable. A good, connected account is found in the still useful *Life of Mahomet*, by Washington Irving. See also W. St. Clair-Tisdall, *The Religion of the Crescent*, London, Society for Promoting Christian Knowledge, 1895, pp. 69 f.

[18] These, especially Yathrib (ancient form, Yathrippa), were designations of Medina before the Prophet removed thither on his *Hijrah* (incorrectly, hegira). It became known forever afterward as *Madīnatu 'n-Nabi*, " City of the Prophet," or for short, *Madīnah*. As the place was long a center of Aramaic speech, however, the name may be more historically traced to a form in Aramaic (one of the Semitic sister tongues of Arabic), *medhīnta*, a word which from " province " or " area " had come to mean " city." As scene of the residence and burial of the Prophet, it is to Muslims the second holiest city, after Mecca.

[19] According to Moslem legend, the place where Moses watered the flocks of Shuʻeib (Jethro). For the interesting Jewish stories of Moses in Midian, see Ginzberg, *Legends of the Jews*, II, 289 f.

[20] A typically favorable mention of Jesus and Mary, for both of whom Moslems have high regard. In the Koran, while his crucifixion and divinity are denied, the Virgin Birth of Jesus is implied and he is called " a Spirit from Him." See Sūrahs 4.169 and 21.91.

[21] The Wailing Wall is only a few yards to the north of that portion of the western wall of the Temple area now especially sacred to Moslems because of the story of the Night-Journey. Here, in and adjacent to the " Wall of al-Burāq," the Prophet's mystic steed, are located a door known as the Door of the Prophet, a ring in the wall by which al-Burāq was haltered, and a small underground mosque called the Mosque of the Prophet, and certain religious property (waqf). The contiguity of the two spots of popular veneration and assembly has given rise to much strife, as in 1929, etc. Insistence by the Arabs upon all traditional privilege and prestige here is symbolic of their fear of being swamped by the hundreds of thousands of Jews who have entered Palestine since 1918, with the financial backing of a world-wide Zionist organization, and often with superiority in Western education and technical training. I have tried to show in an article in *The Moslem World* (Vol. XXII, No. 4, 1932) that, although the statement of our author here is ambiguous, there is much evidence from Moslem sources that the original place of veneration in this connection was the *south* wall of the Temple enclosure. Here is the old southern double gate of the Temple, now closed, and partly covered by the resumption of the city wall contiguous to the Aqsa Mosque (but which used to give access to the sacred area by passages still underneath that structure). By some of the earliest and most important Moslem writers (e. g., Muqaddasi, of Jerusalem itself, who wrote in 985 A. D., and Nāsir-i-Khusrau the Persian, who wrote in 1047) it is said that there were " two gates " of the Prophet, and that " the gate of the Prophet opens toward the qiblah point " (that is, toward the south and Mecca). Folk-tradition is so tenacious, however — and popular feeling is in this case so fervent — that it would doubtless be impossible to remedy the situation.

[22] Leban is curded milk, somewhat like clabber, and is very popular among Near Easterners. It was probably the dish given to the exhausted Sisera by Jael — certainly not *butter!* — in Judges 5.25. In some accounts, a third vessel was offered the Prophet for choice — containing wine, which by reason of not entirely clear injunctions of the Koran, and by popular allegation because of the Prophet's refusal of it here, became forbidden to Moslems.

[23] This brief account thus omits the ascent of Mohammed to Paradise, which is asserted by Miguel Asin Palacios to have influenced Dante; cf. below, p. 28, and see Harold Sunderland's translation, *Islam and the Divine Comedy*, London, J. Murray, 1926. On the Valley of Gehenna, see Note 55. The Koreish (properly, Qureish or Quraysh) were Mohammed's own tribe.

[24] Uncle and father-in-law of the Prophet, and his first successor as Caliph.

[25] A frank citation of one of the severe slanders directed by the hostile Meccans at the Prophet; for Abu Kabshah, here libellously implied to have been the father of Mohammed, was only his freedman.

[26] This is typical of the journeying knowledge of those familiar with the desert marches—as was Mohammed, the former caravan manager for the wealthy widow (later his first wife) Khadījah. The circumstantially detailed portion of the tradition is of course for indisputable proof to those who were inclined to literal acceptance.

[27] "The Excellence or Merits of the Horse."

[28] 'Amr ibn al-'Āsi (or 'Āsī) was the noted conqueror of Egypt, in the first sweeping conquests of the Bible world by the Arabs.

[29] I do not know the identity or location of these two.

[30] The first verse of Sūrah 112 (and standing, of course for that entire brief chapter of the Koran), expressing the uncompromising Islamic doctrine of the Divine unity as opposed to heathen polytheism and Christian trinitarianism. A rak'ah is a performance of a complete cycle of prayer, standing facing Mecca, bowing, kneeling and touching the floor or ground with the forehead, and arising, while repeating the prescribed devotions.

[31] That is, from some distance, at expense and effort.

[32] The Pauline doctrine of original sin has no place in Moslem theology — although Adam literally " fell " from Paradise.

[33] Called a " prince " in the field of tradition—said to have handed down thirty thousand; he died in Basrah in 713 A. D. According to custom, he is addressed below by the name of his eldest son, " O father of 'Abdullah! " Conversely, the son is politely addressed by the name of his father; cf. Saul's reference to David in I Samuel 20. 27, " the son of Jesse."

[34] The Leiden text makes the travellers to be the great caliphs themselves, Abu Bekr, 'Omar, 'Othmān, and 'Ali, the four " orthodox caliphs " who immediately followed Mohammed. 'Abbādān, on the Iraq-Iran border near the Persian Gulf, is now an oil center. It was earlier a flourishing town with many mosques, and figured in the British advance into Persia or Iran in August, 1941. Ramadān is the sacred month observed by fasting from food and drink from sunrise to sunset and by special devoutness.

[35] The ihrām is a seamless white garment assumed by the pilgrim ordinarily as he enters upon a state of consecration (which the word also means) in preparation for his devotions in the sacred territory of Mecca-Medina. This tradition stresses the sanctity of Palestine in that it promises merit for pilgrimaging from it to the holy cities in a state of purification.

[36] Umm Salimah was one of the wives of the Prophet, and the mother of Umm Hakīm, below.

[37] Jābir ibn 'Abdullah, one of the Prophet's Companions, from whom are derived many traditions. The muezzin (properly, mu'adhdhin), a term connected with the word " ear," is he who gives the call to prayer, the adhān, from the minaret of a mosque. Both the Yale and the Leiden texts are somewhat confused by ellipsis and transfer in this paragraph.

[38] One of the most eminent Followers — those associated with the early heroes who were personally acquainted with the Prophet — and one of the founding fathers of religious movements in Islam; d. 728 A. D.

[39] The reference to Elijah and St. George (or al-Khidr, the Green or Everliving One, an important figure in popular Moslem legend, and often confused into one and the same) means that they frequent Jerusalem at the holy season in their spiritual state. Compare the account below in Chapter Seventh. See also Hanauer (cited in note 91), pp. 46-53. Al-Khidr is a saint also to Jews and Christians.

[40] Son-in-law and first cousin of the Prophet, mighty warrior in the early campaigns, the fourth caliph, author of many sententious sayings which are still widely quoted, and the patron saint of the Shī'ites—some sects of whom have even regarded him as possessing divinity.

[41] The Yale text has in the margin: " That is, Blessed House." Although the popular ety-

mology is not correct, the Arabs, despite their almost universal use of " al-Quds," " the Holy," for Jerusalem, were acquainted with its ancient name and with that of the Romans, " Aelia."

[42] See note 10. In the Yale text the words " my reward " are missing.

[43] The nurse is evidently one in the entourage of the Egyptian princess who befriended the infant Moses. The Koran apparently identifies Miriam the sister of Moses with Mary (or Miriam) the mother of Jesus. This is a significant example of the popular and inexact Biblical lore which came to Mohammed and his early followers through Jews and Christians.

[44] See Genesis 2.10 f.; Ezekiel 47.1-12. The four rivers have become the subject of much Jewish and Islamic popular interest and of many attempts at identification. Some of the names have been applied to various streams.

[45] According to fuller accounts of the Night-Journey, the prophets were assembled in the company of Mohammed, who led them in prayer as their *imām*, the one who stands " before " the congregation. The ascension of " my Lord " must be a deeply honorific reference to Jesus, but it seems doubtful. This tradition may have been transferred here from the Chapel of the Ascension (on the Mount of Olives) which is also a Muslim shrine.

[46] For the Judgment scene, cf. Matthew 25.31-46.

[47] A member of the Prophet's own tribe of Koreish, judge (*qādi*) in several important cities, but considered as a fabricator of traditions. The effect here seems to be that the places named are too sacred to be stood upon for fear of some violation. But about the Mount of Olives in this connection *The Book of Arousing Souls* gives conflicting traditions. The four places mentioned after Sinai are stations in the sacred course of the Hajj, between the Ka'bah in Mecca and Mount 'Arafah a few miles away.

[48] Author of a commentary on the Koran, pupil of ath-Tha'labi who wrote the noted *Stories of the Prophets*; died 468/1076 at Nisapur in Persia. The quotations from the Koran regarding the judgment trump are from Sūrahs 30.24 and 6.73. Cf. Poe's poem " Israfel."

[49] That is, if one seeks martyrdom for its superlative rewards in Paradise.

[50] This last sentence is found only in the Leiden text, but that copy also is slightly imperfect in omitting the first few words of the author's personal remarks.

[51] For similar Jewish stories, see Ginzberg, *Legends of the Jews*, IV, 129 and 156.

[52] A Koreishite, eminent Follower, jurisconsult, traditionist; died 124/742. The point to face in prayer is the *qiblah* or " direction " toward Mecca, indicated in mosques by *mihrābs* or recessed niches in the wall facing Mecca from whatever geographical point. In the earlier stages of his ministry, Mohammed prayed toward the Holy City of Jews and Christians (as had Daniel; see Daniel 6.10), later changing the qiblah toward Mecca and the Ka'bah. Therefore, Moslems say in honor of Jerusalem (and Palestine) that it is " first of the two qiblahs, and third of the three sacred places " (after Mecca and Medina). On the veneration of Moslems for the Rock, Le Strange (p. 91) points out the contrasting meagerness of notices by Arab writers on the beginnings of the Mosque al-Aqsa itself and the full accounts of the Dome of the Rock from its foundation (A.H.72 / A.D.691). Although the rites here described are in part for the mosque, we see the same emphasis on the Dome of the Rock. But it may be said that there might well have been no Aqsa Mosque at all without the religious and legendary associations of the Rock, from the time of David (II Samuel 24; I Chron. 21) and probably even before.

[53] The southwest corner of Arabia (cf. note 13), where meet the Red Sea and the Indian Ocean, and where is located the important British stronghold of 'Aden. It has for four centuries been ruled by a line of Zaidite *imāms*. The Imām Yahya (*John*) was killed in 1948. See Amin F. Rihani, *Arabian Peak and Desert*, London, Constable & Co., 1930. On the supposition of the woman that the visitor was the mysterious Elias or al-Khidr, see note 39. On the

Black Marble, see Baedeker, *Palestine and Syria* (1906), p. 57, where it is called "*Balātat el-Jennah*," or "pavement stone of Paradise," and is said to be of jasper.

[54] The title of this chapter is confused by repetition and otherwise.

[55] As will be seen, some Moslem authors thus transfer the name of Gehennah from the Jewish location west and southwest of Jerusalem to the Valley of the Kidron on the east. They place here the scene of the Last Judgment, for which the narrow path, *as-Sirāt*, will be strung from the Temple area over Kidron to the Mount of Olives. This transfer, however, may have been influenced by Jewish and Christian tradition based upon such Old Testament passages as Joel 3.2, on the Valley of Jehoshaphat (the Valley of God-Shall-Judge) and the gathering of the nations.

[56] See I Kings 8.22; II Chron. 6.12-7.1.

[57] Sūrah 19. This chapter of the Koran again attests the high regard of Moslems for the Virgin Mary.

[58] Sūrah 38, a chapter containing an interesting version of the parable of Nathan for conviction of David who had taken Bathsheba, the wife of Uriah the Hittite (II Samuel 11). With this brief reference, our author passes over the pious Caliph 'Omar and his visit to Jerusalem to receive it in capitulation in 636 A.D.—at which time he is supposed to have rediscovered the site of the Temple. The story is given prominent place in other works; see Le Strange, *Palestine under the Moslems*, pp. 139-144.

[59] This is possible from an apocryphal gospel, like those conveniently edited by M. R. James in his *Apocryphal New Testament*, Oxford, 1924; cf. p. 184, "The Book of the Resurrection of Christ, by Bartholomew the Apostle," where it is said that at the time of the ascension "he prayed the Father to bless us."

[60] See note 21. The Gate of the Prophet or of al-Burāq is now walled up, because of the rising of the habitation level of the city by deposit of debris (a familiar process in Oriental towns). Over it is a more recent Gate of the Maghāribah, or the Moors. The disused gate on one of the lower levels of the city was discovered by the American physician Barclay, as described in his book, *The City of the Great King*, Philadelphia, 1858. It is sometimes called Barclay's Gate in his honor, just as the arch in the wall a little to the south is called Robinson's Arch in honor of its discoverer, the great pioneer American archaeologist.

[61] Others, especially later, locate the plain as-Sāhirah just north of the northeast corner of the Holy City. See note 74.

[62] On the marvellous stories in connection with use of the chain, or rod, in judging guilt (in the manner of modern lie detectors!) see Le Strange, pp. 145, 147, 151, 152. In his faulty translation of Shamsu 'd-Dīn as-Suyūti, *Ithāf al-Akhissa fī Fadā'il al-Masjid al-Aqsa* ("Gift for Intimate Friends Concerning the Merits of the Aqsa Mosque," written in 1471), under the English title, *History of the Temple of Jerusalem* (London, 1836, auspices of the Oriental Translation Fund of Great Britain and Ireland), the Rev. James A. Reynolds gives some accounts of trials in which the chain was used. One tells of a Jewish embezzler of money entrusted by a friend. He concealed the gold in a hollow stick, which he asked the complainant to hold for him, while he testified that he had returned the money. Needless to say, this trick "broke the machinery"! It is strange not to find any mention of the judgment chain of Solomon and David in *Legends of the Jews*. Cervantes used the same motif—he who was for five years a galley slave of the Moslems.

[62a] On 'Abdu 'l-Malik, see the Introduction, pp. xx f. On the Houris, mystic maidens of Paradise, see Sūrahs 56.11 f., and 55. See also St. Clair-Tisdall, *The Religion of the Crescent* (cited in note 17), Lecture II, section 8, pp. 106 f., "The Muslim Paradise." The writer of

course has the point of view of Christian apologetics. Moslems give a metaphorical, mystical explanation. The sight of the Houris, as well as the association with the prophets, on the Night-Journey to Jerusalem, was a mystical experience giving a foretaste of the joys to come.

[63] Sūrah 2.55. This verse, in the midst of a confused account of Hebrew history, seems best applied to the conquest of Jericho, as indeed some Moslem commentators say. The feeling that the application was originally to Jericho may well have given rise to the tradition that the Hittah gate of Jerusalem was brought there from the ruined city in the valley. See *Palestine's Pilgrim's Texts*, III, 86 f.

[64] I do not know a reference for this tradition. It may refer to the attempt of the Hebrews to enter Canaan from the South. See Numbers, chapters 13-14, and Joshua 14. 7 f.

[65] That is, at the time of the birth of Jesus, which many Moslem stories say took place in the Temple area itself, in Jerusalem.

[66] Sūrah 57. 13; cf. note 55.

[67] The problem of the location of various places of veneration in the Temple area would require too much space for full discussion here. Le Strange gives (p. 173, with an excellent plan) what he regards as the most accurate information on the shifting names and structures through the centuries. See also pp. 153 f., in his indispensable work. His information on the locations is taken largely from Colonel Sir C. Wilson.

[68] This is supposed to be the great cistern, which is in part excavated under the Aqsa Mosque (Le Strange, p. 198). Le Strange gives (on the page cited and also on pp. 292 f.) some of the versions of the story below. The pool is also called that of Solomon, who is supposed to have made all the underground cisterns of the Haram or Temple area.

[69] A frontier post, and service in the way of Allah there, had special sanctity. The mention here of Asqalon, especially important in the era of struggles with the Crusaders, helps us to understand why later copies of the book included a chapter on the merits of that city.

[70] Sūrah 55.66. Beisān is the Beth-shan of the Old Testament, and a good example of the manner in which the Arabs restored many of the old Semitic names to replace the Classical— in this case Scythopolis. Zamzam is the holy well in Mecca, from which Moslem pilgrims bring back flasks of water like the Christian pilgrim flasks from Jordan.

[71] The second caliph, and conqueror of Jerusalem.

[72] A town in Syria, considerably north of Damascus. Popular etymology, like that of many place names in the Old Testament, asserts that the town was settled by a *hundred* survivors of the overturned Cities of the Plain—i. e., *Salam miyyah*, " a hundred safe."

[73] This story is an excellent example of accretion in popular legend. Note how the details increase in number and wonder as the various forms are recounted.

[73a] The original has in this paragraph, first, " The olives of the *millah*," and below, " I did not know what the *millah* was . . . " (The reference is probably to Gethsemane.) The word (properly, *millatun*, with plural *milal (un)*) means " religion, sect, rite." Under the Ottoman Turkish regime, with each non-Muslim religion and some divisions of such having a representative head who was permitted considerable authority, the word practically meant a *nation* within the empire.

[74] Now called Abu Ghōsh, in honor of a notorious sheikh of the nineteenth century, who with the inhabitants under his control used to " cut the way " of travellers, on the Jaffa-Jerusalem road. (For modern Moslem burials in Jerusalem, see the Introduction, p. xviii.)

[75] Thus with a brief citation of precedents the author shows that circumambulation of the shrines in Jerusalem, in the manner of the pilgrims around the Ka'bah in Mecca, is an open question. Very strict Moslems, like the Wahhābis of contemporary Arabia under rule of Ibn

Sa'ūd, would not agree. In fact, the latter regard as idolatrous the extreme veneration of Jerusalem and of other holy places outside the Hejāz, like the Shī'ite shrines of Najaf and Kerbelah in Iraq.

[76] The name al-Walīd is missing in the Yale text. He is al-Walīd ibn Muslim, celebrated traditionist, born in Damascus, died in the last part of the second century after the Hijrah.

[77] Sūrah 43.44. This verse is generally connected with the Night-Journey tradition by Koran commentators.

[78] The favorite wife of the Prophet, of the number he had after the death of his first wife, Khadījah. She is the source of numerous traditions, giving intimate incidents of the Prophet's life.

[79] Cf. Sūrahs 24.44, 32.7; and Genesis 1.20-21. Kūfah, just below, was a very noted city in Irāq, near old Babylon, and one of the earliest centers of Moslem learning.

[80] An echo of the Heavenly City, Revelation 21.

[81] Leading the prayers and preaching the Friday sermon, as was customarily the duty of the head of government in "totalitarian" Islam, in which there is no separation of church and state until we come to such modern states as Turkey, after World War I. Mu'āwiyah was the founder of the Omayyad dynasty of Damascus (661-750), but this could have been during his governorship of Syria just before. The *minbar* is the mosque pulpit, on which the speaker *sits* on one of the upper steps to deliver the *khutbah* or sermon. Cf. Jesus in the Nazareth synagogue (Luke 4.20-21).

[82] The words, "without just reason," are only in the Yale manuscript, and there between the lines. They may be original, or a later reader's softening of a hard saying.

[83] From Jewish and Moslem traditional accounts of Moses? The account is hardly satisfactory in Ginzberg, IV, 304-310, where Jeremiah summons Moses from his grave, along with others, to devastated Jerusalem to mourn over the ruins of the Temple. I recall, on pointing out Mounts Gerizim and Ebal to a group of Jewish travellers in 1934 and reminding them of the scene in Joshua 24 (cf. Deut. 27), having a rabbi ask, "But where did Moses stand?"(!) He seemed unsatisfied by my tactful reminder of the fact that Moses died and was buried across the Jordan.

[84] See Le Strange, pp. 87 and 198, on the copious dews of the Holy City.

[85] Not an exact quotation; cf. Sūrahs 7.133; 21.71 and 81. Such "memory quotations" of the Old Testament, for instance, are frequent in the New. See C. H. Toy, *Quotations in the New Testament*, New York, Scribner's, 1884. See also Charles C. Torrey, *Documents of the Primitive Church*, Harper & Bros., New York, 1941, p. 25, and (by same author and publishers) *The Four Gospels*, p. 275 (or corresponding page in later edition).

[86] See note 83, and Sūrahs 11.42 and 23.27, and Rodwell's notes in his translation of the Koran (Everyman's Library, p. 219). The sentence seems to mean that in Jerusalem there is the *oven* which boils in preparation for destroying the wicked at the Judgment with a flood of hot water, as happened at the Flood in the days of Noah.

[87] Practically all the following are references to statements in the Koran, which may be found by use of a concordance like Flügel's (Leipzig, 1898), or the index of Rodwell.

[88] These details are doubtless from some of the apocryphal infancy gospels. See note 59, with its reference to James, *The Apocryphal New Testament*. A small underground mosque in the southeast angle of the Haram, near the so-called Stables of Solomon, is called the Cradle of Jesus; see Le Strange, p. 166. On the miraculous palm tree, see Le Strange, pp. 298 f., and the Gospel of Pseudo-Matthew, chapter 20.

[89] On Gog and Magog, see the index volume (VI) of Ginzberg, *Legends of the Jews*, and the index of Rodwell's translation of the Koran.

[90] See notes 59 and 88.

[91] The best reference I can find at present is J. E. Hanauer, *Folk-lore of the Holy Land*, London, The Sheldon Press, new edition, 1935, p. 5. According to popular Moslem cosmology recited there, an angel who supports the world stands on a rock of green emerald, which rests on the back of a great bull, which stands on the back of a whale.

[92] See Psalm 37. 29.

[93] Thus in his brief summary treatment the author avoids the Moslem controversy over whether the one sacrificed was Isaac or Ishmael, traditional progenitor of the North Arabs. See accounts in *The Book of Inciting Desire*, on Abraham and Hebron.

[94] See Sūrahs 34. 10 and 21. 80. Moslem legend has it that David was a master at the art of making mail and other armor, because iron was miraculously softened for him, just as stone was made soft for Solomon, for his wondrous buildings.

[95] The name Jesus is missing in the Yale text, by a copyist's slip. For John, see again the apocryphal gospels cited above.

[96] A giant, mighty-voiced Negro servant of the Prophet, who served as the first to call the faithful to prayer, standing on the flat roof of a house in the simpler days of early Islam.

[97] A fountain for ablutions, performed in a prescribed manner, is provided in the court of, or adjacent to, every mosque. In the desert away from water, clean sand may be substituted.

[98] This is an honest echo of the severities of weather and other discomforts of Jerusalem! Compare the extravagant praises of the city and the land generally in the book.

[99] I. e., *al-Wahhāb*, one of the ninety-nine beautiful names of Allah. However, application of the same term by Westerners to the modern Sa'ūdi Arabians in calling them " Wahhābis " mistakenly follows a precedent set by enemies of the earnest reform movement which still prevails in the peninsula and has influence elsewhere. The word appears in the name of the founder (actually as his father's name repeated by custom in his own), Muhammad *son of 'Abdu 'l-Wahhāb* (1703-1787). The correct and self-applied name of the followers of the strict way of the founder and of his predecessors Ibn Taymīyyah (1263-1328) and Ibn Hanbal (d. 855) is *Muwahhidūn*, " Unitarians," or those who worship God alone, considering devotion to saints or shrines and intercession through saints as kinds of idolatry.

[100] Ad-Dajjāl; see Hanauer (cited above, note 91), pp. 61 and 248.

[101] One of the commanders responsible for the Arab conquest of Palestine and Syria. See accounts of the grant of Hebron to the Dāri clan in the next chapter.

[102] I. e., evidently, that I might be there in whatever form or manner, to enjoy its blessings and to escape the tribulations of the rest of the world.

[103] The Leiden manuscript adds, " and rivers of water," completing the quotation of Sūrah 47. 16-17. On the next phrase, see Revelations 21.

[104] This conclusion of the tradition reflects the great importance of Iraq or Mesopotamia in Islamic history. With Baghdad as the capital, it was the center of the Islamic world during the 'Abbāsid era, 750-1258.

[105] See Genesis 23, and Ginzberg, *Legends of the Jews*, I, 286 f.

[106] This account is an excellent example of the rivalry of various spots in popular tradition. Other accounts recognize the Biblical story of the burial of Jacob near Shechem, and of Rebecca just north of Bethlehem.

[107] Cf. Ginzberg, I, 418 f., 342, and V, 371-372.

[108] This of course refers to the Byzantine Greeks, and their great era of religious architecture after the conversion of Constantine (see the introduction, p. xiii). The ancient structure over the tombs of the patriarchs still reveals its Byzantine architecture, especially in the courses of large, smooth-faced stones. It was a sacred spot before the Hebrews came to Canaan, and then a shrine to them. See the story of Absalom, II Samuel 15. 7. With the

Moslem conquest, it became a mosque—to which it reverted after serving again as a church during the Crusader control of Palestine.

[109] Haran, or Harrān, see Genesis 24, and also the Jacob cycle of stories following thereupon. Haran was one of the most important points of transfer of Classical culture to the Arabs, through both Christian and pagan Syrians. Translated into Arabic through Syriac, the philosophical and scientific works of the Greeks laid much of the basis for Arabo-Islamic cultural development—which in turn brought about the Renaissance in Europe. See Hitti, *History of the Arabs*, Macmillan, London, 1937 and 1940, chapters 24 and 42. Cf. p. 149, n. 2.

[110] See Genesis 12.10 f., and, for the parallel story of Isaac and Rebecca, Genesis 26.6 f.

[111] One purpose of this account is, probably, to explain the veneration of some for the Byzantine site, Rāmet al-Khalīl, or "the High Place of the Friend of God," a few miles north of Hebron, where there are ruins of a church.

[112] The angels Munkar and Nekīr who question the dead, to determine his reward or punishment. Cf. the judgment examination in the Egyptian *Book of the Dead*.

[113] Reynolds (cited in note 62) translates (p. 383) from as-Suyūti: "The death of the Prophets is not like the death of other men; but they are merely translated from one state unto another, and depart from us . . . Thus they continue to exist in a state of being, just as the angels live and exist . . ." See the accounts of visits to the actual tombs underneath the mosque, in the next book. The rites described here are of course for the cenotaphs on the main floor of the mosque.

[114] Cf. note 106.

[115] The Yale manuscript has the names confused into one.

[116] The various accounts of the purported grant have differences in the names and other details. See the Introduction, p. vi. The property later became a *waqf* or pious foundation, but representatives of the Tamīmi family still live in Palestine.

[117] The details here fit historically. The Persians, under Chosroes II of the Sassānid line, captured Jerusalem in 615, seven years before the Hijrah, and held it until its recapture by the Byzantines in 628.

[118] About five miles westward from Hebron, "A land," according to the geographer Muqaddasi, "of riches and plenty, possessing fine domains." Also known as Beit Jibrīn.

[119] The Yale text has Tamīm himself here, probably by reason of his leadership in the clan; and several of the manuscripts exhibit some confusion. It is clear, however, that in this interesting example of the Prophet's "second sight" he approves the choice of Hebron by Abu Hind.

[120] Such materials were often used for important documents. The Arabs also employed papyrus — and it was they who introduced into Europe paper, from the Far East, having developed their own manufactures for it, providentially at the time for the spread of printing in the Western world.

[121] The idea of four villages in Hebron seems to have some traditional connection with the Old Testament name sometimes used for Hebron, *Kiryath-'Arbah*; see Joshua 21.11; 14.15.

[122] Thus asserting that the document had the signatures of the five leading men of the early period — the first four caliphs in order, and Mu'āwiyah, the fifth, who founded the Omayyad dynasty.

[123] The account thus stresses the humanity of the Islamic occupation. The Dāri clan would yet have feudal rights over the territory, whose people would be *ahl adh-dhimmah*, or protected subjects, under them.

[124] The religious law of Islam.

[125] I. e., in June, 1477, according to F. Wüstenfeld, *Vergleichungs-Tabellen* . . . , Leipzig, 1854.

[1] I have omitted here a brief invocation, and transferred the rather long table of contents to the preliminary part of this volume.

[2] On this Biblical genealogical material, rendered here and below in popular style, see Genesis 10-11. I have used Harrān for the place and Haran for the man; and wherever there is a well-known Biblical form of a name, I have used that instead of the Arabic form in the manuscript. See also the popular genealogies in Jewish sources, as given for instance by Ginzberg, *The Legends of the Jews* (cited in note 11 to *The Book of Arousing Souls*). Here will be found the Jewish originals of many of the stories of Old Testament characters, just as those of New Testament characters come from popular Christian books. See note 59, *The Book of Arousing Souls*. In the text of the first chapter, Ar'awa is evidently a variant form of Reu. Such popular lore of course exhibits many variants; e. g., Noah is called the son of Amalek and also the son of Yarid or Yārid. On Gog and Magog, see note 89 to *The Book of Arousing Souls*.

[3] The Tenth of Moharram, a sacred day of fasting and penance said to have been adopted from Judaism; and for the Shī'ah Moslems the martyrdom of Husein, grandson of the Prophet, observed by a realistic "Passion Play." See *'āshūrā'* in index of Philip K. Hitti (Princeton), *History of the Arabs*, Macmillan, New York and London, second edition, 1940.

[4] Northern Mesopotamia. *Al-jazīrah* means also "island," but is used likewise for this district and for the peninsula of Arabia.

[5] The sons of Cain, who in the Biblical account were, after the rehabilitation of Cain, the developers of the arts and crafts. See Genesis 4. 16 f.

[6] By popular accretion, Nimrod, Nebuchadnezzar, Pharaoh, and others become the villains of many stories, just as David, Solomon, and Alexander the Great are the heroes.

[7] Two of the legendary pre-Islamic prophets. In his *Comprehensive Commentary on the Qurán* (London; Kegan Paul, Trench, Trübner & Co., 1896; Trübner's Oriental Series), II, 177, n. 75, E. M. Wherry suggests that the name Āzar may be a conflation between the Talmudic Zarah and the Persian Azar, the planet Mars, the name of which was used for persons among the Persian nobility. But Prof. Charles C. Torrey (p. 68 in his *Jewish Foundation of Islam*; see bibliography) gives the simpler and more plausible explanation that in Sūrah 6. 74 the Koran takes Eliezer the steward of the house of Abraham (Genesis 51. 2) for Terah and gives his name as Āzar.

[8] Cf. Ginzberg, *Legends of the Jews*, I, 187, for an account in which also the restrictions and persecutions of the Pharaoh of Egypt (Exodus 1. 15 f.) are attributed to Nimrod!

[9] Koran, Sūrah 6. 76 f.

[10] Koran, Sūrah 6. 77.

[11] Sūrah 21. 67.

[12] This is another title of the author's noted collection called *Stories of the Prophets*; see note 48, *The Book of Arousing Souls*, and note 1 to the introduction.

[13] Sūrah 26. 69 f.

[14] Sūrah 2. 260 f.

[15] See Sūrahs 21. 52 f., and 32. 81 f., and Ginzberg, *Legends*, etc., I, 197. The portrait of Abraham as the reformer and idol-smasher is so familiar to Jews from their extra-Biblical sources that the unscholarly sometimes forget that the actual accounts do not occur in the

Bible itself. From what follows I have omitted about ten lines of the original, a typical example of Koranic exegesis. The main point for Occidental readers would be a comparison contained therein between Abraham and John the Baptist, with a quotation from Sūrah 9.13 to the effect that Allah gave to him guidance in his childhood as He had to Abraham.

[16] Sūrah 21.59.

[16a] Omitted here are several lines of the original devoted to further interpretation of this interesting story of Abraham as it is given in Sūrah 21.50 f., and citing related verses. The pagans, it is recorded, cling to their error, but make the damaging admission that their idols cannot speak.

[17] Iblīs is Satan. Cf. the account in Ginzberg, *Legends*, etc., cited in note 2.

[18] Sūrah 21.69. In the Jewish account, the furnace was turned into a garden for Abraham, cf. below.

[19] The anachronistic allusion to the Biblical story of the Tower of Babel is obvious.

[20] Cf. story of the ascent of Kai-Kaus (Kavi Usan) in Persian mythology. A convenient reference is *The Mythology of All Races*, Louis Herbert Gray, ed., Boston, Marshall Jones Co., 1917, II, 334 f. Plate XLII gives a good illustration, from a Persian miniature.

[21] Sūrah 14.47.

[22] Sūrah 16.28.

[23] Sūrah 29.25. In the Jewish account, the reason for the conversion of Lot was the patience and victory of Abraham under trial.

[24] Sūrah 21.71.

[25] See note 7. This is based on the story in Genesis 12, and the doublet of it in chapter 26.

[26] Cf. Genesis 16. The gift of Hagar to Sarah by the pharaoh is recorded in the Jewish account. The Moslem story here contains an interesting example of plays on words in personal or place names, such as are often found in the Bible. The Arabic word for Hagar is such that in the popular mind it would have connection with " price, hire, reward."

[27] Be'er-Shebah is explained twice in the Bible, in connection with Abraham and with Isaac, Genesis 21.31 and 26.33. The stem *S-B-'* in Arabic means *seven*; but in other Semitic forms as in Hebrew, with initial *SH-* instead of *S*, it may mean either *seven* or *to swear*. *Sālih* means honest, pious, etc.

[28] A Roman place-name, Legio; which was Megiddo?

[29] A site now known as Nebī Yaqīn, " the Prophet Yaqīn," southeast of Hebron.

[30] See under *tharā* in Lane's Arabic dictionary. Hijr (above) was north of Medina.

[31] Clitoridectomy? Female circumcision has been widely practised by Muslim peoples.

[32] Cf. Genesis 21.

[33] Sūrah 14.40.

[34] These are places visited in the Pilgrimage ceremonies from Mecca, formerly associated with pagan Arabian rites, but afterward with legends of Abraham.

[35] In the customary complimentary fashion of naming a man by the name of his eldest son, Mohammed was so called even after his son al-Qāsim had died, at the age of two. Cf. " Mother of Ishmael " as a term of address for Hagar, below.

[36] The *seil* is to be reckoned with also in the arroyos of the Southwest in America, so like the Near East in general geographical features.

[37] In the Jewish form of the story, the metaphor for the wife is the tent-pin. See Ginzberg, *Legends of the Jews*, I, 263 f.

[38] Sūrah 2.121.

[39] Literally, " the time of ignorance," used more specifically of the age of classical poetry and desert chivalry just preceding Islam, and also more generally for all pre-Islamic history.

[40] The cry of the pilgrim on sighting Mecca from afar, and even earlier, upon first arriving at the border of the sacred territory and entering the state of ceremonial purification or *ihram* for the Hajj. The meaning is said to be: " Here am I, O Lord, in obedience to Thy Command."

[41] Perforce sketchy in details, the text is also unclear and the year 54 should be 72.

[42] Sūrah 37.99 f.

[43] Sūrah 37.112.

[44] Sūrah 11.74.

[45] Sūrah 37.98.

[46] Sūrah 37.101.

[47] The magical steed which bore Mohammed from Mecca to Jerusalem and back in a night. See the story of the Night-Journey, in Chapter Two of *The Book of Arousing Souls*.

[48] The story is told in detail in Jewish sources. See Ginzberg, I, 271 f.

[49] Stones are still thrown in the Pilgrimage rites near Mecca, in the Valley of Mina; and Satan is called " the stoned one," *ash-Shaitān ar-rajim*.

[50] Sūrah 37.101 f., in which also the following quotations are found.

[51] Jewish tradition has it that the place on which Isaac was offered was the spot of the later Temple.

[52] Sūrah 11.72.

[53] Compare the story in Genesis, (17.17, 18.12, 21.6), a most interesting example of popular etymology.

[54] Sūrah 11.72 f.

[55] Sūrah 29.30 f.

[56] Cf. Genesis 25.26. The meaning of the name of Jacob may be nearer, with the inclusion of the divine element " el," or Jacob-el, " God-will-protect." This is another instance of popular Biblical etymology.

[57] Sūrah 2.126.

[58] Chapter 12 of the Koran is the Sūrah of Joseph, who is one of the favorite Biblical characters to Muslim traditionists and poets.

[59] A play on words in Arabic, as if the name *Yūsuf* or Joseph were from the Arabic verb *asifa*, " to regret."

[60] Compare the Biblical account in Genesis 50.

[61] Exodus 13.19.

[62] Genesis 11.32.

[63] Sūrah 29.28 f. Other material in the Koran on Lot and the Cities of the Plain is found in Sūrahs 54.33 f., 37.133 f., 26.160 f., 15.58 f., 27.55 f., 11.79 f., 29.28 f., and 7.78 f. This reveals both what an attraction the story of Lot had for the Prophet, and how he used Biblical material here and there, without consistent treatment.

[64] In the popular Jewish form of the story also, Lot's wife could not keep the secret of the marvellous visitors!

[65] It is still the case that a non-Mohammedan is not allowed to marry a Mohammedan woman. Thus the exclusiveness from tribal origins and the belief in racial superiority of the Jews both operate also among the Mohammedans. The text here is unclear.

[66] The author omits the related story of the escape of *a hundred* from the Overthrown Cities, who migrated to Syria and built the towns of al-Mu'tafikah (*overthrown*) and Sala-mīyyah (*a hundred saved*). See note 72 to *The Book of Arousing Souls*, and Le Strange, pp. 51, 528.

[67] See Le Strange, p. 468.

[68] See Ginzberg, *Legends of the Jews*, I, 328 f., for interesting popular explanations of Isaac's blindness, caused according to one account by injurious smoke from the sacrificial fires of his idolatrous daughters-in-law, the wives of Esau. These stories may be based upon the simple Biblical statement about Isaac, that in his old age " his eyes were dim, so that he could not see." (Genesis 27.1.)

[69] Sūrah 40.56 f.

[70] Cf. Genesis 25.

[71] That is, Be'er-Shebah. See note 27.

[72] See note 29.

[73] I have tried to imitate the original in its character as rhymed prose, which is a feature of the Koran and of many later Arabo-Islamic books as well as of epistolary style.

[74] This story sounds like an echo of that of the return of the Ark of the Covenant from the land of the Philistines, in I Samuel 6.

[75] As mentioned in the introduction, p. v., some of this material has been translated by Sir Guy Le Strange.

[76] January in the Christian Syrian calendar.

[77] This is the Tamīmi waqf or pious foundation, mentioned in the note to p. vi, introduction, and note 116 to *The Book of Arousing Souls*. Other grants were later added to its resources; see Le Strange, *Palestine Under the Moslems*, p. 310.

[78] This is Ibn Hauqal's revision of a famous geographical work on the Arab lands by Istakhri. Both are of the tenth century, Christian era.

[79] Compare the account of the vision of Solomon at Gibeon, probably in the shrine, II Samuel 3.5 f. Also, of course, Jacob at Bethel, Genesis 28.

[80] A modern Moslem descendant of the Prophet told me in Jaffa in 1934 how he had had a dream about Jesus Son of Mary, who smiled and received him with an embrace; and that he hoped before he died to see him in a vision again. In agreement with the well-known apocryphal traditions, he described Jesus as having reddish hair.

[81] Cf. the interesting accounts in Ginzberg, II, 180, 194; III, 5 f., V, 376. No doubt, such Jewish lore was known to the Prophet; cf. below, p. 101.

[82] Reference again to Le Strange's translation of part of the material on Hebron (see p. 325 of his work) prevented my supposing here an example of popular telescoping of history and of belief in extreme longevity. Because of ambiguous identification of Mary or Miriam the mother of Jesus with Miriam the sister of Moses (see 143[43]), some earlier Muslim writers asserted that Miriam was miraculously preserved through the centuries. But the " old woman " of the present account is clearly not the same as that of the preceding, who was to renew her lifetime of 900 years! For rivalry between shrines, compare note 106, p. 147. Al-Muqtadir was caliph in Baghdad in the early part of the tenth century.

[83] A mountain near Medina, where occurred one of the early battles in the struggle of Mohammed and his followers against the Meccans, from whom they had removed on the Hijrah. This section is of course much like parts of *The Book of Arousing Souls*.

[84] *Sunnah* is the custom or practice of the Prophet, used in guidance of life by Moslems. It is effectually a part of the larger field of " Tradition," *Hadīth*, which does not mean ordinary tradition, with derogatory connotation, but tested *reports* or *accounts* of Mohammed's appearance, dress, habits, actions, and words. The plural is *sunan*.

[85] Sūrah 4.124.

[86] Cf. note 7 to *The Book of Arousing Souls*.

[87] Sūrah 64.14.

[88] At the last moment, I saw in the first instalment of Vol. V of the new edition of al-Bukhāri by Muhammad Asad (Leopold Weiss)—Lahore, Arafat Publications, 1938—a solution to a puzzle. My text had here a word missing and one defectively pointed. Access to such helps would have cleared up other problems, including identities of persons mentioned.

[89] A typical quotation from Moslem mystical poetry. I do not know the source.

[90] Sūrah 53. 38. Literally, " paid or fulfilled or performed all his obligations."

[91] Cf. Ginzberg, V, 229. Many interesting popular Jewish notions about Abraham are to be found in Ginzberg (see in the index, in Vol. VII). The trousers or drawers and gray hairs of the next chapter, however, are missing. However, there is the statement (I, 206) that at the birth of Isaac Abraham's grey hair turned black again, and the lines in Sarah's face became smooth.

[92] Another jeu de mots. The form of the name here given Sarah means readiness or easiness in action; but the stem has relation also to words for various kinds of cloth.

[93] A characterization of the Prophet proudly given by Moslems, who hold up his lack of education as proof of his divine inspiration. And, unless clearer light can eventually be thrown upon the sources and means of Mohammed's education in matters religious and Biblical, as well as in grammar and rhetoric, the contents and language of the Koran must continue to be admitted as a marvel. Ahmed may be considered another form of the name Muhammad or Mohammed.

[94] There is a folk-belief among the Jews also (and this is the source for the Moslem) that ancient worthies like Adam and Enoch were given books of revelation. It was this belief which made possible the latter Jewish literature of the Pseudepigraphs, composed under the names of Enoch, the Twelve Patriarchs, etc. These unfortunately are not widely known by Christians, despite their value for the understanding of Judaism, Messianism, and the New Testament.

[95] Sūrah 2. 116 f.

[96] Sūrah 16. 121.

[97] The Hanīfs (hanif is a loan word from Aramaic) were Arabs dissatisfied with their pagan religion and in spiritual search for something better. (The movement doubtlessly influenced Mohammed.) The use of the term for Abraham, a true seeker after God in the midst of pagans, is appropriate.

[98] Sūrah 2. 122.

[99] Sūrah 2. 262.

[100] The universal use of the wooden tooth-stick in Islam, as a means of minor purification, is based upon the sunnah or custom of the Prophet. See Sir William Muir, *The Life of Mohammed* (new and revised edition by T. H. Weir), John Grant, Edinburgh, 1923, p. 532.

[101] Sūrah 16. 121 f.

[102] Sūrah 11. 77.

GLOSSARY

The difficulty of satisfactorily representing Arabic names has led to a practical procedure in this book which it is hoped is fairly consistent. Where clear and convenient, the familiar forms have been used, both in Biblical and in Moslem names.

Without attempting to represent all the peculiar Arabic consonants by diacritics, I have at least indicated spirants by means of h, and have denoted the constrictive laryngeal *'ain* (') as well as the weak glottal stop or *spiritus lenis*, *hamzah* ('). In most cases the vowels which are long have been so indicated, even to the point of writing some words, e.g., *Safīyyah* instead of *Safīyah*, with a transcriptionally superfluous "y." The reader will of course realize that Arabic long "u" is our sound of "oo" as in *boot*, without the common glide of English in the sound of "u" like "ee-yew"; and also that the long "i" is the "European" sound as in *machine*, not as in *write*.

Abu. "Father (of)." In oblique cases the word becomes in the genitive-dative, *abi*, and in the accusative *aba*. But in common translation the nominative form is employed. The "u" is long, but in liaison, as with elision of the vowel of a following article (*al*, "the") it becomes short. Therefore the vowel is left unmarked in all cases in this book. The word is widely used to denote personal characteristics, good or bad, e.g., "father of strength."

Bint. "Daughter (of)." It is of course the feminine of *ibn*, and has a parallel form *ibnah*, *ibnat*.

Caliph. "Successor" of the Prophet as religious and civil head of the Moslem (properly *Muslim*) community. After the conquest, the term became practically equivalent to emperor, but it was frequently used also as designation of religious leaders of special and ofttimes heretical movements in Islam. The Arabic word is *Khalīfah*.

Companions. The intimate and loyal supporters of Mohammed who migrated with him from Mecca to Medina in 622 A.D. Many of them were important in the early struggles of the faith and the campaigns of conquest which followed soon after the death of the Prophet. The Arabic word is, singular, *sāhib*; plural *ashāb*. Another meaning of the same stem is familiar in the East Indian word sahib for master, lord.

Dirham. The name of a coin of varying value, derived from the Greek word *drachma*, especially because the first Moslem coins were minted by Byzantine artisans and even bore Greek inscriptions.

Followers. Children and immediate descendants of those who had been associated with Mohammed as Companions or Helpers. The Arabic word is, singular, *tābi'*; plural, *tābi'ūn*.

Hāfiz. "Holder," or "guarder," particularly one who has memorized the text of the Koran and holds it in memory.

Haram. A *sacred* place, in which desecrating acts or visitors are *forbidden*. A shrine, like the Temple area in Jerusalem is a *Haram*. The word *harem* means the house or tent apartment set aside for the women, into which place all men not immediately related to the women are forbidden entrance.

Helpers. Loyal citizens of Medina who freely threw in their fortunes with the *Muhājirūn* on their removal thither by invitation of a company of Medinites with whom the Prophet met in Mecca. The Arabic word is, singular, *nāsir*; plural, *ansār*.

Hijrah. "Flight," "migration," "removal." It is applied to the migration of Abraham from Mesopotamia to Canaan as well as to that of Mohammed from Mecca to Medina, the year of which latter event, 622, became the year one in Mohammedan reckoning. Those who thus migrate for the sake of their faith are *Muhājirūn* (singular, *Muhājir*).

Ibn. "Son (of)." In its proper form it is (without the final "n" of classical grammar) *ibnu* for the nominative, *ibni* for the genitive-dative, and *ibna* for the accusative.

Ihrām. The seamless white garment assumed by the pilgrim upon entering the sacred territory near Mecca-Medina. It denotes that the pilgrim is now in a state of *purification*, from the same stem as that for *Haram*, which see.

Imām. "Leader," "he who stands *before*" the congregation in worship. The word is also used in a derived sense to honor a person pre-eminent in a field, and among the Shi'ites for the successive heads of the descendants of the caliph Ali.

Islām. This the proper name of the religion, instead of Mohammedanism, means "submission" of one's life and will unto Allah. Mohammed, familiar with the story of Abraham, whom he regarded as his predecessor and the founder of the faith, was no doubt impressed by the Biblical account of his trustful obedience to God in leaving his native country for a strange land. The accent is on the first syllable; and as now pronounced in the Anglicized form both vowels are short. See also *Muslim.*

Mihrāb. A niche, usually beautifully decorated, in the mosque on the side toward Mecca, and indicating the direction of prayer. It is practically equivalent to *qiblah*, but the mihrab more particularly is the place in the mosque which indicates the qiblah or "direction" toward Mecca.

Mohammed. Properly *Muhammad*, "the praised one," a passive particle of the intensive stem. In this book the familiar form has been used to distinguish the Prophet from many others by the same name. In Persian, and notably in Turkish, the word is thinned to the sound *Mehmet*. (Other forms of the name are *Mahmūd* and *Hamīd*.)

Moslem. Properly *Muslim*, one who has submitted his life unto Allah. The "s" has the sound of that in *frustrate*, not that in *reason*, and the "u" has the sound close to that of short "oo" as in *foot*, not that of "u" in cut. See also *Islam.*

Muezzin. Properly *mu'adhdhin*, he who gives the call to prayer for the stated five prayer times daily. The call itself is the *adhān*. The word is related to that meaning *ear*, *udhun*, so that the muezzin is he who makes the people *hear*.

Qādi. " Judge " in the ecclesiastical Moslem court, which is similar to that of the medieval Christian church. From its long use in " Moorish " Spain, the word came to mean in Spanish something like " mayor," written *alcalde* by influence of the emphatic " d " in Arabic.

Rak'ah. The entire ritual of prayer, private or in public, including the positions of standing facing Mecca, bowing, prostrating so that the forehead touches the ground or floor, kneeling, and resuming the standing osition, all the while repeating the prescribed and other devotions.

Sayyid. " Lord, leader "; or a person tracing his descent from the Prophet Mohammed. In common use the term is equivalent to " Sir," or " Mr." Its use with the names of figures in religious history, such as Jesus or Abraham, e. g., *Sayyidunā 'Īsā ibn Miryam*, " our Lord Jesus son of Mary," is one of profound respect, without trinitarian connotations.

Sheikh. Primarily, " old man," but applied generally to heads of tribes and to school-masters in religious schools, and to religious scholars and theologians. The term thus is closely parallel with " elder " and " presbyter."

As-Sirāt. The thin line forming a bridge over which all must walk at the final judgment as a test of their righteousness and acceptance with Allah. In Moslem eschatology, which is largely derived from Jewish and Christian (and like them is influenced by Zoroastrian), the Sirāt is to be set up from the eastern wall of the Temple area in Jerusalem, across the Valley of Kidron or Jehoshaphat, to the Mount of Olives.

Tradition. Accounts of Mohammed's words and acts as reported by his associates and handed down through trustworthy links of a chain of first oral and later written reference. The life of the Prophet is intimately known through this means, although despite the care of the great collectors many traditions remain which were forged. One result of the method of handing down information is the wearisome " So-and-so said that So-and-so said, etc.," in all Moslem books of history and Koran commentary.

Waqf. A pious foundation, in the form of a mosque, school, hospital, hostel for travellers or pilgrims or the poor, or a farm property for charity. The term, meaning " stop," is derived from the sense that the sale or change of ownership has ceased forever. Our nearest (inexact) equivalent is *mortmain*. Because of the commendable spirit of charity among Moslem peoples, such foundations have been so numerous that their governments have included a minister of (pl.) *awqāf*.

BIBLIOGRAPHY

For benefit of those who may wish to pursue further the interesting subject of relationships between Islam and Judaism and Christianity, the following books are cited in English, in addition to the well-known older works in German by Gustav Weil (*Biblische Legenden der Muselmänner*) and Abraham Geiger (*Was hat Mohammed aus dem Judenthume aufgenommen*) and the controversial and apologetic works by the Rev. W. St. Clair-Tisdall:

A. S. Atiyah, *The Crusade in the Later Middle Ages*, London, Methuen 1938.

Richard Bell *The Origin of Islam in Its Christian Environment*, London, Macmillan and Co., Ltd., 1926.

Nabih A. Faris (ed.), *The Arab Heritage*, Princeton, 1944.

Louis Ginzberg, *The Legends of the Jews*, translated from the German by Henrietta Szold, Philadelphia, The Jewish Publication Society of America, 1913 (seven volumes).

Rev. J. E. Hanauer, *Folk-lore of the Holy Land, Moslem, Christian and Jewish*, London, the Sheldon Press (new and enlarged edition), 1935.

The Koran, any convenient English translation, e. g., that of Rodwell or of Palmer. Useful in this connection is E. M. Wherry, *A Comprehensive Commentary on the Quran: Comprising Sale's Translation and Preliminary Discourse* ... London, Kegan Paul, Trench, Trubner & Co., Ltd., 1896 (four volumes). Other translations of the Koran, in addition to those indicated by Rodwell, Palmer, and Sale, have been made by Bell, Marmaduke Pickthall, and A. Yusif Ali, the last two with parallel Arabic text.

Joseph Meyouhas, *Bible Tales in Arab Folk-lore*, translated from the Hebrew by Victor N. Levi, London, Alfred A. Knopf, 1928.

Julian Obermann, "Islamic Origins," in *The Arabic Heritage*, Princeton University Press, 1944.

"Koran and Agada: The Events at Mount Sinai," article in *The American Journal of Semitic Languages and Literatures* (published by the University of Chicago Press), Vol. LVIII, No. 1, January, 1941.

De Lacy O'Leary, *Arabia before Muhammad*, London, Kegan Paul, Trench, Trubner & Co., Ltd., 1927.

Rev. James Robson, *Christ in Islam*, London, John Murray, 1929.

Henry Preserved Smith, *The Bible and Islam, or the Influence of the Old and New Testaments on the Religion of Mohammed* ... New York, Charles Scribner's Sons, 1897.

Charles Cutler Torrey, *The Jewish Foundation of Islam*, New York, Jewish Institute of Religion Press, 1933 (Bloch Publishing Co., agents).

John Walker, *Bible Characters in the Koran*, Paisley, Alexander Gardner, Ltd., 1931.

The nature of Islamic Traditions and the methods by which they were developed and handed down are clarified by Alfred Guillaume's *Traditions of Islam* (Oxford, Clarendon Press, 1924). On pages 47-52 are discussed the Traditions on the religious merits of Syria—including Palestine and Jerusalem.

Useful also are the standard guide books to Palestine which include considerable local tradition regarding Jerusalem, Hebron, and other places holy in common to Muslims, Christians, and Jews. A popular reference work often available in libraries for reading of appropriate articles is the *Dictionary of Islam*, edited by Thomas Patrick Hughes (London, W. H. Allen & Co., reprinted in 1935).

INDEX

Despite the statement regarding transliteration of Arabic names on page 154, inconsistencies became painfully apparent especially during final labors on this volume. However, even to the general reader the index will be a fairly sure guide if the following hints are observed:

Diphthongs are rendered variously—*ai, ei, ay, ey; au, aw* (and once as ō).

Short *a* is sometimes rendered as *e,* as in *Bakr* or *Bekr.*

'Abdullah except when alone or at the end of compound names is abbreviated as *'Abd.* (with a period).

ibn, "son of," when within compound names, is abbreviated by *b* (without a period).

Muhammad, except at the end of compound names, is abbreviated by M (without a period). In contrast, the familiar spelling, *Mohammed,* is used for the name of the Prophet.

Initial *U* with an *'ain* is in more familiar names rendered by *'U,* e.g., *'Omar, 'Othmān.*

al-, the definite article, thus unassimilated or in its various assimilated forms (e.g., *ar-, as-, at-, ath-, ad-, an-, az-*) is placed *before* the names and is to be disregarded in following the alphabetical listing.

Ar: stands for *Arabic:* in denoting within parentheses a more proper transliteration.

'Abbādān (formerly of Iraq, now of Iran), 12, 23, 142[34]

al-'Abbās, 84

'Abbas ad-Dauri, 128

'Abbāsid(s), rulers in Baghdad, 147[104]

'Abd al-Malik, or 'Abdu 'l-Malik, Omayyad caliph, xxii, 144[62a]

'Abd al-Mun'im, 104

'Abd al-Muttalib, g.father of the Prophet, 80

'Abd. b 'Abbās, 73

'Abd. b 'Abd al-Muttalib, father of the Prophet, 80

'Abd. b 'Amr b al-'Āsi, 10, 28, 12, 142[28]

'Abd. b Farrās, 105

Abd. b Hārith, 128, 129

'Abd. . . . b Mas'ūd, 91, 124, 133

'Abd. b M an-Nājjar, 114

'Abd. b 'Omar (or 'Umar), 6, 7, 22, 27, 78, 126

'Abd. b Ribāh, 100

'Abd. b Salām, 16, 37, 118, 119

'Abd. b 'Ubeid b 'Umeir, 85

'Abd. b az-Zubeir, xxii, 78, 79

'Abdu 'l-Malik, *see* 'Abd al-Malik

'Abdu 'r-Rahmān, 21

'Abdu 'r-Rahmān b Yazīd b Aslam, 127

Abel, 83

ablution(s), 32, 131, 147[97]; *see also* ceremonies, rites

Abode of Peace, or Paradise, 14, 37

Abode of the Just, 37, 120

Abraham (Ar: Ibrāhīm): 2, 30, 43, 92, 106, 107, 113, 118, 120, 122, 123, 133, 139[6], 149[15], 153[97]; founder of Islam, xiv, 34, 136; Jewish petitions to, xxix; birth and life of, 47 ff.; wisdom in childhood, 52 f.; makes sport of idols, 54 f., 150[16a]; cast into fire, 35, 50 ff., 84; migrates to Palestine, 27, 30, 31, 35 ff.; from Kūthā-rabba (Babel), 35, 63, 92; offers Isaac (or Ishmael?), 78 ff.; intercedes for people of Lot, 87 f., 93 f., 97 f.; builds the Ka'bah, xiv, 3, 74 ff.; buys burial cave at Hebron, 35 f.; his death, 36, 99 ff.; burial in Hebron, 35, 111; his bier, 108, 114; merits of his shrine, 37, 118 ff., 120, 121; sleeping place of, 97; his wives and descendants, 98 f. (*see also* Hagar, Sarah); his hospitality, 86, 100, 121 ff.; 127 f., 135; his piety and obedience, 86, 121 f., 136; chapters on his qualities, 133 ff.; to be clothed at Judgment, 128 f.;

his palace in Paradise, 129 ff.; companionship of the Just with, 12, 37

Absalom, 147[108]

abu, "father (of)," 154

Abu 'l-'Abbās al-Asamm, 128

Abu 'Abdullah the hāfiz, 128

Abu 'Abd. M b Ahmad al-Bannā', 97, 110, 117

Abu 'Ablah, 25

Abu 'l-Akhwas, 132

Abu 'Amr b al-'Alā', 79

Abu 'Amr b Jābir, 38

Abu 'Amr 'Uthman b Ja'far b Shādhān, 106, 107

Abu 'Āsim, 128

Abu 'l-'Awwām, 7

Abu Ayyūb (al-Ansāri), 5, 133

Abu Bakr al-Ashkāfi, 107 f.

Abu Bakr al-Bazzār, 129

Abu Bakr al-Beihaqi, 128

Abu Bakr b Ahmad, 38

Abu Bakr b Ahmad b Jābir, of Ramleh, 113 f.

Abu Bakr b Faurak, 124

Abu Bekr (or Bakr), first Caliph, 9, 39 f., 119, 125, 141[24], 142[34], 153[88]

Abu Bekr as-Sabbāhi, 97

Abu 'd Dardā', 10

Abu Da'ūd, 5, 13

Abu Dharr (al-Ghaffāri), 3, 135, 139[7]

Abu 'l-Fath M b Ismā'īl al-Farghāni, 109

Abu 'l-Fath Salim ar-Rāzi, 27

Abu Fidā' of Hebron, author The Book of Inciting Desire, xiii, xxii[5], 43

Abu Ghōsh, or village of al-'Aneb, 26, 145[74]

Abu Hāmid, 113 f.

Abu 'l-Hams ar-Rāzi, 114

Abu 'l-Hassan 'Ali . . . al-Wāhidi, 16, 143[48]

Abu 'l-Hassan Mūsā ad-Duweiri, 120

Abu 'l-Hassan Musa . . . ad-Dauri, 114 f.

Abu 'l-Hassan b Muslim, 12

Abu Hātim b Hayyān, 131

Abu Hudheifah (or Hudhaifah), 21

Abu Hudheifah Ishāq b Bishr, 105

Abu Hureirah (or Hurairah), 10, 15, 23, 25, 28, 34, 82, 118, 129, 130, 131, 134

Abu 'l-Husein b Abu Bakr al-Bannā', 117

Abu b Ibrāhīm, 25

Abu Idrīs al-Khaulāni, 15, 135

Abu Ishāq al-Bukhturi, 16, 143[47]

Abu Ishāq ash-Shirāzi, 140[12]

Abu 'l-Ma'ali al-Mushrif (or al-Musharrif) b al-Murajja, author of one of the sources of The Book of Arousing Souls: 1, 12, 14, 16, 17, 18, 19, 34, 66, 139[8]

Abu 'l-Muhājir, 10

Abu Na'īm (or Nu'aim), 126, 127, 129

Abu 'Obeidah (or 'Ubaidah) 'Āmir b al-Jarrāh, one of conquerors of Syria-Palestine, 34, 40, 147[101]

Abu 'Othmān, 18

Abu 'l-Qāsim (Mohammed the Prophet), 71, 150[35]

Abu 'l-Qāsim al-Makki, 102

Abu Qubeis, Mount, 75, 76

Abu Sa'id al-Khudri, 4, 16, 90, 97

Abu 's-Sakan al-Hijri, 102

Abu Sālih, 93

Abu Tufeil, 82

Abu Umāmah al-Bāhili, 11, 27

Abu 'Uqbah 'Abd. al-Marwari, 97

Abu 'l-Walīd b Hammād, 105

Abu Zar'ah, 109

Abu Zeinūr, 113

Abyssinia, or Ethiopia, xviii

Acco, and Acre, see 'Akka

Adam: 4, 45, 90, 91, 123, 126; rebellion and fall of, 90 f.; 142[32]; in Hind (India) and Palestine, 30, 32, 33, 75, 77; revelations to, 46, 135; father of mankind, 46; buried in Hebron (?), 67, 103; coffin of, 105; first to worship at Mecca, 75, 77; built the Ka'bah, 77; his stature, 105

'Aden, 143[53]

adhān, call to prayer: 13, 20, 50, 106, 142[38]; see also mu'ezzin and Glossary

Adler, Cyrus, on "Wailing Wall", xxiv[7]

Aelia, or Jerusalem, 66, 142[41]

'Afrūn, see Ephron

Agada (or Hagada, or Haggadah), xx

Āgar, see Hagar

ahl adh-dhimmah, non-Muslim subjects, 148[123]

ahl al-kitab, people having Scriptures, xvii, xviii, xxi, 78, 84

Ahmad, or Mohammed the Prophet, 134, 153[93]

Ahmad b Hanbal, *see* Ibn Hanbal

Ahmad b Khalaf al-Hamdāni, 26

Ahmad b M b Ka'b, 21

Ahwāz, 47

'Ā'ishah, *see* Āyeshah

'ajwah date, 14

al-'Ajūz, " old woman," 117; cf. 115 f.

'Akka, 23

'Akramah, 62, 84, 86, 96, 130

Aleppo (Ar: Halab), 106

Alexander, believing king, 48, 149[6]

Alexandria, Egypt, 23

'Ali b Abu Tālib, Fourth Caliph, Shī'ite martyr: 12, 14, 25, 27, 34, 40, 60, 76, 84, 115, 128, 129, 130, 142[40]

'Ali b al-Husein, 3, 130

Allah (God), ninety-nine beautiful names of, 99, 147[99]; the Creator, free from finiteness, 125; et passim

almsgiving, merit of, 14, 16, 20, 33

Amalek, son of Methuselah, 46

Amalekites, 69

American Council of Learned Societies, xxx

American School of Oriental Research, xv

'Ammār b as-Sāji, 106

'Amr b al-'Āsi, conqueror of Egypt, 10, 142[28]

'Amr b Qeis, 128

Anas b Mālik, 5, 10, 29, 85, 90, 126, 140[14]

Anastasis, or Church of Holy Sepulchre, xxviii

Ancient (or Everlasting) House, in Paradise, 133

al-'Aneb, or Abu Ghōsh, 26

Angel (s): interceding in Jerusalem, 5, 11, 26, 34; at Well of the Leaf, 24; encompassing Mecca, 27; surround Jerusalem, 28, 30, 33, bow to Adam, 46; in idol temple, 49; at birth and commissioning of Abraham, 50 f.; save Abraham from fire, 59 f.; visit him in Hebron, 67, 85, 86 ff.; guide Adam to Mecca, 75; build the Ka'bah, 77; around Joseph, 90; of the Haram in Mecca, 97; 120, 127; *see also* Gabriel, Israfel, Mālik, Michael

Angel of Death, and Abraham, 100 ff.

Angels of the Tomb, 37, 148[112]

annunciation: of John to Zechariah, 30; of Jesus to Mary, 33; of Isaac to Abraham and Sarah, 30, 85, 86, 93

Ansār, "Helpers", 128; *see also* Glossary

Anti-Christ (Ar: *ad-Dajjal*), 31, 33, 63

Apocrypha of New Testament, 144, 146[88]; *see also* Pseudepigrapha

Apostle of Allah, *see* Mohammed

al-Aqsa, Mosque, in Temple Area, Jerusalem: xxii, 1, 2 f., 4, 32, 134, 139[4], 143[52], 145[68]; devotions in, 19 f.; *see also* Jerusalem, Night-Journey, Temple Area

Arabia: see Arabians, Arabs, Hajj, Hejāz, Ka'bah, Mecca, Medina, Mohammed

Arabians, xviii, xxix

Arabic, Ishmael learns, from Jurham, 73

Arabic names, *see* names in Arabic

Arabs of Palestine, xxix f.

Arabs: Shem father of, 46; *see also* Ishmael

'Arafah, or 'Arafāt: Mount, 16; Day of "Recognition," 81

al-A'raj, 95

Aramaic, 141[18], 153[97]

A'rāq ath-Thārā, appellation of Ishmael

Archives de l'Orient Latin, xiv[2]

Ark of the Covenant, 30, 152[74]

Ark, of Noah, 45

Armenians, descendants of Isaac (!), 84

Arphaxad, 45

ascension: of Jesus, 20, 30; of Mohammed, 20 (*see also* Night-Journey); of Enoch or Idrīs, 46

al-Asbagh b Nabānah, 130

Ascalon, see Asqalon

'Āshūrā', in month of Moharram, 149[3]

al-'Āsi b ar-Rabī', 95

al-Asma'i, philologist, of Basrah, died 828, 79

Asqalon, merits of, as border city, xii, 23, 145[69]

astrologers, 48

Atiyah, Prof. A. S., historian, xxii f.

'Atīyyah b Qeis, 23

'Attā' or 'Atā' (b Abu Ribāh), 84, 85, 89

Aus (or Aws) b Shaddād, 45

authentication of tombs of Patriarch-Prophets, 109

al-awā'il, "the beginnings", xiii, 44 ff.

'Āyeshah (properly, 'Ā'ishah), wife of the Prophet, 27, 146[78]

Ayyūb b 'Utbah, 47

Āzar (or Terah), father of Abraham, 44 ff., 52, 53, 63, 92, 149[7]

al-Azraqi, earlier historian, died 9th century: 3

Baalbek, see Ba'labakk

Babel, or Babylon, 47, 63, 92, 146[79]; Tower of, 150[19]; see also Abraham, Iraq, Kūthā-rabba

Baghdad, 139[8], 147[104]

al-Baghawi, Koran commentator: 52, 55, 80, 85, 86, 88, 94, 95, 121

Ba'labakk, 64, 120, 121

balā', "test, trial", 83

al-Baqar, spring in 'Akka, 34

Barclay's Gate, Jerusalem, 144[60]

Baron d'Anglure, Ogier, xxv

Barzah, 48

basmalah, "in the name of Allah", etc., 38, 40, 139[1]

Basrah, 142[33]

Bathsheba, and David, 144[58]

bedouin and the Prophet, 115 f.

Beershebah (or Shebah; Ar: Bi'r as-Sab'), 63; Abraham and the people of, 66 f., 103, 150[27]

"beginnings, the," al-awā'il, xiii

Behā' ud-Dīn, see Ibn 'Asākir

al-Beihaqi, 7 f., 134

Beirut, 120

Beisān, or Bethshan, 23, 145[70]

Beit 'Ein (or 'Ain) of Hebron, 40

Beit Ibrāhīm, of Hebron, 40

Beit Jibrīl (or Jibrīn), 39, 148[118]

Bernard, J. H., on pilgrimage literature, xxvii

Bethlehem (Ar: Beit Lahm): Saint Jerome in, xxv; merits of, 2, 8, 10, 110, 118

Bethshan, see Beisān

Bethuel, father of Rebecca, 98

Bible: unhistorical nature of some material in, xix f., 149[2]; purported quotations from, 6 f., 17, 25, 28, 31; memory quotations in, 146[85]; 135, 140[10], 143[43]

Biblical characters in the Koran, xviii f.,

31, 140[11]; and see Patriarchs, Abraham, and other familiar names

Biblical names, 149[2]

"Biblical" religions, xxi; see also ahl al-kitāb

Biblioteca Geographorum Arabicorum (ed. De Goeje), xxvi

Bibliothèque Nationale, Paris, xii

Bilāl, mu'ezzin of the Prophet, 32, 147[96]

bint, see Glossary

birds, guide people to water, 71, 73

Black Marble, in Dome of the Rock, 18, 143[53]

Black Stone, of the Ka'bah in Mecca: 68, 74; cause of blackness, 75, 76; witness of divine covenant, 77; and at Judgment, 76

Book: the Koran, 23; "people of the —," see ahl al-kitāb

Book of Brides, Stories of the Prophets by ath-Tha'labi, xiii[1]

books sent down or revealed, see revelation

Bordeaux Pilgrim, xxv, xviii

Brockelmann's history of Arabic literature, xiii[1]

al-Bukhāri, Traditionist, 2, 3, 4, 60, 65, 69, 70, 89, 90, 131, 133, 139[7], 153[88]

bull, or ox, and coffin of Adam, 105

al-Burāq, divine steed: and the "Wailing Wall," xxiv[7], xxviii, 141[21], 144[60]; and the Prophet's Night-Journey, 7 f., 11, 20, 30, 134; and Abraham, 80; 151[47]

Burhān ad-Dīn, see Ibn al-Firkāh

burials, of modern Muslims in Palestine, xxix

Byzantine(s) or Eastern Roman(s), xvii, xxiv f., 5, 147[108], 148[117]

Cain (Ar: Qābīl), 45, 149[5]

calf, of Abraham, 86, 103

Caliph(s), 142[34], 148[122], 152[82]; see also Glossary

call to prayer, see adhān

Canaan, or Palestine, 110, 111

Canaan, son of Cush, 48

Canaan, Dr. Tewfik of Jerusalem, on folk-religion, xxvi[9]

Carmoly, E., on pilgrimage literature, xxvi

catapult (Ar: manjanīq), for Abraham, 59

Catholic Church, or Western Christianity, xxv; see also Crusades cave: (and field) of Machpelah in Hebron, xiv, 97, 102 ff., 107 ff., 110, 114; cave of Abraham's birth, 50 f.

ceremonies of Islam, *see* rites, Hajj, pilgrimage, etc.

ceremonies of pilgrimage: in Palestine, 16, 19 f., 26, 32, 37 f., 145[75]; traditional origin of Meccan, 69 f., 77 f.

Cervantes, 144[62]

Chain, the, in Temple Area: 16, 30; story of, 21, 144[62]; Dome of the, 2, 21

Children (or Tribes) of Israel: evil and idolatry among, 21; forgiveness or banishment by, 22; settlement in land of Jerusalem, 31; 115; *see also* Jews, Hebrews

Christ, *see* Jesus

Christians, xxi, 124, 126; *see also* ahl al-kitāb

Christian pilgrimage to Palestine, xxiv, 145[70]

chronology, popular schemes of, 3 f., 44 f., 68, 75, 112, 113, 152[82]; *see also* folklore, and life, lengthy, of the ancients.

circuit or circumambulation of shrines (Ar: tawāf), xxii, 3, 16, 26, 75, 77, 145[75]

circumcision: 128, 129, 130 ff., 136; female, from example of Hagar, 68, 150[31]

cities, chosen of Allah, 23, 28, 32, 33, 34

Cities of the Plain, or "the Overthrown," 86, 103; 151, notes 63 and 66

clitoridectomy, *see* circumcision, female

clouds: from Rock of Jerusalem, 15; of Judgment, 30; of the Shekinah, 76

cocks; crowing of heard in Heaven, 96, 103

coffin: of Adam, 105; of Joseph, 115 f.

Companions of the Prophet, 38, 78, 84, 119, 123, 142[37]; *see also* Glossary

confusion of tongues, 63

Constantine, Byzantine emperor, xxiv, xxv

Copt(s), Coptic, 98, 128, 129; *see also* Hagar

cosmology, popular ideas of, 31, 147[91]; *see also* creation, and Paradise, rivers of

"Counter-Crusade," xxii f.

Cradle of Jesus, 146[88]

creation: order of cities, 27, 33; from water, 27; of Adam, 46; of the place of the Ka'bah, 75; to be turned to dust, 30

Crucifixion, denied by Muslims, 141[20]

Crusader(s) and Crusades: xxii; motivation of, xxiii; influence on Western civilization, xxv; 139[8]; 145[69]; 147[108]; *see also* "Counter-Crusade"

curse, or invoke evil upon, 35, 120 f.

Cush, son of Shem, 48

ad-Dajjāl, *see* Anti-Christ

dahakat, 86

ad-Dahhāk, 85

Damascus: capital of Omayyad empire, xii; merits of mosque in, 12; among chosen cities, 23, 28; tradition of Abraham's birth there, 47; 122, 139 notes 2 and 8

Dante, 141[23]

Dār as-Salām, *see* Paradise

ad-Dāraqutni, Traditionist, died 995; 13

Dāri, the, from whom the descendants of Tamīm ad-Dāri, xv, 38 f.

darkness, of Judgment Day, 30

dauhah, " tree," 69

David: conqueror of Jerusalem, xix; enlarged its shrine, 4, 12; companionship of the Just with Solomon and, 12; his prayer, 17; in the Koran, 20; his chain of judgment, 21; his kingdom and powers, 30, 32; 102, 112, 147[94]; 149[6]

dates, *see* 'ajwah

death: sudden, of the pious, 102; Angel of, and Abraham, 100 ff.

death and burial, merit of in Jerusalem and Palestine, 25 f., 34

De Goeje, Dutch Arabist, xii, xxvi

De Slane, tr. and ed. Ibn Khallikān, xxiii, 140[9]

devils, 49; *see also* Satan

devotional sincerity of pilgrims, xxviii, 5, 6, 7, 11, 19, 20

devotions, *see* ceremonies, rites, pilgrimage, prayer

dew, of Jerusalem, 28, 33

Dhu 'l-Asābi', 4

Dhu 'l-Qarnein, 112; and *see* Alexander

dirham, *see* Glossary

diviners, 48; *see also* magicians

divinity of Jesus, 141[20]

divorce, 73

dogs, of Lot's people, 96

Dome of the Ascension, 18

Dome of the Rock; 2; built by 'Abd al-Malik, xxii; modern guides to, xxvi, xxix; Solomon's prayer in, 6; Solomon and key of, 17; Black Marble in, 18, 143[53]; distinguish from Mosque al-Aqsa, 143[52]

Dome of the Prophet, 18

dreams, 16, 26, 48 f., 80, 81, 84, 85, 91, 113, 115, 117, 152[80]; see also folklore

dust, all creatures to be turned to, 30

eagles, of Nimrod, 62

Ebal, Mount, 146[83]

Eber, 45

Egypt: story of the deceased from, 26; Abraham in, 63, 92; Jacob in, 89, 91; 98, 110, 118; cloth of, 128, 142[28]; see also Copts

Eisenberg, ed. lives of the prophets, xiii[1]

Elias, or al-Khidr or Saint George, see Elijah

Eliezer, Abraham's steward, 149[7]

Elijah (al-Khidr, Saint George, 14, 18, 142[39], 143[53]

Enoch, or Idrīs, 46

Ephron, sells cave and field to Abraham: xix, 67, 103, 111; see also king (of Hebron), Machpelah

equivocation of the truth, 57 f., 64

Esau (Ar: al-'Is), 35, 36, 88, 98, 104

Ethiopia, see Abyssinia

ethnology, popular, 46 f., 84; see also folklore

etymology, popular, 46, 65, 66, 80, 81, 86 f., 90, 92, 96, 132, 145[72], 153[92]; see also folklore

Eucharist, or "the Table," 12, 30

Eudocia, xxv

Euphrates, 23; see also Paradise, rivers . . . of

Evangel, or New Testament (Ar: injīl), 135

Eve, 91

al-Farra', 3, 139[8]

fasting, merit of, 12, 14, 33; see also Ramadān

al-Fātihah, first sūrah or chapter of the Koran, 11

Fātimah, daughter of the Prophet, wife of 'Ali, mother of Hasan and Husein, 125

fatrah, 47

fadā'il, see merits

Faris, N. A., xx

female circumcision, 68, 150[31]

Fidā', see Abu 'l-Fidā'

figs, of Damascus, 23

fire, Abraham rescued from, 36, 52, 55 f.; see also Hell

fish: upholding the earth, 31 and 147[91]; in the sky, 62

Flood, the, 32, 45, 75, 77, 146[86]; see also Noah

Flügel, concordance to Koran, 146[87]

folklore, and popular religion and custom: xxvi[9], xxviii f.; precedents from Abraham, 136 f.; 141[21], 145[73], 147[91], 149[6]; see also: Adam, life (lengthy, of ancients), chronology, circumcision, cosmology, ethnology, etymology, giant, Gog and Magog, lizard miracles, she-mule, skirt (trailing), threshold

Followers, 78, 84, 142[38]; see also Glossary

fountains or springs, the chosen, 23, 34

forgiveness, by merits of Jerusalem, 11 f., 13 ff., 16, 20, 22, 31, 32, 33, 37; Gate of, 19

Fosdick, Harry Emerson, on Hebron mosque, xiv[2]

Frequented House, see Paradise

Friend of Allah, see Abraham

frontiers, merit of serving on, xii, 23, 145[69]

al-Fulūs, spring or fountain in Beisān, 34

fūsīq, the big lizard (proper form?): 60

Gabriel the Angel (Ar: jabrā'īl; popular, Jibrīl), with the Prophet on the Night-Journey, xxviii, 8 f., 15, 20, 32, 34, 35, 90, 118, 133, 134; with Abraham, 59 f., 67, 68, 70, 85, 104, 124, 132; at Mecca, 68 ff., 76, 83; and the Black Stone, 75; 43, 51, 91, 93, 103

Garrett Collection, Princeton University, xxiii[6]

Gates, in Jerusalem, 19, 20; see also Temple Area

Gehenna, Valley of, see Hell

genealogy, 149[2]

Gerezim, Mount, 146[83]

Gethsemane, 25 f., 145[73a]

ghāra 'l-mā', 66

Ghautah of Damascus, 47

giant, or mighty man, king: in Harrān, 36, 68, 98, 99; *see also* Ephron, Nimrod, Pharaoh

Gibeon, 140[16]; 152[79]

Gihon, river of Paradise, 23

Ginzberg, Louis, *Legends of the Jews,* xviii[4], 140[11], 141[19], 149[2], 153[91]

gnats, and the people of Nimrod, 61

goat, substituted for the sacrificed one, 83

God, the names of, 99, 147[99]

Gog and Magog (Ar: *Yājūj* and *Mājūj*), 30, 46, 146[89]

Greek Orthodox Christianity, xxv; *see also* Byzantine(s)

Greek(s): 5, 36; sons of Shem (!), 46; sons of Isaac (!), 84; inscriptions in Greek at Hebron, 106

grey hairs, of Abraham, 130 f.

Guidance, the Divine (Ar: *al-Furqān* = the Koran), 135

habib, "beloved," 125; cf. *muhabbah*

Habra, and Habrūn, *see* Hebron

Hadith, see Tradition, and same in Glossary

hāfiz, see Glossary

Hagada, *see* Agada

Hagar, 65, 67, 68 ff., 80, 98, 150[26]

Hajj, *see* pilgrimage

al-Hajjāj b Yūsuf, 78, 79

Ham, son of Noah, 45 f.

hamīd, "praised," 87

Hamīd b Zanjaweih, 105

Hamor, of Shechem, xix

Hanauer, J. E., *Folklore of Palestine,* 147[91]

hanif, "rightly inclined," a sincere religious seeker, 122, 136, 137, 153[97]

Haram, see Glossary

Haram, of Hebron, 108 f.

Haram of Mecca (or *Beit Allah al-Haram*), 97; *see also* Mecca

al-Haram ash-Sharīf, see Temple Area (in Jerusalem)

Haran, brother of Abraham, 44, 63, 64, 86, 92, 98, 148[109], 149[2]; *see also* Harrān

Helena, xxv

harem, behind dividing curtain of tent, 86; *see also* haram

Harrān, in Syria, 36, 44 f., 63, 64, 92, 148[109], 149[2]

al-Hasan (son of 'Ali?), 25, 57, 76, 96

al-Hasan al-Basri, grammarian, traditionist, died 728; 14, 78, 142[38]

al-Hasan b 'Abd al-Wāhid b Risq ar-Rāzi, 109

al-Hasan b al-Mufaddil, 95

al-Hauqali, *see* Ibn Hauqal

al-Haushabi, 16

healing, 6, 33, 117

Heaven, *see* Paradise

Hebrew, 89; *see also* Jews

Hebrew conquest, xix, 145[64]

Hebron (Arabic usually:—(Madinat) al-Khalil); second shrine city in Palestine after Jerusalem, xiii; home of Abu 'l-Fidā', second author, xiii; shrine built by Solomon, 36, 111 f.; sanctity, and merits of pilgrimage to, 4, 37, 115, 120, 121; assigned by the Prophet to the Dāri, xv[3], 38; Abraham in, 67 f., 103 ff.; Abraham buried in, 35, 36, 120; visits to and visions of tombs in, 106 ff., 113 ff., 120 f.; gardens of, 110

Hegirah, *see* Hijrah

Heizan the Kurd, 58

Hejāz or Hijāz, cradle-land of Islam, xi, xxii, xxix; 99, 145[75]

Hell: avoided by merits of Jerusalem, 5, 11, 14, 33, 34; and by professing the unity of God, 85; the evil to be committed to, 6; in Jerusalem, 8 f., 19, 22, 29, 30, 31, 32; 144[55], 146[86]

Helpers, *see* Glossary

Hind, or India, 30, 75, 77

Hijāz, *see* Hejāz

al-Hijr, in Arabia, 68, 98

Hijrah: of Mohammed, 40, 44, 47, 112, 141[18], 152[83]; of Abraham, 63, 64 ff.; *see also* Glossary

Himām b Munabbih, 119

Hirā', Mount, 76

Hitti, P. K., xvi, 140[9], 148[109]

Holy Spirit, given to Jesus, 32

hospitality, of Abraham, 121 ff.

Houris of Paradise, 21, 144[62a]

House of Allah, *see* Ka'bah, Mecca

Hūd, ancient prophet, 48, 106, 149[7]; sūrah of, 79

Hudheifah, 25

humility, on pilgrimage, 122

Husein, grandson of the Prophet, martyr, 149[3]; see also Shī'ites

Husein, former king of the Hejāz, xxix

al-Husein b al-Fādil, 83

Iblīs, see Satan

ibn "son," *see* Glossary; abbreviated *within* names in Index as "b"

Ibn 'Abbās, cousin of the Prophet, Companion, traditionist: 3, 4, 11, 12, 21, 25, 28, 36, 47, 62, 68, 70, 71, 72, 76, 77, 78, 81, 32, 83, 84, 85, 86, 93, 94, 95, 112, 115, 118, 121, 123, 127, 128, 132, 133

"Ibn Abu Kabshah," slanderous nickname of the Prophet, 9, 141[25]

Ibn Abu Khutheimah, 46

Ibn 'Amr, 29, 105

Ibn 'Asākir, Abu 'l-Qāsim, historian, 47, 100, 134, 139[8]

Ibn 'Asākir, Behā' ud-Dīn, author of *al-Mustaqsa,* one of the sources, 1, 3, 12, 29, 44, 46, 85, 103, 105, 107, 111, 113, 115, 120, 121, 127, 128, 130, 131, 132, 139[8]

Ibn Batīsh, 140[12]

Ibn al-Firkāh, al-Fazāri, author of *The Book of Arousing Souls:* xxii[5], 1, 40, 139[8]

Ibn Hanbal, founder of Hanbalite school of Islamic law, 128, 147[99]; *see also* Wahhābi(s)

Ibn Hauqal, geographer, 110, 152[78]

Ibn Hayyān, 132

Ibn Ishāq, biographer of the Prophet: 48, 51, 59, 65, 81, 82, 87, 95, 98

Ibn Jarīr, 134

Ibn al-Jureij, 94

Ibn Kathīr, historian, 110

Ibn Khallikān, author of a great biographical dictionary, xxiii, 140 notes 9 and 11

Ibn Mājah, traditionist, 7

Ibn Mas'ūd, Companion, 84, 134

Ibn al-Murraja, *see* Abu 'l-Ma'āli

Ibn 'Omar, Companion, 13, 58

Ibn Sa'ūd, king of Arabia, 145[75]

Ibn Taymīyyah, 147[99]

Ibn Ubeyy Aufi, 118

Ibn Wahb, 133

Ibn Yassār, 60

Ibn Zarārah, 118

Ibn az-Zubeir, *see* 'Abdullah—

Ibrāhīm, *see* Abraham

Ibrāhīm b Ahmad al-Khalanji, 116 f.

Ibrāhīm b Mihrān, 18

idol(s), 49 f., 56, 89, 123

Idrīs, *see* Enoch

Ignorance, time of, *see Jahilīyyah*

ihrām, " purification, taboo," and garment denoting, 2, 13 f., 142[35]; *see also* Glossary

Illīyah, *see* Leah

'Imād ud Dīn b Kathīr, 110

imām, "leader," 4, 40; Mohammed as, for the prophets, 20, 32, 134, 143[45]; Abraham as, 126, 135; *see also* Glossary

Imām Yahya, of Yemen, 143[53]

'Imrān, father of Miriam (and of Moses and Aaron), 15; the wife of 'Imrān, 32

India, *see* Hind

inscriptions, of tombs in Hebron, 105, 106

intercession: merit of, in Jerusalem, 12; *see also* Angels, forgiveness, merits

Iran(ian), 140 notes 9 and 17; 141[21]; *see also* Persia(n), Persians

Iraq (Ar: 'Irāq), ancient Mesopotamia: 35, 92, 145[75], 147[104], 149[4]; *see also* Abraham, Babel, Kūthārabba

Irving, Washington, 140[17]

'Isā b Maryam, *see* Jesus

Isaac (Ar: Ishāq), 31, 35, 37, 38, 68; the sacrificed one(?), 78 f., 84 ff., annunciation of, 85 ff.; life of, 98 f.; blind, 98 f., 152[68]; 91, 99, 100, 102, 104, 106, 111, 114, 114, 118, 120, 147[93], 151[51]

Islam: strength of, xi, xxi; scholars and literary men of, xxi; 95, 104, 132, 140[9]; church and state in 146[81]; marriage in, 151[65]; 153[88]; sources and background of, xvii f., 140[11], and *see also* ceremonies, rites, Koran, Mohammed, and the Glossary

Ishmael (Ar: Ismā'īl): traditional ancestor of northern Arabs, xiv, 3, 69, 79; builder of the Ka'bah with Abraham, xiv, 3, 68 f.; his birth, 65, 68; his life, 67 ff.,

98; the sacrificed one (?), 78 ff.; 89, 99, 106, 131

Ismā'īl b Abu Krālid, 129

isnād, chain of reference in Tradition, 1, 139[3]

Israel: name of Jacob, 37, 88; *see also* Children of—

Israfel, Angel, 16, 31, 85, 93

Istakhr, 112

Istakhri, geographer, 152[78]

'Iyād, a judge, author of *Kitāb ash-Shifa'*: 123, 124

Jabal Abu Qubeis, at Mecca, 75, 76

Jabbour, J., xxiii[6]

Jābir b 'Abdullah, 13, 142[37]

Jabrā'īl *see* Gabriel

Jacob (Ar: Ya'qūb): 35, 36, 37, 85, 86, 87 ff., 91 ff., 98, 104, 106, 107; his bier, 108, 113; 111, 117, 118, 120, 151[56], 152[79]; *see also* Israel

Jael and Sisera, 141[22]

Ja'far b Musāfir, 26

Jaffa (Biblical Joppa), 120, 152[80]

al-Jāhilīyyah, the time of "ignorance" of true religion before Islam, 75, 150[39]

Jamāl ad-Dīn Ahmad, of Jerusalem, author of another *Muthīr*, xxiii[6]

al-Janad, in Yemen, 4, 140[13]

Japheth (Ar: Yāfāt), son of Noah, 46

al-Jazīrah, province, 45, 76, 149[4]

jebel, "mountain," *see jabal* and Mount—

Jehoshaphat, Valley of, see Valley of the Kidron, Judgment Path

Jeremiah, 146[83]

Jericho, 145[63]

Jeroboam, king of Israel (example of state manipulation of religion, I Kings 12.26 f.), xxii, 144[62a]

Jerome, Saint, xxv

Jesse, father of David, 112

Jupiter, star, 53

Jerusalem (Ar: *al-Quds ash-Sharīf*): sanctity to Muslims, xi, 13, Roman *Aelia*, xxiv; the Prophet's Night-Journey to, xxviii, 7 f., 118; merits of, 4, 6, 10, 23, 24, 28, 133, 134; paved by David and Solomon with silver and gold, 12; waters and rivers of, 15, 23 f., 29, 30, 34; the

Judgment in, 6, 16, 29, 63, 144[55], 146[86]; created after Mecca and Medina, 27; in the Koran, 21, 29; first *qiblah* of the Prophet, 18, 30, 137, 143[52]; all believers to go there, 32; discomforts of, 33, 34, 147[98], protected from Anti-Christ, 33; Isaac buried there, 84; Adam buried there, 105; 106, 111, 139[8], 143[52], 145[63]; *see also* Dome of the Rock, pilgrimage, Temple Area, and Biblical characters connected with Jerusalem. (In devotional literature, often means Palestine in general.)

Jesus, son of Mary (Ar: *'Īsā b Maryam*): in the Koran, xviii, 32, 141[20]; xix; on pilgrimage to Jerusalem, xxiv; Mohammed honors, 8, 10, 32, 143[45] (e); born in Jerusalem, 30, 145[65]; to slay Anti-Christ, 31; miracles of, 32; return for Judgment, 63; abrogates law of Moses, 112; "brother" of Mohammed, 118; word and spirit of Allah, 32, 123, 141[20]; 139[3]; 143[45], 146[81], 152[80]; *see also* divinity of—

Jethro, or Shu'eib, 8, 141[19]; *see also* Midian

Jewish Church, History of the, xiv[2]

Jews and Judaism: xvii, xviii; excluded from Roman Palestine, xxiv; pilgrimages of, xxiv; contend the sacrificed one was Isaac, 79, 84; Jewish convert, 79; worshipped idols, 89; 112, 124, 136, 139 notes 3 and 10; 149 notes 2 and 3; later Pseudepigraphical literature of, 153[94]; Jewish history, 44, 68; *see also* Children of Israel, and Islam, sources and background of

Jews, Legends of the, see Ginzberg

Jibrīl, *see* Beit—

jihād, "holy war," xxiii, 11

jinn, spirits, conceived of as good or bad: aid Solomon, 17; in Jerusalem, 30; and the fire of Abraham, 59; built Hebron shrine, 110, 112

Joab, conqueror of Jerusalem for David, xix

John the Baptist, xxviii, 30; given wisdom in childhood, 32, 149[15]

Jordan, river, 30; region of, 35, 36, 92

Joseph (Ar: Yūsuf): reputed tomb at Hebron, 33, 116 ff., 152[82]; truthfulness,

58; life of, 89 ff.; description of, 91; 106, 151 notes 58 and 59

Judah, 112

Judgment, after Resurrection: 6, 15, 25, 28, 30, 31, 33; Black Stone to witness at, 76; 120, 143[46], 146[86]

Judgment Path or Bridge (Ar: as-Sirāt): 11, 25, 31, 144[55]; see also Glossary

Jūdi, Mount, 45, 76, 120

Jurham, tribe, 71, 72, 98

Justinian, xxv

Ka'b al-Ahbar, Jewish convert, source of traditions: xxi, 3, 5, 6, 15, 16, 20, 21, 24, 25, 28, 35, 36, 37, 59, 60, 62, 66, 82, 84, 90, 100, 102, 103, 111, 112, 119, 120, 140[10]

Ka'b b al-Mālik, 98

Ka'bah, in Mecca: central shrine of Islam, xiv, xxii, 3, 14, 27; traditionally built by Abraham and Ishmael, xiv, 3, 68 ff., 75 ff.; ceremonies of the Hajj at, xxii, 16, 75, 145[75]; built by Angels, 77; a ruby from Paradise, 75, 77; horns of the goat in, 79, 83; history of, 78; see also Hajj, haram, Mecca

Kafar-Barīk, Lot buried in, 97

al-Kalbi, 78, 86, 89

Kai-Kaus, 150[20]

al-Karāshi, 116

Kerbelah and Najaf, Shī'ite shrine cities, 145[75]

Khadījah, first wife of the Prophet, 142[26], 146[78]

Khālid b Ma'dān, 23, 28

al-Khalīl, or Khalīl Allāh, "the Chosen Friend of Allah," (see Abraham); meaning of, 88, 124 f., 139[6]; see also Hebron

al-Khattābi, 4

al-Khidr, or Saint George, see Elijah

khillah, see al-Khalīl, meaning of

Khorasān, 117

Khuleid b Du'laj, 6, 25

khutbah, "sermon," 146[81]

Kidron, see Valley of the—

king: of Hebron, 35; the first, Nimrod, 48; kings of whole earth, believing and heathen, 48, 112; see also giant, pharaoh

kingdom: of David, 32; of Solomon, 6, 33, 112; of Allah, 34; of Nimrod, 48 ff.

Khanūkh, see Enoch

al-Kisā'i, author of lives of the prophets: xiv[1], 57, 76; see also ath-Tha'labi

Kohut Fellowship, at Yale University, xxx

Koran (Ar: Qur'ān): indebtedness to Hebrew and Christian Scriptures and popular sources, xvii f., xx f.; revealed partly in Palestine, 27; elliptical and dramatic style of, xviii; "memory quotations" from, 146[85]; Flügel's concordance to, 146[87]; 92, 123; translators of, see Bibliography; see also al-Fātihah, and various Biblical characters

Koreish (Ar: Qureish), tribe of Mohammed, 9, 141[23], 143[52]

Krenkow, F., xv[2]

Kūfah, of Iraq, 27, 130, 146[79]

Kūtha, or Kūthārabba, in ancient Babylon, modern Iraq: Abraham migrated from, 30, 35, 47 f., 63, 103

labbeika! the pilgrim's cry, 78, 151[40]

al-Lajjūn, 66, 103, 150[28]

La Monte, J. L., on Crusades, xxiii

Landberg Collection at Yale University, xi

law: of Moses, established by Solomon and abrogated by Christ, 112; of Islam, shar' or sharī'ah, 11, 148[124]

Law, the (Ar: at-taurāt), = the Old Testament, 31, 135

Leaf, Cistern or Pool of the, see Well of the—

Leah (Ar: Illīya or Līya): 35, 37, 104, 106, 107, 111, 120

learned, the (Ar: 'ulemā', plural of 'ālim): 5, 45, 78, 84, 91, 103, 105, 109, 113, 114, 121, 138[8], 140[9]

learning, merit of, 5

leban (properly laban), milk, and in some regions curded milk: 8, 76, 134, 141[22]

Lebanon, Mount, 76

Legends of the Jews, see Ginzberg

legends, popular, see folklore

Legio, see al-Lajjūn

Le Strange, Sir Guy, xiv, xxii, xxvi; on shrines in Temple Area, 145[67]

life: lengthy of the ancients, 36, 44 f., 61,

68, 84, 87, 88, 92, 98, 99, 102, 110, 115 f.; parable of life, 45

light, as divine manifestation, 20, 28, 29, 32, 36, 48, 49, 111, 112

lighting lamps, merit of, 5, 6, 14

living in Jerusalem, merits of, 28, 29, 33, 24

Lïya, see Leah

lizard, the transgressor, 59

Lot (Ar: Lūt): 21, 36, 48; believes through Abraham, 63, 64; destruction of his people, 86, 92 ff., 103, 151[63]; his tomb near Hebron, 97 f.; his wife, 87, 94 f.

Lot, Sea of, = the Dead Sea

love: of Allah toward Abraham, 123 ff.; of the Prophet for his family, 125

Machpelah, see cave and field of—

magicians, 49, 96; see also diviners

Magog, see Gog and Magog

Mahaliel, 46

Majīd, "praised," 87

Makhūl, 11, 111

Makki, 111

Makki b 'Abdullah of Jerusalem, 111, 118

Mālik b Anas, founder of Malikite school of Islamic law, 109, 130, 140[14]

Mālik, Angel of the Fire, 30

Mamre, see Hebron, Machpelah

Ma'mūn, 'Abbāsid caliph, 139[8]

man, superior to woman, 38

manjanīq, "catapult," 59

manuscripts and texts, Arabic collections: xi, xii, xiii[1], xv, xvi, xxiii[6], xxvi

Maqrīzi, historian, xv

Marble, the Black, 18, 143[53]

al-Martūm, of Hebron, 40

martyrs and martyrdom, 4, 13, 16; see also 'Ali, Husein, Shī'ites

al-Marwah, 16, 70, 71

Mary, mother of Jesus (Ar: Maryam): in the Koran, 20, 32, 141[20], 152[82]; mihrāb of, 20; favored and brought sustenance, 22, 30, 32, 33; Zechariah cared for, 31; annunciation to, 33, 99; a prophetess, 99; 143[43], 144[57], 152[82]

Masrūq, 84

mats, Hebron known for manufacture of, 39

Mecca (Ar: Makka(tu)): xi, 3, 4, 23, 28; beginnings of the Ka'bah in, xiv, 3; the Prophet's Night-Journey from, 7 f., 31; first of Allah's creation, 28; Abraham and Ishmael in, 68 f., 97, 98; number of prophets in, 68 f., haram of, 97; 139[4]; see also Ka'bah, Hajj, pilgrimage, ceremonies, rites, Mohammed, Zamzam

Medina (Ar: Madīnah): second holiest city in Islam, xi, 2, 4, 23, 28, 32, 40; created after Mecca and before Jerusalem, 27; former name Yathrib, 8, 141[18]; see also Hijrah, Helpers

Meimūn b Mihrān, 77

Meimūnah, wife of the Prophet, 4, 6

"memory quotations" from sacred scriptures, 146[85]

menstruation, 67, 75, 86; see also folklore

"Merits" (Ar: faḍā'il): of Jerusalem and Palestine, xxii, xxiii[6], xxvii; see also birth, death, prayer, fasting, living, almsgiving, pilgrimage, and various place-names

Mesopotamia, see Iraq

messengers, see Angels

Michael, the Angel, (Ar: Mikhā'īl): 32, 67, 85, 93, 103

Michaud, on the Crusades, xxvi

Midian, and trees of Moses, 8, 141[18]

migration, see Hijrah

mihrāb(s), in Temple Area, 19 f.; see also Glossary

millah, in Jerusalem, 145[73a]

Mina, place of Hajj sacrifices, 83, 84, 85; see also ceremonies, rites

minbar, "pulpit," 28, 130, 137, 146[81]

al-Minhal, 128

al-Minhal b 'Omar, 60

miracles, 28, 43, 49, 55, 85; see also names of great characters of religion

mi'rāj, see Night-Journey

Miriam (Ar: Maryam): sister of Moses, 15; mother of Jesus, see Mary; 143[43], 152[82]

miswāk, toothbrush, 137, 153[100]

Mohammed the Prophet (Ar: Muhammad): xvii; his learning partly from Jews and Christians, xvii f., regarded Abraham as founder of his religion, xiv, ff.; as prophet and leader, xxi; relics of, xxviii;

Night-Journey of, 7 f.; slanderous nick-name of, 9, 141[25]; Dome of, in Temple Area, 19; on the Black Stone, 76; on Joseph, 89, 91; on duty of kindness and piety, 97; Gate of, 19 f.; Hijrah of, 44, 141[18]; on story of old woman of Israel, 115 f.; second sight of, 39; on the big lizard, 59 f.; on Abraham and Ishmael, 70, 71, 72, 74, 78; most handsome of men, 91; on the people of Lot, 93; on the Copts, 98; 95, 112, 118, 120, 123, 124, 128, 129, 133, 137; the unlettered prophet, 134, 153[93]; guide to his people, 152[84]; *see* in Glossary Muhammad, Islam.

Mohammedan Saints and Shrines in Palestine, xxvi[9]

Mohammedanism, properly *Islām*, xvii, and Glossary

Moharram (Ar: *Muharram*), first month, 45, 50, 149[3]

Molinier, Augustus, xxvi

Moses (Ar: *Mūsā*): 28, 92; staff of, 34; his mother a prophetess, 99; law of, 112; 113, 115, 116, 123, 141[19], 143[43], 146[83]; Nabi Mūsa festival, xxiv

Moslems, properly *Muslims*: numbers of, xi; veneration of for Palestine, xi, xxi ff., xxvi, xxix f.; 122, 136; *see also* Glossary

Mosque (Ar: *Masjid*): Mosque al-Aqsa, *see* al-Aqsa; of 'Omar, *see* Dome of the Rock; of al-Yaqīn, 67; *see also* cities, by name

mosques, the most sacred, 4 f., 10, 12, 32

Mosul, in Syria, 45

Mt., *see* Mount, and under names

Mount Ohod (near Medina northward), 119[152], 152[83]

Mount of Olives, 2, 6, 17, 18, 20, 21, 25, 76, 120, 142[45]; *see also* as-Sāhirah

Mount Thabīr, near Mecca, 83

mountains: prayer unacceptable on certain, 16, 143[47]; the chosen, 34; the Ka'bah built from five, 76; smoothed for Abraham, 85; those sacred, 120

moustaches, of Abraham, 130

Mu'amil b Ismā'īl, 26

Mu'ādh b Jabal, 28

Mu'āwiyah (b Abu Sufyān), first Omayyad caliph, 28, 40, 80, 146[81], 148[122]

muezzin(s), 13, 21, 32, 142[37]; *see also* adhān, and Glossary

al-Mughār, in Palestine, 66

muhabbah, "friendship, love", 125: cf. *habīb*

Muhammad b 'Abd as-Salām, 122

M b Ahmad an-Nahawi, 106

M b Ahmad . . . al-Anbāri, 107

Muhammad 'Ali, of India, xxix

M b Bakrān b M al-Khatīb, 106, 107, 132

M b Ishāq, *see* Ibn Ishāq

M b Ka'b al-Qarzi (?), 85, 112

M b Shihāb az-Zuhri, 18, 143[52]

M b Shu'eib, 12

Muhammad the Prophet, *see* Mohammed

Muir, Sir William, 153[100]

Mujāhid, 3, 56, 70, 78, 86, 87, 91, 95, 96, 129

al-Muqaddasi, historian, 141[21], 158[118]

Muqātil, 14, 28, 29, 30, 55, 58, 62, 83, 84, 85, 86, 132

Muqātil b Suleimān, 97, 106

al-Muqtadir, 'Abbāsid caliph, 117, 152[82]

al-Mushrif (or al-Musharrif), *see* Abu 'l-Ma'āli

al-Mustari, Jupiter (star), 53

Muslim(s), xvii; *see also* Moslems, Islam, Abraham, Mohammed, Hanīf

Muslim, traditionist, 4, 131, 133, 139[7]

al-Mu'tamir b Suleimān, 129

Muthīr al-Gharām: title of second work in this volume, xi, 43; title of work by Jamāl ad-Dīn Ahmad al-Maqdisi, xxiii[6]

Muwahhidūn of Arabia, 147[99]; *see also* *Wahhābi*(s), Unity of God

mythology 150[20]

Nabi Mūsa festival ("Prophet Moses"), xxiv

Nāfi', 105

Najaf and Kerbalah, 145[75]

Nahor, brother of Abraham, 44, 86

names in Arabic, 154; *see also* etymology, popular

an-Nasā'i, 3, 7, 76, 140[9]

Nāsir-i-Khusraw, Iranian poet, pilgrim, xxvi, 141[21]

Nathan, parable of, 144[58]

Nauf al-Bakāli, 15

an-Nawawi, tradition and jurist, died 1278:
44, 47. 60, 91, 92, 102, 112, 113, 131

Nazarenes, or Christians, 136

Nebuchadnezzar, xii, 48, 112, 149[6]

New Testament, Apocrypha of, 144[59]

Nicholson, R. A., 140[9]

Night-Journey (Ar: *mi'rāj*) of the Prophet:
xxviii. 7 ff., 16, 20, 27, 30, 34, 90, 118,
133, 134, 139[4], 143[45], 140[17], 141[21],
144[62a], 146[76]

Night of Heeding (or reflecting, or of pouring water for animals on eighth day of the
Hajj—popular etymology of Arabic *tar-
wiyah*), 80, 81

Nile, river, 23; Joseph buried in, 92, 115
f., 118

Nimrod (Ar: *Numrūd*): 47, 48; and Abraham, 52 ff., 64; his impious ascent, 62 f.;
see also giant, king, pharaoh

Noah (Ar: *Nūh*), 4, 32, 44, 45, 105

Nuheilan, 18

an-Nuweiri, encyclopedist, died 1332: 49

Obermann, J., xvii f., xx f.

offering, *see* sacrifice

Ogier, Baron d'Anglure, xxv[8]

Ohod, *see* Mount—

old woman of the Children of Israel, 115
f.; cf. 117

olive-gardens (Gethsemane?), 26, 145[73a]

olives, Jerusalem place of, 23

Olivet, *see* Mount of Olives

'Omar (Ar: 'Umar), second caliph: 2, 19;
worshiped in Jerusalem, 20, 144[58]; on the
leaf from Paradise, 23 f.; Oratory of, on
Mount of Olives, 25; authenticated grant
of Hebron, 39 f.; 84, 119, 142[34], 145[71];
Mosque of, in Jerusalem, *see* Dome of
the Rock

'Omar b 'Abd. b al-'Azīz (Omayyad caliph,
"Omar II"), 79

Omayyads, caliphs in Damascus, xii, xxii,
146[81]; *see also* Mu'āwiyah

'Oqbah (Ar: 'Uqbah), Companion, 9

'Othmān (Ar: 'Uthmān) b 'Affān, third
caliph, 40, 142[34]

'Othmān al-Khorasāni, 12

Ottoman (Turkish: *Usmānlu*) Turks, 145[73a]

oven, *see tannūr*

Overthrown Cities, see Cities of the Plain,
Lot

Palacios, Miguel Asín (y), on Dante and
the Night-Journey, 141[23]

Palestine (Ar: *Filastīn* — Jerusalem often
equivalent to): sanctity to Muslims,
Christians, and Jews, xi, xiv, xvi, xvii, xxi,
xxii, xxiii, xxx; Byzantine building up of,
xxiv f.; Muslim conquest of, xxi, xxiv,
xxix f., 4, 39, 147[101]; Muslim and Christian Arabs of, xxi, xxix; pious foundations in, xxix; Zionist and Arab clashes
in, vi, xxiv[7], xxix, 141[21]; 140[17], 142[35];
see also Hebron, Jerusalem, pilgrimage

Palestine Pilgrim Texts Society, xxvi; *see
also* pilgrimage literature, xxvii, xxviii

Palestine Oriental Society, xv[2], xvi

Palestine under the Moslems, see LeStrange

Palestinians, Christians and Muslim Arabs,
xxi, xxix f.

palm tree(s), of Paradise, 15; of Medina, 8,
23; of Mary, 30; *see also* tree(s)

Palmyra, *see* Tadmor

paper, manufacture of, 148[120]

Paradise (Ar: *al-Jannah*, "the Garden"):
the good to be rewarded with, 6, 11, 13;
divisions of, 14, 75, 90; "Abode of Peace,"
Dār as Salām, 14; the Rock of Jerusalem
from, 14 ff.; the "Frequented House" in,
14, 75, 77; rivers and waters of, 15, 23
f., 34; visions of or entrance into before
death, 16, 23 f.; cities of, 28; mountains
of, 34; over Jerusalem, 14, 23, 28, 32;
under Jerusalem, 31 (and *see* Well of the
Leaf); over Mecca, 14; Abraham clothed
and fed from, 51; the Ka'bah from, 75;
the goat from, 83, 118; "Dwellings of the
Just," 120; Abraham in, 128 ff., 133, 136;
description of, 133 f.; Muslim concept of,
144[62a]; 146[80]; the Prophet's ascension to,
see Night-Journey

pardon, *see* forgiveness

Patriarchs and ancients: 34 ff., 44 ff.; their
burial in Hebron, 103 ff.; their tall stature,
105; *see also* prophets, life, lengthy

Paul, Saint, xxiv;—and original sin, 142[32]

Paula, Saint, xxv, xxvii

pearl, palace of in Paradise, 129 f.

Peleg, 45

Persians (the Sassanids): in Palestine, 39, 148[117]; sons of Shem (!), 46

Persia (n), xix, 140 notes 9 and 17, 142[34]; *see also* Iran (ian)

pharaoh (Ar: *fir'aun*): nurse of the wife of, 15;—and Sarah, 64, 150[25]; 149 notes 6 and 8; *see also* giant, king

pilgrimage (Ar: to Mecca at stated season, *Hajj*; to Mecca otherwise and to other holy places, *'umrah* or *ziyārah*): xxiv f.; Biblical custom, xxiv; the Hajj, xxii, xxiv (traditional connection of Abraham, Hagar, and Ishmael with, 68 ff., 136); to shrines in Palestine, xxiv f., 4, 5, 6, 11 f.; of Judaism and Christianity, xxiv f., 145[70]; influence on Western civilization, xxv; literature of, xxv f.; devotional attitude in, xxvii f.; merit of combining, to Jerusalem and to Mecca, 12, 13 f.; to tombs of Patriarch-Prophets in Hebron, 34 f., 118 ff.; proprieties of, 37 f., 122, 142[35]

pillars, 3, 76; *see also qawā'id*

popular religious belief and custom, xxiii; *see also* folklore

prayer (Ar: *salāt*; informal private devotions, *dū'ā*): value of at various places, 4, 6, 10 f., 12, 29, 23; the five daily, 11; unacceptable places for, 16, 143[37]; value anywhere, 17; of Solomon at Temple dedication, 6; of David, 17; of Jesus, 20; of Mohammed with the Prophets in Jerusalem, 20 (and see also *imām*); swiftness of Allah's answering, 21; at the tombs of the prophets in Hebron, 37 f.; merit of in the sight of Allah, 127; 131, 137, 142[30]; call to prayer, *see adhān*

Prophet Mohammed, *see* Mohammed

prophetesses, 99

prophets (Ar: *anbiyā'*; singular, *nabi*): Patriarchs and other ancients considered as, xiv, xvii, xviii, xxiv, 44 ff., 79, 83, 84, 87, 88, 89, 90, 92, 111, 140[11]; in Paradise, 11, 13; numbers of in Palestine, 12, 15, 30; pray with Mohammed, 20, 27, 30, 134; Abraham as prophet, 52 f.; numbers buried in Hebron, 67, 97, 103, 133; their

tombs, 34 f.; mistreated by their people, 93; fathers of their people, 95; their state in death, 148[113]

Prophets, stories or lives of, *see* ath-Tha'labi and al-Kisā'i

proprieties of pilgrimage, 37 f., 122

protection (for non-Muslim subjects), 98, 148[123]

Psalms: quoted, 31; 135, 147[92]

Pseudepigrapha (cf. Apochrypha), 153[94]

pulpit, *see minbar*

Qābīl, *see* Cain

qādi, judge, 16, 107, 123, 124; *see also* Glossary

qādūm, prepuce, 131

al-Qarzi, *see* Muhammad b Ka'b

al-Qāsim b Abu Umāmah, 131

Qat, or Qut, in Palestine, 66

Qatādah, 56, 57, 81, 84, 86, 94, 96, 118

qawā'id, plural of *qā'idah*, " pillar," 76

Qazwīn in Khorasān, 23

al-Qazwīni, author 3, 5, 6, 13, 140[9]

Qeturah, wife of Abraham, 99

qiblah, focal direction of prayer: the Rock in Jerusalem, 17, 18, 30; the Ka'bah in Mecca, 101, 113, 122, 137, 141[21], 143[52]; *see also mihrāb* in Glossary

Qisas al-Anbiyā', *see* ath-Tha'labi and al-Kisā'i

quotation or citation, method of in Traditions, xvi, 139[3]

Qur'ān (xvii), *see* Koran

al-Qutubi, 57

rabbis, teaching of the, xxvii ff.

ar-Rabī' b Anas, 79

ar-Rādi-bi'llāh, 'Abbāsid caliph, 157

Rāfi' b 'Amr, 14

Rajab, seventh month, 45

rak'ah, 11, 34, 37, 142[30]; *see also* Glossary

ram, 85; *see also* goat

Ramadān, month of daylight fasting, 12, 13, 14, 18; 142[34]; *see also* fasting

ar-Ramah, or Ramet al-Khalīl, 111, 147[111]

Ramleh, 26, 66, 106, 107

rau', "fear," 87

Rebecca (Ar: Ribqah), 35, 37, 38, 98, 104, 106, 107, 111, 120, 147[106] rebellion: 34; of Adam, 97; against Abraham, 127

reckoning, *see* Judgment and Resurrection

refuge in Jerusalem, 6, 34

relics, of prophets and saints, xxviii

remonstrance, of Abraham, 48, 52 ff., 136

Repentence, Gate of, 22

Resurrection for Judgment, 6, 15, 16, 25, 28, 30, 31, 37, 44, 58, 63, 105, 120, 123, 124, 128, 129, 137; *see also* Hell, Jerusalem, Paradise

Reu, 45, 149[2]

revelation: historic, xviii; to Abraham, 35, 44; to David, 31; to Solomon, 36, 111 ff.; to the ancients, 46; *fatrah* or interval in, 47; to Nimrod, 49; to women prophets, 99; Moses, 115; to Mohammed, see Mohammed, Koran, Night-Journey; 43, 44, 48, 104, 125, 127, 131, 132, 135, 153[94]

Reynolds, J. A., 144[62]

rhymed prose, 105, 152[73]

Riant, le Comte, xiv[2]

Rihani, Amin F., 143[53]

rites and ceremonies of Islam, 72, 174, 137, 139, 150[34], 151 notes 40 and 49; *see also* ceremonies, circuit, Hajj, pilgrimage, prayer, rak'ah, etc.

rivers of Paradise, 143[44]; *see also* Paradise

Robinson's Arch, 144[60]

Rock, the, in Jerusalem: 6, 14 f., 17, 20; Mohammed's first *qiblah*, 18; door to Paradise, 18; center of the world, 29; Israfel to blow trumpet over, 31; Paradise under, 31; first disclosed from the Flood, 32; source of waters, 63; 105, 118; *see also* Dome of the Rock

rocks in Temple Area, 19

Roman Catholic Church, *see* Catholic Church

Roman Jerusalem, xxiv; *see also* Aelia

Romans, descended from Isaac (!), 84

sacred law: 11, 31; established by Noah, 46; *see also* law

sacred mosque (of Mecca), *see* Haram

sacrifice: of Solomon, 7 f., of prophets in Jerusalem, 30; of Nimrod, 61; begun by Abraham, 137

sacrificed one, *see* Ishmael, Isaac

as-Safā, 16, 69 f.

Safīyyah, wife of the Prophet, 6; in Jerusalem, 20, 21

Sahīh of al-Bukhāri and of Muslim, 3, 69, 124, 126, 128, 131, 133, 139[7]

Sahil b 'Abdullah, 12

as-Sāhirah, plain or plateau of (= Mount of Olives), 20, 25, 144[61]

Sa'īd b Jubeir, 83, 84, 94, 95, 129

Sa'īd b al-Musayyib (or -Museiyyib), 60, 78, 123, 130, 131

Saint Antonius, xxvii

St. Clair-Tisdall, xix, 140[17]

Saint George, or *al-Khidr*, *see* Elijah

Saint Jerome, xxv

Saint Paula, xxv, xxvii

sāj wood (= teak), 105

sakkat, 87

Saladin (Ar: Salāh ad-Dīn): xxiii, 139[8]; *see also* Map of Palestine

Salamīyyah, 23, 145[72]

Sālih, ancient prophet, 48, 106, 149[7]

as-Sālih, ash-Sheikh, appellation of Abraham, 66, 104

Sālim b Thaubān, 130

Sa'lūk, descends to tombs of Hebron, 108

Samrah b Jandab, 133

as-Sanālihi, 80

Sarah: first to be buried at Hebron, 35;— and the giant or king, 36, 64, 68, 148[110]; believes through Abraham, her husband and cousin, 63, 64; her beauty and trials, 64; —and Hagar, 65 f., 68 ff.; tried by Satan, 82; bears Isaac, 84; annunciation to—, 86; 92, 98; a prophetess, 99; 100, 103, 104, 106, 111, 120, 132, 137

Sa'sa'h, Companion, 34

Satan (Ar: Shaitān, or Iblīs): xix; and catapult for Abraham, 59, 150[17]; tries Abraham, Ishmael, and Sarah, 81, 82; stoned on Hajj, 82, 151[49]

Sa'ūdi Arabia, 147[99]; see also Wahhābi(s)

Savage, H. L., xxv[8]

sayyid, *see* Glossary

scales of Judgment, 16

Scripture, people of, see *ahl al-kitāb*

Scriptures: Latin (the Vulgate), xxv; of the ancients, 48

Scythopolis, *see* Beisān
second sight (divining), 39, 48, 65, 148[119]
seil, "flash-flood," 72, 150[36]
Semite, Semitic, 141[18]
as-Seyyidah, wife of Ishmael, 98
Sepulchre: Church of the Holy—, xxviii; *see also* tombs
Serug, 45
Seth, 135
Sha'bān, the eighth month, 113
ash-Sha'bi, 78, 79
Shaddād b Aus, 7 f.
Shāfi'ite school of Islamic law, xii, 140[17]
ash-Shām, 3, 139[2]; *see also* Syria
ash-Sharafi b Qattā'i, 105
Sharīk b Hubāshah, entered Well of the Leaf, 23 f.
shaving, first by Abraham, 131
Shebah, *see* Beersheba
Shechem, xix
sheikh, see Glossary
Shekinah (Ar: sakīnah): 30; Gate of the, 19; guided Abraham to Mecca, 75 f.; 139[5]
Shem (Ar: Sām): 3, 4, 45 ff., 105, 140[11]
she-mule, why barren, 60
Shī'ites, 142[40], 145[75], 149[3]
shrines of Palestine, *see* Hebron, Jerusalem, Temple Area, etc.
Shu'eib, or Jethro, *see* Midian
Shu'eib b al-Jabbā'i, 61
as-Siddīq, "trustworthy," appellation of Abu Bakr, 39; of Joseph, 38, 39
Sihon, river of Paradise, 23
Siloam (Ar: Silwān), 2, 23 f., 34
Sinai, Mount, 16, 76
sins, protection from, 32; punishment of, 22; *see also* forgiveness
as-Sirāt, see Judgment-Path, and Glossary
Sisera and Jael, 141[22]
skirt, origin of trailing—, 71; *see also* folklore
slaughter of the innocents, by Nimrod, 48
snow in Palestine, 107
Société de l'Orient Latin, xxvi
Sodom, Lot and people of, 92
sodomy, 92 f.
Solomon (Ar: Suleimān): xii, xxviii, 30; enlarged the Jerusalem shrine, 4, 12; prayer at Temple dedication, 6 f., 19, 31, 33; companionship of the Just with David and, 12; his throne, 19; his magic powers, 31; built first mosque at Hebron, 36, 111 ff.; believing king, 48, 112; description of, 112; wisdom and powers of, 112; a prophet, 112; his age, 113, 140[16], 145[68], 149[6]
Stanley, Dean, *Jewish Church*, xiv[2]
star: of Abraham, 48, 50; Jupiter and Venus, 53
as-Suddi, 14, 56, 57, 60, 80, 81, 84, 85, 86, 94, 96, 99
Sufyān ath-Thauri, 12, 128, 142[33]
Sughār, Lake (= Dead Sea), 77
sultān, ruler, emperor, 117
sunnah ("path" of example and custom of the Prophet, part of Tradition): 40, 123, 140[9], 152[84]
Sūq Thamānīn, 45
Sūrah, "chapter" of the Koran, 139
Sūrah, heavenly prototype of the Ka'bah, 77
Sūs, 47
Suwād, 47
as-Suyūti, 148[113]
Syria (Ar: *ash-Shām*, or *Sūriyah*): often includes Palestine, e.g., 24, 34, 63, 99, 103, 139[2]; Arabian contacts with, xviii; divinely honored cities of, 12, 23; 92, 112
at-Tabari, historian, Koran commentator, 47, 64, 65, 70, 84, 140[12]
Table, *see* Eucharist
Tadmor (Ar: *Tadmur*), Palmyra, xiii
Talaq b Habīb, 128
talla-hu li-'l-jabīn, 81
Tamīmi clan, of the Dāri: granted Hebron by the Prophet, xv, 38 f., 147[116], 152[77]; leader, Tamīm ad-Dāri, 38 f., 148[119]
tannūr, "oven," 29, 146[86]
tawāf, see circuit (of a shrine)
Teibah, 8
Temple and Temple Area: xxii, xxiii, xxvi; modern guides to, xxvi, xxix; modern burials in, xxix; shrines in, 2, 19 f., 141[21], 145[67]; 113, 139 notes 4 and 5, 144[55], 146[83]
temple of idols, 49 f.

Terah, *see* Āzar

Thabīr, Mount, 83

ath-Tha‘labi, author the *Book of Brides* on stories of the prophets: xiii[1], 45, 46, 47, 51, 54, 56, 60, 61, 64, 66, 70, 77, 80, 84, 86, 90, 91, 92, 93, 97, 99, 112, 123, 135, 143[48], 149[12]; *see also* al-Kisā’i

threshold, metaphor for "wife," 73, 74, 150[37]; *see also* folklore

throne of Allah: the Rock of Jerusalem, 15, 34; in Paradise, 75, 128, 129, 130

throne of Solomon, 19

at-Tīn, Mount of, 120

at-Tirmidhi, traditionist, 76, 133

Tobler, Titus, xxvi

Tomb(s): of the Patriarch-Prophets in Hebron, xiv, xxiv, 2, 34 f., 47, 103 ff., 106 ff., 110; of Christ, *see* Sepulchre, Church of the Holy

Torah (Ar: Taurāt), or Old Testament, 135; *see also* Law

Torrey, C. C., xv, xix, 146[85], 149[7]

tower, of Nimrod, 52, 62 f.

Toy, C. H., 146[85]

Traditions of Islam, 97, 100, 109, 139 notes 3 and 7, 152[84]; *see also* Sunnah

tree(s): of Moses in Midian, 8; of Paradise, 23 f.; *see also* palm—

Tribes of Israel, 111; *see also* Children of Israel, Hebrews

Tribes, Gate of the, 19

trousers, or drawers, 130 ff.

Turkey, 146[81]

Turks, 46; *see also* Ottoman Turks

‘Ubādah b as-Sāmit, 15, 22

Ubayy b Ka‘b 15, 59, 63

‘Ubeid Allah b Anas, 129

‘Ubeid b ‘Umeir, 127, 129

‘Umar, *see* ‘Omar

‘Umar b Dīnār, 92

Umm Hakīm, step-daughter of the Prophet, 13

Umm Ismā‘īl, *see* Hagar

Umm Salimah, wife of the Prophet, 13, 142[36]

Umm Sharīk, 60

Unity of God, 51, 53, 54 ff., 85, 142[30], 147[99]; *see also* Wahhabi(s)

Unūs, Enoch or Enosh (?), 46

Ūrushalīm, or Rūshalīm (= Jerusalem), 14, 28, 142[41]

‘Usāmah, Abyssinian freedman, beloved of the Prophet, 125

‘Uthmān, *see* ‘Othmān

Valley of the Kidron, or Jehoshaphat: 19, 144[55]; *see also* Judgment Path

Venus, star, 53

Virgin Birth of Jesus, 141[20]

visions, *see* dreams

Vita Prophetarum, xiii

vow(s), 32, 80

Wabh b Munabbih, xxi, 15, 18, 21, 25, 28, 36, 86, 92, 105, 112, 119, 127, 140[10]

Wādy es-Sab‘a, see Beersheba

Wahhābi(s) of Arabia (properly, *Muwahhidūn*): 145[75], 147[99]

"Wailing Wall," or Western Wall of Temple Area, xxiv[7], xxix; 139[5], 141[21]; *see also* al-Burāq

Wakī‘ b al-Jarrāh, 26

al-Walīd (b Muslim), 27, 146[76]

waqf, see Glossary

al-Wasīlah, in Paradise, 130

Well of the Leaf, 2, 23 f., 145[68]

Wilson, Col. Sir C., 145[67]

wind(s), from Rock of Jerusalem, 15; of creation, 27

woman, inferior to man, 38

Wright, Thomas, xxvi, xxvii

Yahya b Sa‘īd, 131

Yājūj and Mājūj, *see* Gog and Magog

al-Yaqīn, 67, 98, 103, 150[29]

Yāqūt, geographer, 140[13]

Ya‘qūbi, xxii

Yarid, father of Noah, 46

Yasārah = Sarah, 132

Yathrib, *see* Medina

ya weilata! ("Alas!"), 87

Yazīd ar-Raqāshi, 23

Yemen: Jews in, xviii, a pilgrim from, 18; 140[13], 143[52]

Yūsuf b Māhik, 79

Zaidites, 143[53]

Zamzam, well in Mecca: 23, 34, 69 ff., 80, 106, 145[70]

Zechariah, 2, 30, 31; Mihrāb of, 19

Zeid b Aslam, 17, 61, 85

Zemzem, *see* Zamzam

Zionism, xxiv[7], xxix, 141[21]

ziwār, "girth-rope," 8

Ziyād b Abu Saudah, 22

Zoroastrianism, xix; *see also as-Sirāt* in Glossary

az-Zubeir, *see* 'Abdullah b—

az-Zuhrah, *see* Venus

az-Zuhri, 84, 98

Arabic works cited in the original and not mentioned in translation text or notes

Fadā'il al-Quds wa-'sh-Shām, by al-Muqad-dasi: 88

Jāmi'u 'l-Usūl, by Majdu 'd-Din . . . ibn al-Athīr, one of three noted scholar brothers, died 1310: 45, 46, 47, 67, 84, 88, 91, 113

Kitāb al-Badī' fī Tafdīl Mamlakat al-Islām, by Abu 'Abdullah Muhammad ibn Ahmad al-Bannā': 97, 110

Kitāb ash-Shifā', by the Qadi 'Iyād, of North Africa and Spain, died 1149: 123

Al-Muwatta' of Mālik ibn Anas: 130

Nihāyat al-Arab fī Funūn al-Adab, by an-Nuweiri: 49

Tahdhīb al-Asmā' wa-'l-Lughāt, by an-Nawawi: 44, 47, 60, 112

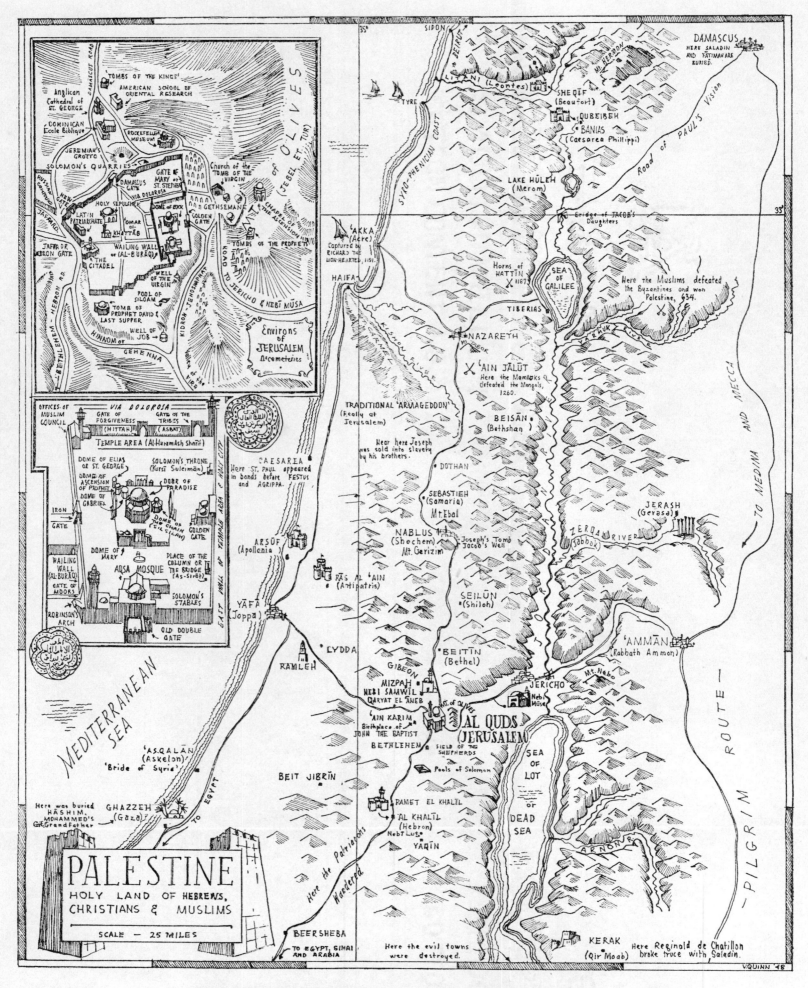

HISTORICAL AND RELIGIOUS MAP OF PALESTINE

Drawn by Vincent Paul Quinn

The Medallions placed with the inset maps represent the obverse and reverse of a silver coin of al-Malik al-ʿĀdil (brother of Saladin), whom Richard the Lion-Hearted proposed to marry to his sister in order to seal a lasting truce between Christian and Muslim contenders for the Holy Land. The legend of the obverse (upper) reads: *Al-Malik al-ʿĀdil Abu Bakr ibn Ayyūb Seif ad-Dīn;* the reverse (lower) reads: *The Leader Aiding the Religion of Allah, the Commander of the Believers.*

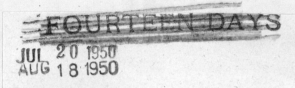